Anonymous

Memorial Addresses and After-Dinner Speeches

New-York's season of public entertainments. The most notable addresses

delivered in the metropolis during the winter of 1891-'92

Anonymous

Memorial Addresses and After-Dinner Speeches
New-York's season of public entertainments. The most notable addresses delivered in the metropolis during the winter of 1891-'92

ISBN/EAN: 9783337254483

Printed in Europe, USA, Canada, Australia, Japan

Cover: Foto ©ninafisch / pixelio.de

More available books at **www.hansebooks.com**

THE TRIBUNE MONTHLY.

OL. IV.   APRIL, 1892.   NO. 4.

Memorial Addresses

--AND--

After-Dinner Speeches.

EW-YORK'S SEASON OF PUBLIC ENTERTAINMENTS.

HE MOST NOTABLE ADDRESSES DELIVERED IN THE ME-TROPOLIS DURING THE WINTER OF 1891-'92.

LIBRARY OF TRIBUNE EXTRAS.

THE TRIBUNE ASSOCIATION,
NEW-YORK.

MEMORIAL ADDRESSES AND AFTER-DINNER SPEECHES.

NEW-YORK'S SEASON OF PUBLIC ENTERTAINMENTS.

GENERAL SHERMAN.

ORATION OF CHAUNCEY M. DEPEW.

AT THE MEMORIAL SERVICES HELD IN HARMANUS BLEECKER HALL, ALBANY, BEFORE THE NEW-YORK LEGISLATURE ON MARCH 29.

Senators and Members of Assembly: The passions of civil war usually survive centuries. We cannot yet impartially and calmly estimate the ability and services of Hamilton and Jefferson. Their names still stand for antagonistic principles and antagonized followers. But the issues of the Rebellion were buried with its dead. That struggle was unique, both in magnitude and settlement. It was an earthquake which rent asunder a continent and plunged into cavernous depths millions of men and money, and the shackles of slaves. It closed, and the survivors, freed from the causes of contention, were united for the upbuilding of the new Nation. Prior to the war we were singularly provincial and insular, but we have since grown to be as radically liberal and cosmopolitan. Then our judgments of statesmen and measures were governed by considerations which were territorial or inherited. Now those who were in the front and heat of the great battle can fairly view and freely weigh the merits of those friends and foes. We can eliminate our feelings, our prejudices and our convictions upon the purposes for which they fought, and contrast Grant and Lee, Sherman and Joe Johnston, Sheridan and Beauregard, as to the genius and ability with which they planned and played the game of war, with equal candor and better light than the historian of the future. Yesterday General Sherman was the last of that triumvirate of great captains, Grant, Sherman and Sheridan, who were the most distinguished soldiers of our country, and of our times, and a familiar figure in our midst. His presence revived and embodied the glories and the memories of the marches and the victories of the heroes who fought, and of the heroes who had died, for the preservation of the Union. To-day we commemorate his life and deeds; and the Civil War is history.

THE SPIRIT OF CROMWELL AND THE COVENANTER

General Sherman's ancestors had been noted for many generations for their culture, ability and intellectual power. His father was a Judge of the Supreme Court of Ohio, and his grandfather of a Connecticut Court, while the grandfather of the Connecticut Judge was a Puritan clergyman, who came to Massachusetts in 1634, in company with a warrior relative, Captain John Sherman, the ancestor of Roger, the signer of the Declaration of Independence. Much has been said, but the whole can never be written, of the influence of the Puritan stock upon the formation and development of the United States, and the destinies of mankind. They alone of all colonists emigrated, not to improve their worldly condition, but to secure liberty of conscience, and to live under a Government of just and equal laws. All through the career of General Sherman the spirit of Cromwell and the Covenanter was the motive-power of his action. His principle of war was to use up and consume the resources of the enemy. The destruction of Atlanta and the devastating march through Georgia and the Carolinas were upon Puritan lines. The enemies of his country were as much to his mind the enemies of the Lord as were the Cavaliers of Prince Rupert to Cromwell and his Ironsides. He was by nature the most genial, lovable and companionable of men, but the mailed hand and merciless purpose followed any attack on the things he held sacred. This appears not only in his campaigns, but also in his dispatches to Generals Grant and Halleck. "I will make the interior of Georgia feel the weight of war." "The utter destruction of its roads, houses and people will cripple their military resources." "I attach more importance to these deep incisions into the enemy's country, because this war differs from European wars in this particular: We are not only fighting hostile armies, but a hostile people, and must make old and young, rich and poor, feel the hard hand of war as well as their organized armies." And in his letter demanding the surrender of Savannah he says: "Should I be forced to assault, or the slower and surer process of starvation, I shall then feel justified in resorting to the harshest measures, and shall make little effort to restrain my army, burning to avenge the National wrong, which they attach to Savannah and other large cities which have been so prominent in dragging our country into civil war."

This was the language of the Puritan soldier. It was born and bred in the children of the people who first separated Church from State, and went to the stake for believing and declaring that the will of God could be one way and the will of the King the other, and their allegiance was to the Lord. It was the same conscience which beheaded Charles the First, and afterward threw the tea into Boston Harbor. Marston Moor, Lexington and the March to the Sea were fruits of the same tree. Sherman was a soldier, educated by the Government of the United States, and the Republic was his love and his religion. The intensity of his passion for the Nation would in other times and surroundings have made him a General in the Parliamentary Army, or the leader of a New-England colony.

SHERMAN'S REPLY TO SUMNER.

I shall never forget a dramatic scene at a notable gathering in New-York, when Charles Sumner indirectly attacked President Grant, as a failure in civil affairs, by ridiculing Miles Standish. General Sherman was a stranger to a New-York audience, and none knew that he could speak. Few men would have dared reply to the world-famed orator. But he had assailed the two tenderest sentiments of General Sherman—his love and admiration for Grant, and his pride in his profession of a soldier. Without any opportunity for preparation, but without hesitation, he immediately arose to meet this unexpected and surprising attack. Defence, under such conditions, would with most untrained speakers have degenerated into abuse, but with Sherman it became the most impressive eloquence. It was a direct and simple statement of his faith in his friend, and a description of the merits and mission of the soldier, which was like the brilliant dash and restless momentum of a charge of cavalry through the broken squares of the enemy. It was a speech Captain Miles Standish might have made after two hundred and fifty years of American opportunity, and the mighty soul of the Puritan captain seemed inspiring the voice and the presence of his advocate.

The same qualities made him the most amiable and lovable of men, and the most rigid of disciplinarians. His heart was easily touched and his sympathies aroused by the distress or want or sorrow of others, but he was the incarnation of the vengeance of the law upon military crimes. A corps commander of the Army of the Potomac once said to him: "General Sherman, we had trouble in enforcing strict obedience to orders, because the findings of the Court Martials had to be sent to President Lincoln for approval in extreme cases, and he would never approve a sentence of death. What did you do?" "I shot them first," was the gruesome reply.

General Sherman was destined from his birth for the career which has become one of the brightest pages in his country's history. The hero among the early settlers of the Ohio valley was that brave and chivalric Indian chief, Tecumseh, who had commanded the admiration of the whites by his prowess, and their goodwill by his kindness. He fought to exterminate, but he could as quickly forgive as he fiercely and savagely struck. The qualities of this wild warrior became part of the characteristics of his namesake. It was ruthless and relentless war with the enemy in the field, but no commander ever granted more generous terms to the vanquished, or was so ready to assist with purse and influence a fallen foe.

His father, Judge Sherman, died suddenly, leaving his widow with little means, and a family of seven children. The helplessness of the American family when thrown upon their own resources, and the ready and practical sympathy of American communities, so extended as to convey, not charity but compliment, has no better example than in the story of this household, and the success in life of its members. The Bench and the Bar felt that the boys were the wards of the profession. Ohio's leading lawyer and United States Senator, the Hon. Thomas Ewing, said: "Give me one, but the brightest," and the brothers and sisters of the future captor of Atlanta answered: "Take Cump, he is the smartest." The profound jurist and keen observer of character saw the future General in this quick, nervous, intelligent, pugnacious boy, with his Indian warrior name, and appointed him to the West Point Military Academy. His fertile and versatile mind pushed its inquiries into too many directions, and explored fields too diverse for that methodical and accurate mastery of the curriculum which makes a valedictorian, but not always a man. Nevertheless, he stood sixth in his class and was its most original and attractive member. He had a fondness for topographical studies, and a keen eye and natural trained instinct for the opportunities for defence and attack which could be utilized in the places where he was stationed and the country over which he travelled.

EARLY OBSERVATIONS IN THE SOUTH.

His first service was in Florida, and his duties carried him, during his six years in the South, through South Carolina, Alabama, Georgia, and the adjoining counties of Tennessee. The great debate as to the powers of the General Government and the reserved rights of the States was at its height. General Jackson had placed his iron heel upon John C. Calhoun and registered the mighty oath, "By the Eternal, the Union of these States must and shall be preserved." South Carolina was specially independent and defiant. Threats of disunion met Sherman at every social gathering. Webster's masterly and unequalled argument and eloquence had converted the North and thousands of broad-minded men in the South to the idea that the United States was a Nation, with the right to use all the resources of the country to enforce its laws and maintain its authority. The possibility of these questions being decided by the arbitrament of war was ever present to the suggestive thought of this young lieutenant. The line of the Tennessee River, the steep ascent of Kenesaw Mountain, the military value of Chattanooga and Atlanta, were impressed upon the intellect of the maturing strategist, to materialize twenty years afterward in the severance and ruin of the Confederacy by his triumphal March to the Sea.

Sherman had been brought up and trained in the school of Hamilton, of Webster, and of Henry Clay. His Bible was the Constitution. He had imagination, but no sentiment; passion, but no pathos. Believing slavery to have guarantees in the Constitution, he would have unsheathed his sword as readily against a John Brown raid as he did at the firing upon Fort Sumter. His imagination led him to glorify and idealize the Republic. Its grandeur, its growth, and its possibilities captured and possessed his heart and mind. The isolation and loneliness of the life in frontier forts destroys many young officers. Their energies are exhausted and their habits and principles demoralized by dissipation, or their faculties paralyzed by idleness. But the card table or the carouse had no attraction for Sherman. His time on the Plains was fully occupied. He was building railroads across the continent on paper, and peopling those vast regions with prosperous settlements long before they had any roads but the paths of the buffalo, and any inhabitants but roving tribes of wild Indians. He could never understand the lamentation, so common, over the extermination of the buffalo. The patient oxen drawing the plough through the furrow, and the lowing herds winding home at sunset, seemed to him to have replaced the wild and useless bison with the sources of individual and National wealth and happiness. He would have destroyed the Indians, because with their occupancy of extensive and fertile territories, which they would neither cultivate nor sell, and the wars with them, which frightened settlers from their borders, they retarded the development and checked the majestic march of his country to the first place among the nations of the earth.

This intense Nationalist and accomplished soldier was selected by the State of Louisiana to be the Superintendent and organizer of her State Military School. The veteran who could bring to the business of banking little more than unswerving integrity and failed, and whose directness of purpose and transparent candor were disgusted with the law, found in this field of instruction a most pleasant and congenial occupation. He was at the head of a university which was fitting youth for careers in civil life, and training them, if needs be, to fight for their country. The institution grew so rapidly, and wisely, that the attention of the State authorities was attracted to its able and brilliant principal. He did not suspect treason, and they were organizing rebellion. To capture this born leader of men was to start with an army. Social blandishments, political pressure, and appeals to ambition were skilfully applied to his purposes and principles. Suddenly the truth burst upon his frank nature. He was poor, and had a large and helpless family. He held an honorable, congenial, lucrative and permanent position. The future, if he abandoned his place, was dark and doubtful, but the Union was in danger, and he did not hesitate a moment. His letter of resignation to the Governor of Louisiana reads like a bugle-call of patriotism: "As I occupy a quasi-military position under the laws of the State, I deem it proper to acquaint you that I accepted such position when Louisiana was a State in the Union, and when the motto of this seminary was inserted in marble over the main door, 'By the liberality of the General Government of the United States. The Union esto perpetua.' Recent events foreshadow a great change and it becomes all men to choose. If Louisiana withdraws from the Federal Union, I prefer to maintain my allegiance to the Constitution as long as a fragment of it survives. . . . On no earthly account will I do any act or think any thought hostile to or in defiance of the old Government of the United States."

KNEW IT WAS NO PICNIC CAMPAIGN.

Events move rapidly in revolutions, and the situations are always dramatic. Captain Sherman is in Washington, offering his services to the Government, Lincoln is President, Seward Secretary of State, Chase Secretary of the Treasury, John Sherman the new United States Senator from Ohio, and old General Scott in command of the Army. Nobody believes there will be war. It is the general conviction that, if the Southern States are rash enough to attempt to secede, the rebellion will be stamped out in three months, and the campaign will be a picnic. Alone in that great throng of office-seekers and self-seekers stands this aggressive and self-sacrificing patriot. He understands and appreciates better than any man living the courage, resources and desperate determination of the South. "They mean war," he cries; "they will soon have armies in the field officered and led by trained and able soldiers. It will require the whole power of the Government and three years of time to subdue them if they get organized before you are on them." Congressmen laughed at the wild talk of the dramatic alarmist, old army officers significantly tapped their foreheads, and said "Poor Sherman, it is too bad"; and the President answered, coldly: "Well, Captain, I guess we will manage to keep house."

The Confederate Army had concentrated at Manassas, threatening Washington. There were few West Point officers available, and Captain Sherman was commissioned a colonel and given command of a brigade at Bull Run. He was the one earnest man among the crowd of triflers in uniform and citizen's dress who flocked to the field. Congress adjourned to see the rebels run, and Congressmen led the tumultuous flight from the battle to Washington. Holding in hand all there was of his brigade which had not stampeded, exposing himself with reckless courage, and keeping a semblance of discipline which did much to prevent pursuit by the victorious enemy, Colonel Sherman rode into Washington so freely to acknowledge the faults on the field, and so vigorously denounce the utterly inadequate preparations for civil war that he again fell into disrepute, was again assailed as a madman and banished to the West. But Ohio never lost confidence in him and demanded and secured his appointment in the long list of brigadier-generals.

The senseless clamor which frightened the Cabinet and the War Office by shouting "On to Richmond," was not appeased by the disgrace and slaughter of Bull Run and Manassas. The frightful recoil, which had followed obedience to the popular cry, only infuriated the politicians. If they could not put down the rebellion in a day, they could at least punish those who had insisted upon the power of the Confederacy. There was a significant display of that singular quality of human nature which leads people who have been warned against a rash act, to turn in defeat and disappointment and rend the prophet who foretold the result. Sherman, from the more commanding position of his superior rank, was once more announcing the strength, power and resources of the rebels in Kentucky and Tennessee. He boldly proclaimed that the forces collected to hold those States were so absurdly inadequate that another and more fatal Bull Run was sure to follow, unless the means were equal to the emergency. The Government, the press and the people united in condemning his terrorizing utterances, and for the third time he was sent into retirement as a lunatic. Accumulating perils and providential escapes from hopeless disasters speedily demonstrated that this madman was a seer, and this alarmist a general.

SHERMAN'S OPPORTUNITY.

Then, for the glory of the American army and the incalculable advantage of the Union cause, came the opportunity for the most brilliant soldier and magnetic commander in our annals. The control of the Mississippi, the allegiance of the Border States, and the existence of the Western army, were in gravest peril at Shiloh. Sherman was at the front on those two desperate days, holding his men by his personal example and presence. He was as much the inspiration of the fight as the white plume of Henry of Navarre at Ivry. Though wounded, he still led, and though three horses were shot under him, he mounted the fourth. General Halleck, then Commander-in-Chief of all the National forces, reported to the Government that "General Sherman saved the fortunes of the day on the 6th, and contributed largely to the glorious victory of the 7th."

Critics and historians will forever discuss the men and the movements of the Civil War. As time passes and future events crowd the record, most of the figures of that bloody drama, now so well known to us, will disappear. It requires, even after the lapse of only a quarter of a century, an effort and a history to recall many names which were then household words. But Sherman's march to the sea, like the retreat of Xenophon and his ten thousand Greeks, will, through all ages, arouse the enthusiasm of the schoolboy, the fervor of the orator, and the admiration of the strategist. When at last, with a picked army of 60,000 veterans, Sherman was encamped at Atlanta, he had grasped and materialized the factors of success in the dream of his youth. He bombarded the President and the Commanding General with letters and telegrams: "I can divide the Confederacy, destroy the source of its supplies, devastate its fertile regions, and starve its armies." "Give me the word 'go,'" burdened the wires and the dispatch boxes. The Cabinet said: "Your army will be lost, floundering in the heart of the enemy's country, and cut off from your base of supplies." The headquarters staff said: "Turn back upon the course you have traversed and destroy Hood's army, which threatens your communications and your rear, and then we will discuss the question with you." Sherman detached that most remarkable general, Thomas, with a force sufficient, in his judgment, to take care of Hood, and that superb officer vindicated the trust reposed in him by pulverizing the rebel army.

At last the President gave an approval so reluctant that it threw the responsibility upon General Sherman, and Grant gave his assent. Said General Sherman to me, in one of the confidences so characteristic of his candid mind: "I believed that this permission would be withdrawn, and sent immediately a detachment to destroy the wires for sixty miles. I never felt so free and so sure as when the officer returned and reported the work done. Years afterward I discovered an official memorandum that, 'owing to the sudden interruption by the rebels of communications with Atlanta, a message countermanding the assent to General Sherman to march across the country to Savannah could not be delivered.'" Upon such slender threads hang the fate of campaigns and the fame of illustrious men.

THE MARCH TO THE SEA.

The armies of Tennessee and of Georgia had the dash and daring, the free and breezy swing and ways, and the familiarity with their officers, characteristic of the West. They idolized their fatherly but cyclonic commander. This superb specimen of the pure Puritan stock, born and bred in the West, careful of every detail which promoted their comfort and efficiency, and careless of the form and dignity which hedge in authority, won their love and admiration. Most veteran armies, with their lines of communication and supplies abandoned, and marching into the enemy's country, ignorant of the food and forage which might be found, or the forces which might cross their path, would have murmured or hesitated. But the soldier, who with only a day's rations in his haversack called out to his grim and thoughtful general as he rode by: "Uncle Billy, I suppose we are going to meet Grant in Richmond," expressed the faith of his comrades. If Richmond was their objective point, nor mountains, nor rivers, nor hostile peoples, nor opposing armies, could prevent Sherman from taking them there triumphantly. The capture of Atlanta had aroused the wildest enthusiasm among the people. For the thirty days during which the victors were lost in the interior of the Confederacy the North listened with gravest apprehension and bated breath. Then the conquering host were on the shores of the sea, Savannah was laid at the feet of President Lincoln by their General as a Christmas present, the Confederacy was divided and its resources destroyed, and William Tecumseh Sherman became "one of the few, the immortal names, that were not born to die."

Having placed his army across all the roads by which General Lee could escape from Richmond, Sherman left his quarters to visit Lincoln, then with Grant at City Point.

In April, 1861, Captain Sherman had informed the President in the White House that "he might as well attempt to put out the flames of a burning house with a squirt gun as to put down the Rebellion with 75,000 men, and that the whole military power of the North should be organized at once for a desperate struggle"—to be laughed out of Washington as a lunatic. Four years had passed. Two millions of men had been mustered in, 500,000 had been killed in battle or died in the hospital, or had been disabled for life, and in March, 1865, General Sherman stood in the presence of the President. It was the original faculty of Mr. Lincoln that he could so acknowledge a mistake as to make it the most delicate and significant compliment. "Mr. President," said Sherman, "I left in camp 75,000 of the best troops ever gathered in the field, and if Lee escapes Grant they can take care of him." "I shall not feel secure, nor that they are safe," said the President, "until I know you are back again and in command." "I can capture Jefferson Davis and his Cabinet," said General Sherman. "Let them escape," was the suggestion of this wisest of Presidents; "and, above all, let there be no more bloodshed, if that is possible." General Joseph E Johnston and the last army of the Confederacy in Sherman's hands, the terms of reconstruction and reconciliation which he had heard from Lincoln in that final and memorable interview, submitted as the condition of surrender, the President's assassination and its dread consequences, the contemptuous repudiation of his terms by Secretary Stanton, the grand review of his soldiers by the Cabinet and Congress at Washington, the indignant refusal of the proffered hand of the Secretary of War in the presence of the Government and the people, the farewell to and muster out of his beloved army, and one of the most picturesque, romantic and brilliant military careers of modern times came to a close. Its ending had all the striking and spectacular setting of its course, and its adventures, achievements and surprises will be for all time the delight of the historian and the inspiration of the soldier.

HIS LIFE'S IDEAL CLOSE.

The later years of most heroes have been buffeted with storms, or have come to a tragic end. Caesar in the supreme hour of his triumph, fell at the foot of Pompey's statue, pierced by the daggers of his friends. Napoleon fretted out his great soul in the solitude of St. Helena. Wellington lost popularity and prestige in the strifes of parties. Washington was worried and wearied into his grave by the cares of office and the intrigues of his enemies—enemies as he believed, also of his country. Grant's death was hastened and his last days clouded by the machinations of politicians and the crimes of trusted associates. But General Sherman, in retirement, led a ideal life. Only Von Moltke shares with him the peaceful pleasures of content and of his people's love.

The Fathers of the Republic were fearful of military influence and apprehensive of dangers to liberty and perils to the life of the young Republic. Some of them even distrusted Washington and a dictatorship. After him they set aside all the Revolutionary generals and selected statesmen for Presidents. But with confidence in the power and perpetuity of the Nation came the popular strength of the successful soldier. None of our heroes have been able to resist the fascinations and the dangers of the Chief Magistracy except General Sherman. All of our great captains would have led happier lives, and left their fame less obscured, if they had spurned the temptation. In nearly every canvass since Jackson, one or both of the great parties have had military candidates. General Sherman had such peculiar and striking elements of popularity that party leaders begged and besought him to carry their standard. His election would have been a certainty, and he knew it. But his answer was: "I will not accept nominated, and I will not serve if elected." "In every man's life occurs an epoch when he must choose his own career, and when he may not throw off the responsibility, or tamely place his destiny in the hand of his friends. Mine occurred in Louisiana when, in 1861, alone in the midst of a people blinded by supposed wrongs, I resolved to stand by the Union as long as a fragment of it survived on which to cling. I remember well the experiences of Generals Jackson, Harrison, Taylor, Grant, Hayes and Garfield, all elected because of their military services, and all warned, not encouraged, by their sad experiences. Not the least of the dramatic memories which will distinguish this most sincere and original actor in the drama of life will be that he will remain forever the only American who refused the Presidency of the United States. Though declining political preferment for himself, he rejoiced in the honors bestowed upon any member of his old army. "I am proud," he said, "that Ben Harrison is our President; that Foraker, Hovey, Fitler and Humphreys are Governors of the great States of Ohio, Indiana, Illinois and Kansas, all 'my boys,'" and he would have been wild with delight if he could have added Slocum, Governor of New-York.

HIS DAILY WALKS TRIUMPHAL PROCESSIONS.

His daily walks were a series of triumphal processions. The multitudes never obtruded upon his privacy, but separated as he approached, and united when he passed, to express their individual and collective affection and gratitude. The encampments of the Grand Army were fame in his absence, but his presence called together from fifty to 100,000 comrades to greet "Uncle Billy," and rend the heavens with the chorus of "Marching Through Georgia." His versatile genius met instantly and instinctively the exacting requirements of an impromptu address before a miscellaneous audience. He possessed beyond most men the quick sympathy with the occasion, the seriousness and humor, the fervor and story, the crisp argument and delicacy of touch which make the successful after-dinner speech. He was the most charmingly unconscious of conversationalists. In his effacement of himself and cordial recognition of others, picturesque narration of adventure and keen analysis of character, droll humor and hot defence or eulogy of a friend, his talk was both a panorama and a play. He was always a boy, with a boy's love of fun, keen interest in current events, and transparent honesty in thought and expression.

He loved the theatre, and the stage, feeling the presence of a discriminating but admiring friend, was at its best when General Sherman was in the audience. He was delightfully happy in the applause and praise of his countrymen and countrywomen. He felt that it came from their hearts, as it went to his. Through his course as a cadet at West Point and his career as a young officer he revealed his innermost soul in frequent correspondence with the daughter of his adopted father, who became afterward his wife, and whose wisdom, devotion and tenderness made his home his haven and his heaven. No impure thought ever occupied his mind or unclean word passed his lips. There was something so delicate and deferential in his treatment of women, the compliment was so sincere both in manner and speech, that the knightly courtesy of Bayard had in him the added charm of a recognition of woman's equal mind and judgment.

He lived in and with the public. There was something in the honesty and clear purpose of crowds which was in harmony with his ready sympathy and unreserved expression and action on every question. He delighted in large cities, and especially in New-York. The mighty and yet orderly movements of great populations were in harmony with his constant contemplation of grand campaigns. His penetrating and sensitive mind found rest and recreation in the limitless varieties of metropolitan life. He so quickly caught the step of every assemblage that he was equally at home among scientists, and Sunday-school teachers, alumni associations and National societies, club festivities, chambers of commerce celebrations and religious conventions. He never hesitated to respond on any and all these occasions to call for a speech, and always struck a chord which was so in unison with the thought of his audience as to leave a lasting impression. After the most serious and important of consultations or meetings, the small hours of the night would often find him the honored guest, a boon companion among bohemians, or old comrades, but in all the freedom of story and repartee, of humor or recitation, neither he

nor they ever for an instant forgot that they were in the presence of General Sherman.

He was entirely free from the intense and absorbing passion for wealth which characterizes our times. He knew little of and cared less for the processes of money-getting. The one place in the country where fortunes were never estimated was his house, and his was the only presence where riches, their acquirement and their uses were never discussed. He was satisfied with his well-earned pay from the Government, and did not envy those who possessed fortunes. In his simple tastes and childlike simplicity, as he lived and moved in the midst of the gigantic combinations and individual efforts to secure a larger share of stocks and bonds and lands, he stood to the financial expansions and revulsions of the day as did the Vicar of Wakefield to the fashionable society of his period.

This soldier, citizen and patriot, this model husband, father and friend, held a place in every heart, and a seat by every fireside in the land. His death carried a sense of personal bereavement to every household, and plunged the country in mourning. The imposing catafalque has attracted the curiosity of thousands as it has borne to the tomb eminent citizen or soldier, but the simple caisson rumbling over the pavement, and carrying General Sherman to the side of his beloved wife and adored boy in the cemetery, drew tears from millions. His name and his fame, his life and his deeds are among the choicest gifts of God to this richly endowed Republic, and a precious legacy for the example and inspiration of coming generations.

JAMES RUSSELL LOWELL.

AN ADDRESS BY GEORGE W. CURTIS.

HE SPEAKS OF THE POET AND DIPLOMATIST BEFORE THE NEW BROOKLYN INSTITUTE.

An eloquent tribute to the career of James Russell Lowell was paid by George William Curtis in an address February 22 at the meeting of the members of the Brooklyn Institute of Arts and Sciences, in Association Hall, Brooklyn. The bequest of one of the founders of the Institute provides for an address on Washington's Birthday, upon some eminent American. It was expected that Mr. Lowell would be the speaker this year, until his death occurred, last August. As his birth, in 1819, was upon the same day as Washington's, in 1732, it was decided to ask Mr. Curtis to speak upon the double anniversary and make Mr. Lowell his theme. The hall was filled with 1,500 people, among them many well-known men.

When Mr. Curtis made his way to the platform, accompanied by General John B. Woodward, president of the Institute, and Drs. Hall and Backus, there was loud applause, which was repeated when he arose to speak, and it frequently punctuated his address. General Woodward made a brief speech of introduction. Mr. Curtis spoke as follows:

The birthday of Washington not only recalls a great historic figure, but it reminds us of the quality of great citizenship. His career is at once our inspiration and rebuke. Whatever is lofty, fair and patriotic in public conduct, instinctively we call by his name; whatever is base, selfish and unworthy, is shamed by the lustre of his life. Like the flaming sword turning every way that guarded the gate of Paradise, Washington's example is the beacon shining at the opening of our annals and lighting the path of our national life.

But the service that makes great citizenship is as various as genius and temperament. Washington's conduct of the war was not more valuable to the country than his organization of the government, and it was not his special talent but his character that made both of those services possible. In public affairs the glamor of arms is always dazzling. It is the laurels of Miltiades, not those of Homer or Phidias or Demosthenes, which disturb and inspire the young Themistocles. But while military glory stirs the popular heart it is the traditions of national grandeur, the force of noble character, immortal works of literature and art, which nourish the sentiment that makes men patriots and heroes. The eloquence of Demosthenes aroused decadent Greece at last to strike for independence. The song of Koerner fired the resistless charge of Lutzow's cavalry. A pamphlet of our Revolution revived the flickering flame of colonial patriotism. The speech, the song, the written word, are deeds no less than the clash of arms at Cheronea and Yorktown and Gettysburg.

It is not only Washington the soldier and the statesman, but Washington the citizen, whom we chiefly remember. Americans are accused of making an excellent and patriotic Virginia gentleman a mythological hero and demi-god. But what mythological hero or demi-god is a figure so fair? We say nothing of him to-day that was not said by those who saw and knew him, and in phrases more glowing than ours, and the concentrated light of a hundred years discloses nothing to mar the nobility of the incomparable man.

It was while the personal recollections and impressions of him were still fresh, while as Lowell said, "Boston was not yet a city and Cambridge was still a country village," that Lowell was born in Cambridge seventy-three years ago to-day. His birth on Washington's birthday seems to be a happy coincidence, because each is so admirable an illustration of the two forces whose union has made America. Massachusetts and Virginia, although of very different origin and character, were the two colonial leaders. In Virginia politics as in the aristocratic salons of Paris on the eve of the French Revolution there was always a theoretical democracy; but the spirit of the State was essentially aristocratic and conservative. Virginia was the Cavalier of the Colonies, Massachusetts was the Puritan. And when John Adams, New-England personified," said in the Continental Congress that Washington ought to be General, the Puritan and the Cavalier clasped hands. The union of Massachusetts and Virginia for that emergency foretold the final union of the States, after a mighty travail of difference, indeed, and long years of strife.

The higher spirit of conservatism, its reverence for antiquity, its susceptibility to the romance of tradition, its instinct for continuity and development, and its antipathy to violent rupture; the grace and charm and courtesy of established social order, in a word the feminine element in national life, however far from actual embodiment in Virginia or in any colony, was to blend with the masculine force and creative energy of the Puritan spirit and produce all that we mean by America. This was the consummation which the Continental Congress did not see, but which was none the less for cast when John Adams summoned Washington to the chief revolutionary command. It is the vision which still inspires the life and crowns the hope of every generous American, and it has had no truer interpreter and poet than Lowell. Well was he born on the anniversary of Washington's birth, for no American was ever more loyal to the lofty spirit, the grandeur of purpose, the patriotic integrity, none ever felt more deeply the scorn of ignoble and canting Americanism, which invest the name of Washington with imperishable glory.

THE POET'S LIFE-LONG HOME.

The house in which Lowell was born has long been known as Elmwood, a stately house embowered in lofty trees, still full, in their season, of singing birds. It is one of the fine old mansions of which a few yet linger in the neighborhood of Boston, and it still retains its dignity of aspect, but a dignity somewhat impaired by the encroaching advance of the city and of the architectural taste of a later day. The house had its traditions, for it was built before the Revolution by the last loyal Lieutenant-Governor of Massachusetts, whose stout allegiance to the British Crown never shaken, and who left New-England with regret when New-England, also not without natural filial regret, left the British Empire. It is a legend of Elmwood that Washington was once its guest, an after the revolution it was owned by Elbridge Gerry a signer of the Declaration of Independence, wh occupied it when he was Vice-President.

Not far away from Elmwood, Lowell's lifelon home, is the house which is doubly renowned as th headquarters of Washington and the home of Long fellow. Nearer the colleges stands the branchin elm, twin heir with the Charter Oak, of patriot story, under which Washington took command o the Revolutionary army. Indeed, Cambridge is al Revolutionary ground and rich with Revolutionar tradition. Lexington common is but six miles away Along the West Cambridge road galloped Pau Revere to Concord. Yonder marched the militi to Bunker Hill. Here were the quarters in whic Burgoyne's redcoats were lodged after the surrende at Saratoga. But peaceful among the storied scene of war stands the university, benign mother of edu cated New-England, coeval with the Puritan settle ment which has given the master impulse to Amer ican civilization.

The American is fortunate who, like Lowell, is bor among such historic scenes and local associations and to whose cradle the good fairy has brought th gift of sensitive appreciation. His birthplace wa singularly adapted to his genius and his taste. Th landscape, the life, the figures of Cambridge constantl appear both in his prose and verse, but he lays littl stress upon the historic reminiscence. It is the pic turesqueness, the character, the humor of the lif around him which attract him. This apparent in difference to the historic charm of the neighborhoo is illustrated in a little story that Lowell tells on hi first visit to the White Mountains. In the Franconi Notch he stopped to chat with a recluse in a sawmil busy at work, and asked him the best point of viev for the Old Man of the Mountain. The busy workmar answered: "Dun no; never see it." Lowell continues "Too young and too happy to feel or affect the Juve nalian indifference, I was sincerely astonished and I expressed it. The log-compelling man attempted n justification, but after a little while added, "Com from Bawsn?" "Yes," with peculiar pride. "Goodl to see in the vicinity of Bawsn?" "Oh, yes," I said I should like—nwl I should like to stan' on Bunke Hill. You've been there often, likely?" "N-o,' unwillingly seeing the little end of the horn in clea vision at the terminus of this Socratic perspective "Awl, my young fren', you've l'arned now that wut man kin see any day he never does see; nawthin pay nawthin vally!"

HIS EARLY LITERARY BENT.

Lowell entered college at fifteen and graduated a nineteen, in 1838. His literary taste and talent were already evident, for in literature even then he was an accomplished student, and he was the poet of his class, although at the close of his last year he was rusticated at Concord, a happy exile where he saw Emerson, and probably Henry Thoreau and Marga ret Fuller, who was often a guest in Emerson's house It was here that he wrote the class poem which gave no melodious hint of the future man, and disclosed the fact that the child of Cambridge, although a student, was as yet wholly uninfluenced by the moral and intel lectual agitation called derisively transcendentalism.

Of this agitation John Quincy Adams writes in his diary in 1840: "A young man, named Ralph Waldo Emerson, a son of my once-loved friend, William Emer son, and a classmate of my lamented son, George, after falling in the every-day avocation of a Unitarian preacher and schoolmaster, starts a new doctrine of transcendentalism, declares all the old revelations superannuated and worn out, and announces the ap proach of new revelations and prophecies. Garrison, and the non-resident abolitionists, Brownson, and the Marat Democrats, phrenology and animal magnetism, all come in, furnishing each some plausible rascality as an ingredient for the bubbling cauldron of religiou and politics." There could be no better expression of the bewildered and indignant consternation with which the old New-England of fifty years ago regarded the awakening of the newer New-England, of which John Quincy Adams himself was to be a character istic leader, and which was to liberate still further American thought and American politics, enlarging religious liberty, and abolishing human slavery. Like other Boston and Harvard youth of about this time, or a little earlier, Charles Sumner, Wendell Phillips, Edmund Quincy, Lothrop Motley, Oliver Wendell Holmes, Lowell seemed to be born for studious leis ure or professional routine, as yet unheeding and unconscious of the real forces that were to mould his life. Of these forces, the first and most enduring was an early and happy passion for a lovely and high-minded woman who became his wife, the Egeria who exalted his youth and confirmed his noblest aspirations; a heaven-eyed counsellor of the serener air who filled his mind with peace and his life with joy.

AN EXTRAORDINARY RANGE OF READING.

During these years Lowell greatly impressed his college comrades, although no adequate literary record of the promise which they felt survives. When he left college and studied law the range of his reading was already extraordinarily large, and his observation of nature singularly active and comprehensive. His mind and memory like the Green Vaults of Dresden were rich with treasures accumulated from every source. But his earliest songs echoed the melodies of other singers and foretold no fame. They were the confused murmuring of the bird while the dawn is deepening into day. Partly his fastidious taste, his conservative disposition, and the utter content of happy love, lapped him in soft Lydian airs which the angry public voices of the time did not disturb. But it was soon clear that the young poet whose early verses sang only his own happiness would yet fulfill Schiller's requirement that the poet shall be a citizen of his age as well as of his country.

One of his most intimate friends, the late Charles F. Briggs, for many years a citizen of Brooklyn, and known in the literary New-York of forty years ago as Harry Franco, said of him with fine insight, that Lowell was naturally a politician, but a politician like Milton, a man that is to say with an instinctive grasp of the higher politics, of the duties and relations of the citizen to his country, and of those moral principles which are essential to the welfare of States as oxygen to the breath of human life. "He will never narrow himself to a party which does not include mankind," said his friend, "nor consent to dally with his muse when he can invoke her aid in the cause of the oppressed and suffering." This was the just perception of affectionate intimacy. It foretold not only literary renown but patriotic inspiration and consequent political influence in its truest and most permanent form. In Lowell's mind as in Milton's, as in the spirit of the great Dutch revolt against Spain, of the later German defiance of Napoleon, and of the educated young heroes of Union and liberty in our own civil war, the words of Sir Philip Sidney to Hubert Languet, presently glowed with quickening truth; "To what purpose should our thought be directed to various kinds of knowledge unless room be afforded for putting it into practice so that public advantage may be the result?" It was not a Puritan nor a Republican who wrote the words, but they contain the essential spirit of Puritan statemanship and scholarship on both sides of the ocean.

The happy young scholar at Elmwood, devoted to literature and love and unheeding the great movement of public affairs, showed from time to time that beneath the lettered leisure of his life there lay the conscience and moral virility that give public effect to genius and accomplishment. Lowell's development as a literary force in public affairs is unconsciously and exquisitely portrayed in the prelude to Sir Launfal in 1848:

"Over his keys the musing organist
    Beginning doubtfully and far away,
First lets his fingers wander as they list,
    And builds a bridge from Dreamland for his lay:
Then as the touch of his loved instrument
Gives hope and fervor, nearer draws his theme,
First guessed by faint auroral flushes sent
    Along the wavering vista of his dream."

THE ANTI-SLAVERY CAUSE.

In 1844-'45, his theme was no longer doubtful or far away. Although Mr. Garrison and the early abolitionists refused to vote as an act sanctioning a Government which connived at slavery, yet the slavery question had already mastered American politics. In 1844 the Texas controversy absorbed public attention, and in that and the following year Lowell's poems on Garrison, Phillips, Giddings, Palfrey, and the capture of fugitive slaves near Washington, like keen flashes leaping suddenly from a kindling pyre, announced that the anti-slavery cause had gained a powerful and unanticipated ally in literature. These poems, especially that on "The Present Crisis," have a Tyrtean resonance, a stately rhetorical rhythm, that makes their dignity of thought, their intense feeling and picturesque imagery, superbly effective in recitation. They sang themselves on every anti-slavery platform. Wendell Phillips winged with their music and tipped with their flame the darts of his fervid appeal and manly scorn. As he quoted them with suppressed emotion in his low, melodious, penetrating voice, the white plume of the resistless Navarre of eloquence gained loftier grace, that relentless sword of invective a more flashing edge.

The last great oration of Phillips was the discourse at Harvard University on the centenary of the Phi Beta Kappa. It was not the least memorable in that long series of memorable orations at Harvard of which the first in significance was Buckminster's in 1809, and the most familiar was Edward Everett's in 1824, its stately sentences culminating in the magnificent welcome to Lafayette, who was present. It was the first time that Phillips had been asked by his Alma Mater to speak at one of her festivals, and he rightly comprehended the occasion. He was never more himself, and he held an audience called from many colleges and not predisposed to admire, in shuddering delight by the classic charm of his manner and the brilliancy of his unsparing censure of educated men as recreant to political progress. The orator was nearly seventy years old. He was conscious that he should never speak again upon a greater occasion nor to a more distinguished audience, and as his discourse ended, as if to express completely the principle of his own life and of the cause to which it had been devoted, and the spirit which alone could secure the happy future of his country if it was to justify the hope of her children, he repeated the words of Lowell:

"New occasion bring new duties, time makes ancient good uncouth.
They must upward still and onward who would keep abreast of truth.
Lo! before us gleam her camp fires, we ourselves must pilgrims be.
Launch our Mayflower and steer boldly through the desperate winter sea.
Nor attempt the future's portal with the Past's blood-rusted key."

HIS VOCATION THE MAKING OF VERSE.

When Lowell wrote the lines he was twenty-five years old. He was thoroughly stirred by the cause which Edmund Quincy in reply to Motley's question, "What public career does America offer?" had declared to be "the noblest in the world." But Lowell felt that he was before all a poet. When he was twenty-seven, he wrote: "If I have any vocation, it is the making of verse. When I take my pen for that, the world opens itself ungrudgingly before me; everything seems clear and easy, as it seems sinking to the bottom would be, as one leans over the edge of his boat in one of those dear coves at Fresh Pond. But when I do prose it is in vita Minerva. I feel as if I were wasting time and keeping back my message. My true place is to serve the cause as a poet. Then my heart leaps before me into the conflict." Already the musing organist had ceased to dream and he was about to strike a chord in a strange and unexpected key and with a force to which the public conscience would thrill in answer.

Lowell was an intense New-Englander. There is no finer figure of the higher Puritan type. The New-England soil from which he sprang was precious to him. The New-England legend, the New-England language, New-England character and achievement, were all his delight and familiar study. Nobody who could adequately depict the Yankee ever knew him as Lowell knew him, for he was at heart the Yankee that he drew. The Yankee early became the distinctive representative of America. He is the Uncle Sam of comedy and caricature. Even the sweet-souled Irving could not resist the universal laugh, and gave it fresh occasion by his portrait of Ichabod Crane. Those who preferred the cavalier and counted as a national type, traced the Yankee's immediate descent from the snivelling, sanctimonious, and crafty zealots of Cromwell's Parliament. Jack Downing and Sam Slick, the coarser force and stories broadly exaggerated this conception, and in our great controversy of the century, the anti-slavery movement was derided as the super-serviceable, sneaking fanaticism of the New-England children of Tribulation Wholesome and Zeal-in-the-land-Busy, whom the Southern sons of gallant cavaliers and gentlemen would teach better morals and manners. The Yankee was made a bye-word of scorn and identified with a disturber of the national peace and the enemy of the glorious Union. Many a responsible citizen, many a prosperous merchant in New-York and Boston and Philadelphia, many-a learned divin·, whose honor it was that they were Yankees, felt a half-hearted shame in the name and grudged the part play·d by their noses in the conversation. They seemed perpetually to hear a voice of contempt saying, "Thy nose b·wrayeth thee."

THE REPRESENTATIVE YANKEE FIGURE.

This was the figure which, with the instinct of genius, with true New-England pride and the joy of conscious power, Lowell made the representative of liberty-loving, generous, humane, upright, wise, conscientious, indignant America. He did not abate the Yankee a jot or a tittle. He magnified his characteristic drawl, his good-natured simplicity, his provincial inexperience. But he revealed his unbending principle, his supreme good sense, his lofty patriotism, his unquailing courage. He scattered the clouds of hatred and ignorance that deformed and caricatured him, and showed him in his daily habit as he lived, the true and worthy representative of America, with mother wit preaching the gospel of Christ, and in plain native phrase applying it to a tremendous public exigency in Christian America. The Yankee dialect of New-England, like the Yankee himself, had become a jest of farce and extravaganza. But, thoroughly aroused, Lowell grasped it as lightly as Hercules his club and struck a deadly blow at the Hydra that threatened the national life. Burns did not give to the Scottish tongue a nobler immortality than Lowell to the dialect of New-England.

In June, 1846, the first Biglow Paper, which, in a letter written at the time, Lowell called "a squib of mine," was published in "The Boston Courier." That squib was a great incident both in the history of American literature and politics. The serious tone of our literature from its grave colonial beginning had been almost unbroken. The rollicking laugh of Knickerbocker was a solitary sound in our literary air until the gay note of Holmes returned a merry echo. But humor as a literary force in political discussion was still more unknown, and in the fierce slavery controversy it was least to be anticipated. Banter in such a stern debate would seem to be blasphemy, and humor as a weapon of anti-slavery warfare was almost inconceivable. The letters of Major Jack Downing, a dozen years before the Biglow Papers, were merely extravaganza to raise a derisive laugh. They were fun of a day and forgotten. Lowell's humor was of another kind. It was known to his friends, but it was not a characteristic of Lowell the author. In his early books there is no sign of it. It was not a humorist whom the good-natured Willis welcomed in his airy way, saying that posterity would know him as Russell Lowell. Willis thought, perhaps, that another dainty and graceful trifler had entered the charmed circle of literature that pleases but not inspires.

EFFECT OF THE BIGLOW PAPERS.

But suddenly, and for the first time, the absorbing struggle of freedom and slavery for control of the Union was illuminated by humor radiant and piercing, which broke over it like daylight, and exposed relentlessly the sophistry and shame of the slave power. No speech, no plea, no appeal was comparable in popular and permanent effect with this pitiless tempest of fire and hail, in the form of wit, argument, satire, knowledge, insight, learning, commonsense and patriotism. It was humor of the purest strain, but humor in deadly earnest. In its course, as in that of a cyclone, it swept all before it, the press, the church, criticism, scholarship, and it bore resistlessly down upon the Mexican War, the pleas for slavery, the Congressional debates, the conspicuous public men. Its contemptuous scorn of the public cowardice that acquiesced in the aggressions of the slave power startled the dormant manhood of the North and of the country.

"The North hain't no kind of business with nothin',
  An' you've no idee how much bother it saves,
We ain't none riled by their frettin' and frothin',
  We're used to layin' the string on our slaves;
Sez John C. Calhoun, sez he.
          Sez Mister Foote,
       I should like to shoot
The hull gang, by the great horn spoon, sez he.
"The mass ough' to labor an' we lay on sofies,
  That's the reason I want to spread Freedom's aree.
It puts all the cunningest on us in office,
  An' reclizes our maker's orig'nal idee,
Sez John C. Calhoun, sez he.

That's as plain, sez Cass,
  As that some one's an ass,
It's ez clear us the sun is at noon, sez he.
"Now don't go to say I'm the friend of oppression,
  But keep all your spare breath for coolin' your broth;
For I allers hev strove (at least that's my impression)
  To make cussed free with the rights of the North,
Sez John C. Calhoun, sez he.
    Yes, says Davis of Miss,
    The perfection o' bliss
Is in skinning that same old coon, sez he."

Such lines, as with a stroke of lightning, were burnt into the hearts and conscience of the North. Read to-day they recall as nothing else can recall the intensity of the feeling which swiftly flamed into civil war.

ESSENTIALLY AND PURELY AMERICAN.

Apart from their special impulse and influence the Biglow Papers were essentially and purely American. It is sometimes said that the best American poetry is only English poetry written on this side of the ocean. But the Biglow Papers are as distinctively American as Tam o'Shanter is Scotch or the Divine Comedy Italian. They could have been written nowhere else but in Yankee New-England by a New-England Yankee. With Uncle Tom's Cabin they are the chief literary memorial of the contest, a memorial which as literature, and for their own delight, our children's children will read, as we read to-day the satires that scourge the long-vanished Rome which Juvenal knew and the orations of Burke that discuss long-perished politics. So strong was Lowell's anti-slavery ardor that he proudly identified himself with the Abolitionists. Simultaneously with the publication of the first Biglow Paper, he became a corresponding editor with Edmund Quincy of "The Anti-Slavery Standard," the organ of the American Anti-Slavery Society, and in a letter to his friend, Sydney Howard, esq., the editor of the paper, he says, "I was not only willing but desirous that my name should appear, because I scorned to be indebted for any share of my modicum of popularity to my abolitionism without incurring at the same time whatever odium might be attached to a complete identification with a body of heroic men and women whom not to love and admire would prove me to be unworthy of those sentiments, and whose superiors in all that constitutes true manhood and womanhood I believe never existed."

But his anti-slavery ardor was far from being his sole and absorbing interest and activity. Lowell's studies, more and more various and incessant, were so comprehensive that, if not like Bacon, all knowledge, yet he took all literature for his province, and in 1855 he was appointed to the chair of modern languages and belles lettres in Harvard University, succeeding Longfellow and Ticknor, an illustrious group of American scholars which gives to that chair a distinction unparalleled in our schools. His love and mastery of books were extraordinary, and his devotion to study so relentless that in those earlier years he studied sometimes fourteen hours in the day, and pored over books until his sight seemed to desert him. But it was no idle or evanescent reading. Probably no American student was so deeply versed in the old French romance, none knew Dante and the Italians more profoundly; German literature was familiar to him, and perhaps even Ticknor in his own domain of Spanish lore was not more a master than Lowell. The whole range of English literature, not only its noble Elizabethan heights, but a delightful realm of picturesque and unfrequented paths, were his familiar park of pleasance. Yet he was not a scholarly recluse, a pedant or a bookworm. The student of books was no less so acute and trained an observer of nature, so sympathetic a friend of birds and flowers, so sensitive to the influences and aspects of out-of-door life, that, as Charles Briggs, with singular insight, said that he was meant for a politician, so Darwin, with frank admiration, said that he was born to be a naturalist. He was as much the contented companion of Izaak Walton and White, of Selborne, as of Donne or Calderon. His social sympathies were no less strong than his fondness for study, and he was the most fascinating of comrades. His extraordinary knowledge, whether of out-door or in-door derivation, and the racy humor in which his knowledge was fused, overflowed his conversation. There is no historic circle of wits and scholars, not that of Beaumont or Ben Jonson, where haply Shakespeare sat, nor Pope's nor Dryden's nor Addison's, nor Dr. Johnson's Club, nor that of Edinburgh; nor any Parisian salon or German study, to which Lowell's abundance would not have contributed a golden drop, and his glancing wit a glittering repartee. It was not of reading merely, it was of the reading of a man of Lowell's intellectual power and resource, that Bacon said "reading maketh a full man."

THE PROSE OF A POET.

He had said in 1846 that it was as a poet that he could do his best work. But the poetic temperament and faculty do not exclude prose, and like Milton's swain "He touched th tender stops of various quills." The young poet early showed that prose would be as obedient a familiar to his genius as the tricksy Ariel of verse. Racy and rich, and often of the most sonorous or delicate cadence, it is still the prose of a poet and a master of the differences of form. His prose indeed is often profoundly poetic, that is, quick with imagination, but always in the form of prose not of poetry. It is so finely compact of illustration, of thought and learning, of wit and fancy, and permeating humor, that his prose page sparkles and sways like a phosphorescent sea. "Oblivion," he says, "looks in the face of the Grecian muse and forgets her errand." And again: "The garners of Sicily are empty now, but the bees from all climes still fetch honey from the tiny gard n plot of Theocritus." Such concentrated sentences are marvels of felicity and, although unmetred are as exquisite as songs. Charles Emerson said of Shakespeare, "he sat above this hundred-handed play of his imagination pensive and conscious," and so Lowell is remembered by those who knew him well. Literature was his earliest love and his latest delight, and he has been often called the first man of letters of his time. The phrase is vague, but it expresses the feeling that while he was a poet, and a scholar, and a humorist, and a critic, he was something else and something more. The feeling is perfectly just. Living all summer by the sea we watch with fascinated eyes the long-flowing lines, the flash and gleam of multitudinous waters, but beneath them all is the mighty movement of unfathomed ocean on whose surface only these undulating splendors play. Literature, whether in prose or verse, was the form of Lowell's activity, but its master impulse was not esthetic but moral. When the activities of his life were ended, in a strain of clear and tender reminiscence he sang:

"I sank too deep in the soft-stuffed repose,
That hears but rumors of earth's wrongs and woes;
Too well these Capuas could my muscles waste,
Not void of toils, but toils of choice and taste.
These still had kept me could I but have quelled
The Puritan drop that in my veins rebelled."

PATRIOTISM WAS HIS PASSION.

Literature was his pursuit, but patriotism was his passion. His love of country was that of a lover for his mistress. He resented the least imputation upon the ideal America, and nothing was finer than his instinctive scorn for the pinchbeck patriotism which brags and boasts and swaggers, insisting that bigness is greatness and vulgarity simplicity, and the will of a majority the moral law. No man perceived more shrewdly the Amer can readiness of resource, the Yankee good nature, and the national rectitude. But he was not satisfied with an easy standard. To him the best, not the thriftiest, was most truly American. Lowell held that of all men the American should be master of his boundless material resources, not their slave, worthy of his unequalled opportunities, not the sycophant of his fellow Americans nor the victim of national conceit. No man rejoiced more deeply over our great achievements or celebrated them with ampler or prouder praise. He delighted with Yankee glee in our inventive genius and restless enterprise, but he knew that we did not invent the great muniments of liberty, trial by jury, the habeas corpus, constitutional restraint, the common school, of which we were common heirs with civilized Christendom. He knew that we have Niagara, and the prairies and the great lakes, and the majestic Mississippi; but he knew also with another great American that still

"Earth proudly wears the Parthenon
As the best gem upon her zone.
And morning opes with haste his lids
To gaze upon the Pyramids."

As he would not accept a vulgar caricature of the New-Englander as a Yankee, so he spurned Captain Bobadil as a type of the American, for he knew that a nation may be as well-bred among nations as a gentleman among gentlemen, and that to bully weakness or to cringe to strength are equally cowardly, and therefore not truly American.

Lowell's loftiest strain is inspired by this patriotic ideal. To borrow a German phrase from modern musical criticism it is the leit motif which is constantly heard in the poems and the essays, and that inspiration reached its loftiest expression, both in prose and poetry, in the discourse on Democracy and the Commemoration Ode. The genius of enlightened Greece breathes audibly still in the oration of Pericles on the Peloponnesian dead. The patriotic heart of America throbs forever in Lincoln's Gettysburg address. But nowhere in literature is there a more magnificent and majestic personification of a country whose name is sacred to its children, nowhere a profounder passion of patriotic loyalty, than in the closing lines of the Commemoration Ode. The American whose heart, swayed by that lofty music, does not thrill and palpitate with solemn joy and high resolve, does not yet know what it is to be an American.

ALSO A PUBLIC CRITIC AND CENSOR.

Like all citizens of high public ideals Lowell was inevitably a public critic and censor, but he was much too good a Yankee not to comprehend the practical conditions of political life in this cuntry. No man understood better than he such truth as lies in John Morley's remark: "Parties are a field where action is a long second best, and where the choice constantly lies between two blunders." He did not therefore conclude that there is no alternative, that "naught is ev.rything and everything is naught." But he did see clearly that while the government of a republic must be a government of party, yet that independence of party is much more vitally essential in a r. public than fidelity to party. Party is a servant of the people, but a servant who is foolishly permitted by his master to assume sovereign airs, like Christopher Sly, the tinker, whom the Lord's attendants obsequiously salute as master:

"Look how thy servants do attend on thee;
Each in his office ready at thy beck."

To a man of the highest public spirit like Lowell, and of the supreme self-respect which always keeps faith with itself, no spectacle is sadder than that of intelligent, superior, honest public men prostrating themselves before a party, professing what they do not believe, affecting what they do not feel, from abject fear of an invisible fetich, a chimera, a name, to which they alone give reality and force, as the terrified peasant himself made the spectre of the Brocken before which he quailed. The last patriotic service of Washington, and none is more worthy of enduring commemoration on this anniversary, was the farewell address, with its strong and stern warning that party government may become a ruthless despotism, and that a majority must be watched as jealously as a king.

With his lofty patriotism and his extraordinary public conscience Lowell was distinctively the Independent in politics. He was an American and a republican citizen. He acted with parties as every citizen must act if he acts at all. But the notion that a voter is a traitor to one party when he votes with another was as ludicrous to him as the assertion that it is treason to the White Star steamers to take passage in a Cunarder. When he would know his public duty Lowell turned within, not without. He listened, not for the roar of the majority in the street, but for the still small voice in his own breast. For while the method of republican government is party, its basis is individual conscience and common-sense. This entire political independence Lowell always illustrated. He was born in the last days of New-England Federalism. His uncle, John Lowell, was a leader in the long and bitter Federalist controversy with John Quincy Adams. The Whig dynasty succeeded the Federal in Massachusetts, but Lowell's first public interest was the anti-slavery agitation, and he identified himself with the abolitionists. But he retained his individual view and did not sympathize with the policy that sought the dissolution of the Union, and which refused to vote. In 1850 he says in a private letter to his friend Gay, alluding to some differences of opinion with the Anti-Slavery Society, "there has never been a oneness of sentiment." that is to say complete identity, "between me and the society," and a passage in a letter written upon election day, November, 1850, illustrates his independent position: "I shall vote the Union ticket (half Free Soil and half Democratic), not from any love of the Democrats, but because I believe it to be the best calculated to achieve some practical result. It is a great object to overturn the Whig domination, and this seems to be the only lever to pry them over with. Yet I have my fears that if we get a Democratic Governor he will play some trick or other. Timeo Danaos et dona ferentes, if you will pardon stale Latin to Parson Wilbur."

HE WAS NEVER A PARTISAN.

This election is memorable because it overthrew the Whig domination in Massachusetts and made Charles Sumner the successor of Daniel Webster in the Senate. It restored to the State of Samuel Adams the same political leadership before the Civil War that she had held before the Revolution. The Republican party, with whose anti-slavery impulse Lowell was in full accord, arose from the Whig ruins, and whether in a party or out of a party, he was himself the great illustration of the political independence that he represented and maintained. As he allowed no church or sect to dictate his religious views or control his daily conduct, so he permitted no party to direct his political action. He was a Whig, an Abolitionist, a Republican, a Democrat, according to his conception of the public exigency, and never as a partisan. From 1863 to 1872 he was joint editor with his friend, Mr. Norton, of "The North American Review," and he wrote often of public affairs. But his papers all belong to the higher politics, which are those of the man and the citizen, not of the partisan, a distinction which may be traced in Burke's greatest speeches, where it is easy to distinguish what is said by Burke the wise and patriotic Englishman, for such he really was, from what is said by the Whig in opposition to the Treasury Bench.

But whatever his party associations and political sympathies, Lowell was at heart and by temperament conservative, and his patriotic independence in our politics is the quality which is always unconsciously recognized as the truly conservative element in the country. In the tumultuous excitement of our popular elections the appeal on both sides is not to party, which is already committed, but to those citizens who are still open to reason and may yet be persuaded. In the most recent serious party appeal, the orator said: "Above all things, political fitness should lead us not to forget that at the end of our plans we must meet face to face at the polls the voters of the land with ballots in their hands demanding as a condition of the support of our party fidelity and undivided devotion to the cause in which we have enlisted them." This recognizes an independent tribunal which judges party. It implies that beside the host who march under the party color and vote at the party command, there are citizens who may or may not wear a party uniform, but who vote only at their own individual command, and who give the victory. They may be angrily classified as political Laodiceans, but it is to them that parties appeal, and rightly, because except for this body of citizens the despotism of party would be absolute and the republic would degenerate into a mere oligarchy of "bosses."

A TRIBUTE TO INDEPENDENCE.

There could be no more signal tribute to political independence than that which was offered to Lowell in 1876. He was a Republican Elector, and the result of the election was disputed. A peaceful solution of the difference seemed for some months to be doubtful, although the Constitution apparently furnished it, for if an elector, or more than one, should differ from his party and exercise his express and unquestionable constitutional right, in strict accord with the constitutional intention, the threatened result might be averted. But in the multitude of electors Lowell alone was mentioned as one who might exercise that right. The suggestion was at once indignantly resented as an insult, because it was alleged to imply possible bad faith. But it was not so designed. It indicated that Lowell was felt to be a man who, should he think it to be his duty under the undisputable constitutional provision, to vote differently from the expectation of his party, he would certainly do it. But those who made the suggestion did not perceive that he could not feel it to be his duty, because nobody saw more clearly than he that an unwritten law with all the force of honor forbade. The constitutional intention was long since superseded by a custom sanctioned by universal approval, which makes the Presidential Elector the merest ministerial agent of a party, and the most wholly ceremonial figure in our political system.

By the time that he was fifty years old Lowell's conspicuous literary accomplishment and poetic genius with his political independence, courage and ability, had given him a position and influence unlike those of any other American, and when in 1877 he was appointed Minister to Spain, and in 1880 transferred to England, there was a feeling of blended pride and satisfaction that his country would be not only effectively but nobly represented. Mr. Emerson once said of an English Minister, "he is a charming gentleman, but he does not represent the England that I know." In Lowell, however, no man in the world who honored America and believed in the grandeur of American destiny but would find his faith and hope confirmed. To give your best, says the Oriental proverb, is to do your utmost. The coming of such a man was the highest honor that America could pay to England. If we may personify America we can fancy a certain grim humor on her part in presenting this son of hers to the mother country, a sapling of the older oak more sinewy and supple than the parent stock. No eminent American has blended the Cavalier and the Puritan tradition, the romantic conservatism and the wise radicalism of the English blood, in a finer cosmopolitanism than Lowell. It was this generous comprehension of both which made him peculiarly and intelligently at home in England, and which also has made him more than His Excellency the Ambassador of American Literature to the Court of Shakespeare, as "The London Spectator" called him upon his arrival in London, for it made him the representative to England of an American scholarship, a wit, an intellectual resource, a complete and splendid accomplishment, a social grace and charm, a felicity of public and private speech, and a weight of good sense, which pleasantly challenged England to a continuous and friendly bout in which America did not suffer.

HIS LIFE IN ENGLAND.

During his official residence in England Lowell seemed to have the fitting word for every occasion and to speak it with memorable distinction. If a memorial of Dean Stanley were erected in his chapter House, or of Fielding at Taunton, or of Coleridge in Westminster Abbey, or of Gray at Cambridge, the desire of literary England turned instinctively to Lowell as the orator whose voice would give the best expression, and whose character and renown the greatest dignity, to the hour. In Wordsworth's England, as president of the Wordsworth Society, he spoke of the poet with an affectionate justice which makes his speech the finest essay upon Wordsworth's genius and career, and of Don Quixote he spoke to the Workingman's College with a poetic appreciation of the genius of Cervantes and a familiarity with Spanish literature which was a revelation to British workmen. Continuously at public dinners, with consummate tact and singular felicity, he spoke with a charm which seemed to disclose a new art of oratory. He did not decline even political speech, but of course in no partisan sense. His discourse on Democracy, at Birmingham, in October, 1884, was not only an event, but an event without precedent. He was the Minister of the American Republic to the British Monarchy, and, as that Minister, publicly to declare in England the most radical democratic principles as the ultimate logical result of the British Constitution, and to do it with a temper, an urbanity, a moderation, a precision of statement and a courteous grace of humor, which charmed doubt into acquiescence, and amazement into unfeigned admiration and acknowledgment of a great service to political thought greatly done—this was an event unknown in the annals of diplomacy, and this is what Lowell did at Birmingham.

PERHAPS HIS GREATEST SERVICE.

No American orator has made so clear and comprehensive a declaration of the essential American principle, or so simple a statement of its ethical character. Yet not a word of this republican, to whom Algernon Sydney would have bowed and whom Milton would have blest, would have jarred the Tory nerves of Sir Roger de Coverley, although no English Radical was ever so radical as he. The frantic French Democracy of '93, gnashing its teeth in the face of royal power, would have equality and fraternity, it every man were guillotined to secure it. The American Republic, speaking to monarchical Europe a century later by the same voice with which Sir Launfal had shown the identity of Christianity with human sympathy and succor, set forth in the address at Birmingham the truth that Democracy is simply the practical application of moral principle to politics. There were many and great services in Lowell's life, but none of them all seem to me more characteristic of the man than when, holding the commission of his country, in his own person representing its noblest character, standing upon soil sacred to him by reverend and romantic tradition, his American heart loyal to the English impulse, which is the impulse of constitutional liberty, for one memorable moment he made monarchical England feel for republican America the same affectionate admiration that she felt for him, the republican American. His last official words in England show the reciprocal feeling. "While I came here as a far-off cousin," he said, "I feel that you are sending me away as something like a brother." He died, the poet, the scholar, the critic, the public counsellor, the ambassador, the patriot, and the sorrowing voice of the English Laureate and of the English Queen, the highest voices of English literature and political power, mingling with the universal voice of his own country, showed how surely the true American faithful to the spirit of Washington and of Abraham Lincoln reconciles and not exasperates international feeling.

A FASCINATING AND INSPIRING FIGURE.

So varied, full and fair is the story of Lowell's life, and such services to the mind and heart and character of his country we commemorate on this hallowed day. In the golden morning of our literature and National life there is no more fascinating and inspiring figure. His literary achievement, his patriotic distinction, and his ennobling influence upon the character and lives of generous American youth, gave him at last power to speak with more authority than any living American for the intellect and conscience of America. Upon those who knew him well so profound was the impression of his resource and power that their words must seem to be mere eulogy. All that he did was but the hint of this superb affluence, this comprehensive grasp; the overflow of an exhaustless supply, so that it seemed to be only incidental, not his life's business. Even his literary production was impromptu. "Sir Launfal" was the work of two days. "The Fable for Critics" was an amusement amid severer studies. The discourse on Democracy was largely written upon the way to Birmingham. Of no man could it be said more truly that

"Half his strength he put not forth."

But that must be always the impression of men of so large a mould and of such public service that they may be properly commemorated on this anniversary. Like mountain summits, bright with sunrise, that announce the day, such Americans are harbingers of the future which shall justify our faith and fulfil the promise of America to mankind. In our splendid statistics of territorial extension, of the swift civilization of the Western world, of the miracles of our material invention; in that vast and smiling landscape, the home of a powerful and peaceful people, humming with industry and enterprise, rich with the charm of every climate from Katahdin, that hears the distant roar of the Atlantic to the Golden Gate through which the soft Pacific sighs, and in every form of visible prosperity we see the resplendent harvest of the mighty sowing, 200 years ago, of the new continent with the sifted grain of the old. But this is not the picture of a National greatness, it is only its glittering frame. Intellectual excellence, noble character, public probity, lofty ideals, art, literature, honest politics, righteous laws, conscientious labor, public spirit, social justice, the stern, self-criticising patriotism which fosters only what is worthy of an enlightened people, not what is unworthy—such qualities and such achievements, and such alone, measure the greatness of a State, and those who illustrate them are great. citizens. They are men whose lives are a glorious service and whose memories are a benediction. Among that great company of patriots let me to-day, reverently and gratefully, blend the name of Lowell with that of Washington.

CHARLES STEWART PARNELL

A GREAT MEETING IN THE ACADEMY OF MUSIC.

CHAUNCEY M. DEPEW DELIVERS AN ELOQUENT ORATION ON THE LIFE OF THE DEAD IRISH LEADER.

Eleven years ago Colonel Henry A. Gildersleeve, now Judge, stood upon a platform in the Madison Square Garden and introduced for the first time to an American audience Charles Stewart Parnell, who in company with John Dillon had come to the United States to plead the cause of the suffering people of Ireland, a large part of which country was then overshadowed by famine. On November 15 Judge Gildersleeve again presided at a meeting, this time in the Academy of Music, but it was not the living personality, but the cold marble bust of the dead Irish leader that was close by. Around it was a wreath, the gift of the Polish societies of New-York, the sad history of whose own country is in many respects similar to the sad history of Erin. A large portrait of Parnell was also on view, together with a wreath, sent from the women of Cork specially for the occasion. The wreath was made of laurels and shamrocks, the latter plucked from the grave of Parnell in Ireland's National cemetery at Glasnevin, Dublin. The memorial meeting was organized by the Municipal Council of the Irish National League aided by the different county societies and all the other Irish organizations of the city John McConvill was chairman of the Committee of Arrangements. It was a full house, and although a memorial meeting is not exactly an occasion for cheers and applause, the irrepressible Celt found it impossible to keep still when the familiar face and stately figure of Chauncey M. Depew, who was to deliver the oration on Parnell, appeared upon the platform, escorted by Judge Gildersleeve and some members of the committee, and sat down, awaiting his turn to speak. The platform was draped in purple, and in a conspicuous place was the touching request of the Irish leader as he lay dying: "Give my love to my colleagues and the people of Ireland.'

SOME OF THOSE PRESENT.

Among those present were Governor-elect William McKinley, jr., of Ohio; ex-Senator James Daly, William J. Knoud, Michael Breslin, Judge James Fitzgerald, ex-Judge Edward Browne, John W. Goff, Congressman Campbell, ex-Judge Van Hoesen, Colonel W. L. Brown, J. P. Farrell, R. M. Walters, Dr. Philip E. Donlin, T. St. John Gaffney, Roderick J. Kennedy, Matthew Carroll, Mrs. Marguerite Moore, Lawrence F. Fullam, Daniel Riordan, R. D. Walsh, of Chicago; Lieutenant Moran, Captain D. C. McCarthy, and Colonel James Cavanagh, of the 69th Regiment; John J. Rogers, John Torney, Barnard O'Beirne, ex-Congressman Quinn, B. G. McSwyny, Assistant District-Attorney Lynn, Stephen McFarland, Edward O'Flaherty, Michael Giblin, John J. Murphy, Stephen McPartland, Civil Justice Murray, ex-Police Justice Murray, ex-Congressman McAdoo and William P. Mitchell.

Bayne's 69th Regiment Band furnished the music. By permission of Walter Damrosch, of the Symphony Orchestra, Miss Inez Carusi played some selections on the harp. The orchestra played a funeral march, composed and dedicated to the

Parnell Memorial Committee by William Barton Stone, and a quartette sang Cardinal Newman's hymn, "Lead, Kindly Light."

John McConvill opened the meeting in a brief and stirring speech and introduced Judge Gildersleeve as chairman. Judge Gildersleeve's introductory speech was also brief and eloquent, and was well received.

MR. DEPEW WARMLY WELCOMED.

Chauncey M. Depew, on rising to make the oration of the evening, was applauded again and again. Mr. Depew said:

Ladies and Gentlemen: We are here to pay tribute to the memory of a man who made an indelible impress upon his times and performed incalculable services for his country. In this audience are Irishmen of all creeds and widely divergent views on questions affecting Ireland, who for the evening and the occasion lay aside their antagonism to plant a flower upon the grave of one of the most eminent of their race. (Applause.)

The weaknesses and the errors of great leaders are an inseparable part of the elements which effect their fortunes while living, but, when they are dead, the sum of their services to their people is their monument. A career crowded with battles, persecutions, imprisonments, defeats and triumphs, concentrating in one individuality the hopes and fears, the passions and resentments of a nation for centuries, could not end without leaving behind controversies which time and opportunity alone can heal. But we have not met to discuss or settle the party differences of the hour. It is our purpose to recognize and gracefully remember the wisdom, the patriotism, the courage and the superb generalship with which Charles Stewart Parnell organized and led his countrymen to within sight of the promised land of self-government. The historian of this period cannot write the chronicles of Germany without Bismarck, of France without Gambetta, of Italy without Cavour and Garibaldi, of Ireland without Parnell. (Applause.)

The history of modern Ireland begins with the century. Prior to that is a fearful story of wars, confiscations, executions and transportations of whole populations from their lands and homes. It is a monotony of horrors. All European countries have been ravaged by the armies of foreign invaders and devastated by civil strifes, but with conquest or exhaustion has come peace. Then has followed recuperation and prosperity. Commerce has revived, manufactories have flourished, internal improvements have been made, new cities have been founded, and old ones have increased in inhabitants and importance, and there has been solid growth in population and wealth.

A SAD AND SOLITARY EXCEPTION.

Ireland forms the solitary exception to the beneficent power of peace. Her industries have one by one been paralyzed until few manufactures remain and those are confined to limited territory. Her population has been reduced nearly one-half in the last fifty years. Her story is the paradox of nations. When most at rest she has suffered the most misery. These results must be due to either the conditions of climate and soil, the temper and capacity of the people, or bad government. The land is not to blame. The Emerald Isle was fashioned by God to be an earthly paradise. Its fertile fields invite agriculture and abundantly reward the husbandman. Its noble harbors ought to shelter prosperous commerce, and hospitably entertain the mercantile marine of the world, and its innumerable locations for the successful development of varied industries should attract capital and enterprise.

It is not the fault of the Irish people. Driven from home they have settled all over the globe, and are everywhere distinguished for industry, enterprise and thrift. They take leading positions in the professions and in business. They show special aptitude for politics, and win distinction in public life. Then her condition must be due to what Mr. Gladstone had recently characterized as centuries of wrong, and every Parliamentary leader in England for a half century has, under the pressure of the evidence of Royal Commissioners, or when telling the truth to undermine the party power, denounced in language as vigorous as the passionate utterances of Irish patriots.

The forms of self-government without the spirit of liberty work greater injustice than absolutism.

The autocrat can be forced to listen to the cry of his people, but when they are misrepresented, or not represented at all, in the federal congress, they have no voice. There was no possibility of the Imperial Parliament hearing or knowing or caring for the wrongs or aspirations of Ireland until Parnell. (Applause.) He compelled Parliament to hear and know and care. Parnell was born 100 years after Grattan, and he entered the British Parliament just a century after Grattan became a member of the Irish Parliament. It was a century of fruitless struggles, of fearful famine, of patient waiting, breaking out occasionally into fierce revolt, to be repressed with relentless ferocity, of wholesale evictions of tenant farmers and vast emigrations to foreign lands.

Grattan was the most eloquent speaker of a period famous for its orators, and a commanding genius when the country was rich in men of genius. His unequalled appeals for liberty have been the inspiration of the patriots of many lands and alien tongues. He was himself the first-born across the seas of the ideas of the American Revolution. The man who took up the traditions of his failure and crystallized them into the forces of success after the lapse of ten decades, had neither eloquence nor genius, but he possessed the tireless energy, the grasp of his surroundings and the directness of aim which command the business senates of our day. (Applause.)

A TRIBUTE TO O'CONNELL.

The nineteenth century was ushered into immediate contact with its needs and possibilities by the superb figure of Daniel O'Connell. He began in 1800 his glorious struggle for Catholic emancipation. Four-fifths of his countrymen were denied the suffrage, and two-thirds, on account of their religious faith, were not permitted the ordinary rights of person and property. He stood at the head of his people more like a prophet of the Old Testament, who led by faith, than a modern reformer. Napoleon with the assistance of a vast and complicated machinery conscripted an army of hundreds of thousands of men, but O'Connell attracted an audience of half a million people. He felt and enforced the lesson of liberty, that all men are equal before the law. The majestic power of such a following behind such a leader conquered the prejudices and convinced the judgments of Sir Robert Peel and the Iron Duke. The victor of Waterloo surrendered to the united demand of Ireland voiced by her greatest son. It was a signal triumph of moral force and constitutional method, where revolution had always failed. The Liberator, as his countrymen lovingly named him, found his victory incomplete, the redemption of his people impossible under the operation of land laws which were the legal cover for every form of persecution and injustice.

With the suffrage so restricted that there was no popular representation, the Irish delegation was filled with members blindly obedient to one or the other of the two great English parties, and indifferent or hostile to the interests of the vast non-voting population whom they misrepresented. It was not in the power of O'Connell or of any man to inform the British Parliament or the English constituencies of the real condition of Ireland, when the large majority of Irish members denied the existence of wrongs to be righted or evils to be remedied. O'Connell saw that the only possible relief was to have all Irish questions relegated to an Irish Parliament, and he boldly struck for a repeal of the Union. His object was not to dismember the Empire, but to secure the administration of Irish domestic affairs to the Irish people—a thought evidently suggested by the success of the Federal principle in the United States. The despair of O'Connell was the birth of Home Rule. It was the desperate groping in the dark for that idea, which, perfected by disheartening defeats and discouraging betrayals, is to-day the aspiration of most Irishmen, and the belief of the majority in England, Scotland and Wales. (Applause.)

The patriot and statesman saw the impending famine. The combined operation of laws which suppressed manufacturing and varied industries, and drove a whole population to agriculture, which permitted neither freedom of transfer nor security of tenure, and subjected whole countries to rack rents and evictions by absentee landlords, was culminating in one of the most frightful calamities which ever befell a nation. He made one last, grand and pathetic appeal. Parliament was deaf, his colleagues from Ireland were indifferent, and O'Connell died of a broken heart.

Three millions of people dependent on public relief, a million dead from starvation and fevers, one-half the population of the country seeking in exile homes and an opportunity to live are the cold figures which crystallize for the historian results, but the horrid details are beyond the power of language to describe, or the imagination to grasp. From the depths of this misery sprang revolution, heroic efforts, desperate conspiracies, every form of patriotic endeavor, or wild unreasoning vengeance to be suppressed by an ever present and overwhelming force. It was the opportunity of the office-hunter and adventurer, of the Keoghs and Sadliers, to secure by popular favor power which could be bartered for place or pelf.

PARNELL AS A LEADER.

In a representative Government, composed of different States, existing under divers conditions, the pride of Empire, the sense of security, the feeling of nationality, will always combine the united force of the whole against the effort of any part to violently disrupt the State. While the fight lasts and the fever of nationality is on, they will be blind and deaf to the just demand of the dissatisfied member. The necessity of the disaffected and injured Commonwealth is a competent and incorruptible leader, and a united and loyal representation in the Federal Congress.

Such a commander, with devoted followers, will know no party, except that which recognizes his demands, will permit no measures to pass until the petition of his people has been heard and its prayer answered. This ideal leader was Charles Stewart Parnell. (Cheers.) The time was not yet ripe for this new force. It was a needed preparation, both for the Irish people and the Imperial Parliament, that the old methods should be fairly tried under a leader of ability and integrity. He was found in that picturesque and most interesting personality, Isaac Butt. He tried to consolidate Irish representation for Home Rule. He was compelled to accept candidates who cared more for their Liberal or Tory affiliations than for Irish measures. He was surrounded by members who feared the social ostracism of London society, and longed for the rich places in the British Civil Service. Yet this brilliant, courageous, undaunted patriot, struggling with poverty, besieged by bailiffs, sacrificing his professional income to his public duties, rose from every defeat, to begin anew with unabated ardor and hope, his battle for justice and liberty.

His fight was within the lines of his party, and he never succeeded in convincing its managers that Ireland had wrongs to redress, or of teaching them that coercion was not the way to settle Irish questions and give peace to the Emerald Isle. At the hour when the prospect was darkest, and the Irish were despairing of their cause, there appeared upon the field a champion who presented none of the externals of heroism or leadership. No herald trumpeted his coming, no applause greeted his arrival. His comrades had not noticed his presence, the enemy was not aware of his existence. He hated publicity, but was destined to be the most conspicuous figure in the Empire. He disliked to speak, and whenever possible avoided the forum or the platform, but he was to effectively voice the demands and principles which had taxed the resources of the greatest orators of a nation justly famed for eloquence. He was cold in manner, undemonstrative, self-poised, imperturbable, neither elated nor depressed, and yet he became the idol of the most impulsive of peoples.

The weakness of leaders is their jealousy of talent among their followers. Many a cause has been imperilled or lost and many a party driven from power because the chief could not endure the praise bestowed upon his lieutenants. Parnell welcomed ability, and gave its possessor every opportunity for distinction. His superiors in eloquence, like Sexton and Redmond, in literature, like McCarthy and O'Connor, in journalism or popular appeal, like Sullivan, or O'Brien, or Dillon, or Harrington, were given the places where they could best serve. If he had ambitions other than for his country, they were never apparent. If he had likes or animosities, they never stood in the way of a useful man occupying his proper place.

GOD SAVE IRELAND.

The inspiration which started him in his career and guided him in his work was the motto of the Manchester martyr, "God Save Ireland." He saw that for Irishmen to plot against the Castle or hurl themselves on the bayonets of the soldiery was madness. He proclaimed that any man who committed a crime was a foe to Ireland. He found that Home Rule was a subject for debate, which the House of Commons would wearily listen to and both parties unite to

kill. And yet he resolved to win by moral force and constitutional methods.

He became master of the rules of the House, and then used them to stop its business. With only three who dared follow, he attacked 600 and odd, entrenched in the forms, the usages, and the traditions of centuries. "No measure shall pass until the demands of Ireland are granted," was his battle cry. Tories were shocked, Liberals indignant. Radicals amazed, and the Speaker paralyzed. Isaac Butt feared the result, and withheld his support. Shaw thought the movement was not respectable, and most of the Irish members agreed with him.

Parliamentary procedure is the growth of generations of representative government. It is the pride and glory of England. It preserves the constitution, and crystallizes into law the opinions of the people. It permits the weight of popular sentiment to so balance parties as to put power into the hands of the one which, for the time, best voices public opinion. To interrupt the smooth and accustomed working of this venerable machinery was accounted little less than sacrilege, and believed to be flat treason. Obstruction buried for the moment partisan animosities and ambitions, and brought together all elements to crush the obstructionist. Though threatened with the unknown perils and punishment and the frightful possibilities of being named by the Speaker, though menaced with suspension, and put under the ban of personal and social ostracism, though treated with derision in the House and contempt in the press, the undismayed and unruffled leader stood with his little band across the path of public business, demanding justice for Ireland.

He baffled the statesmen who had led the House of Commons for generations by showing them that they could neither stop nor suspend nor expel, for he was acting strictly within their own rules and fighting with weapons from their own armory. Then said Mr. Gladstone: "When you show us that a majority of the members from Ireland want legislation, we are prepared to listen and act." This proposition could not be satisfactorily answered. Parnell believed that the people of Ireland were with him, but he knew, as did the House, that their representatives were not. Senates do not go behind Senates to canvass their constituents, and Parnell recognized the fatal force of Mr. Gladstone's proposition. Party leaders, as a rule, are eminent and powerful within recognized lines, and by the skilful handling of men and measures.

Great crises develop original genius for the emergency, like Abraham Lincoln. They win triumphs by methods which the veteran soldier has learned neither in school nor on the field, and which he either derides or distrusts. Parnell was the most resourceful of men, with unlimited confidence in himself, and the rare faculty which inspires unquestioning obedience in others. He said to the Irish people, if you believe in me, you must be represented in Parliament by members who will act with me, and who can neither be misled, nor intimidated, nor bought. Give your answer to Mr. Gladstone's challenge. The response has no parallel in the history of the electorate under free governments. It was, "Select your own candidates. Mr. Parnell, and we will elect them." Experience had demonstrated that under the pressure and temptations at Westminster and the disintegrating influences at home, something more than a common sentiment was required to keep constituencies solid and members constant. For this purpose Parnell took control and perfected the machinery of the Land League, which had been organized by Michael Davitt.

THE DIFFICULT LAND QUESTION.

It is difficult for Americans to appreciate the Irish land question. Real estate with us is sold and exchanged as freely as any other commodity. A bargain with regard to the soil has all the incidents of other commercial transactions. But the land system of Ireland had made a large majority of the population the tenants of a few landlords. The laws were wholly on the side of the landowners and administered by their agents. The comfort and misery of millions of human beings, the peace or unrest of the Kingdom, was not dependent upon legislation, but on the whim or wisdom of irresponsible and unrelated individuals. The necessities of a spendthrift in London, losses at the gambling table at Homburg, or the irritation of the lord against his vassals, would raise rents beyond the possibility of their being earned, and evict thousands to die by the roadside without compensation for improvements or opportunity for defence.

It is a frightful commentary on the situation that during the famine which carried over a million of men.

women and children to their graves, there was plenty
j food produced in Ireland, but it all went for rent,
while the potatoes, the sole resource of the tenant,
rotted in the ground. The ship from America laden
with provisions for the starving passed at the entrance
of the harbor of Cork three vessels sailing out and
filled with export wheat. The British Parliament, the
most conservative of bodies, and ruled by landed proprietors, became so impressed with these conditions
that between 1870 and 1890 it enacted several of the
most sweeping acts ever put upon the statute book
for the relief and protection of the tenantry of Ireland.
(Applause).

Thus in gaining control of the Land League, Parnell
had the deepest interests of the people as the foundation for political sentiment and personal loyalty.
When he entered Parliament at the head of 83 out of
103 representatives from Ireland, he held in one hand
party power and in the other the homes and the fortunes of his people. He had returned in triumph. The
Commons were bewildered. The calm and confident
leader, who had defied them with three followers, now
faced them with the larger number of the Irish members behind him. "I have come with the majority
you demanded," he said, "will you listen now?" From
that hour the Irish question became the foremost factor
in British politics, and Parnell the most powerful member of the House of Commons. The time-worn policy
of coercion put him in Kilmainham jail, and it became
not the cell of a criminal, but the palace of an un-
crowned king. The Ministry which imprisoned him
negotiated with him as with a conqueror.

The question was not on what terms will we set you
free, but on what conditions will you accept release?
He did not mince matters. He demanded, and was
accorded, the settlement of arrears of rent, the amend-
ment of the land act, the abandonment of coercion and
the retirement of Mr. Forster, the coercion Minister.
As Parnell, fresh from prison, entered the House, Mr.
Forster, the defeated Minister, in a memorable speech,
placed upon the brow of the victor this wreath: "I
think we may remember what a Tudor king said to a
great Irishman in former times, 'If all Ireland cannot govern the Earl of Kildare, let the Earl of Kildare
govern Ireland." In like manner, if all England cannot govern the honorable member for Cork, then let
us acknowledge that he is the greatest power in Ireland to-day."

The Tories hailed his alliance with delight. The
members who had denounced him as an arch-con-
spirator, and believed him to be in league with assas-
sins, now embraced him as an associate and bid high
for his support. Local self-government became a conservative war cry. The principle which has been the
contemptuous football of parties, became the chief
plank in their platforms. (Applause.)

INSENSIBLE TO FLATTERY.

But Parnell was insensible to flattery and unmoved
by promises. He wanted measures and not pledges.
He was cordial with the party which was at the
moment most likely to adopt and pass his bills, but he
cared nothing for either party. He became the
potential force in the Government. He made and un-
made Cabinets. He hurled the Gladstone Ministry
from power and defeated that of Lord Salisbury.
He compelled the adjournment of Parliament and an
appeal to the country. The conversion of Mr. Gladstone to Home Rule for Ireland is the most momentous
event in the English politics of our generation. He
went to defeat and out of power on the issue, and has
steadily kept it as the test of faith. The splendor of
this statesman's acquirements and achievements ob-
scures his defects and weaknesses.

He has had, in his time, no equal as the leader of the
Opposition. Peerless as an orator, resourceful, versatile, aggressive, positive, fertile in attack, and skilful

in retreat, he soon puts his adversaries in the
wrong, and regains the confidence of his countrymen.
It is only in power that he shows uncertainty of policy.
When he is burdened with the responsibilities of government, it often happens that it is only after he has made
up his mind that he is in doubt. But in the heat of
battle and the fury of the fight this hero of many fields
does not waver, and Home Rule is in desperate struggle
until an Irish Parliament convenes on Dublin Green.
He saw that Parnell represented the Irish people, and
formulated a Home Rule bill to meet their demands.
His defeat, coming, as it did, through the defection of
cherished friends, intensified his ardor and confirmed
his purpose. He made the principle of Home Rule the
cardinal doctrine of his party, and challenged Tories
and Liberal Unionists to go to the country upon the
issue.

Ireland no longer fights with one arm tied and the
other held back by false friends. Parnell freed them
both. Ireland no longer struggles alone, her cause is
the stake of one of the great parties of England, and
made so by Parnell. (Applause.)

Where all others had failed, he succeeded. The
weary waiting, the almost hopeless struggle of a century for local self-government, has nearly ended, and
the victory is practically won, because, with the existing and growing sentiment and party support in England, Scotland and Wales, backed by a united front
from Ireland, the first act of the Parliament to be
elected next year will be a complete and satisfactory
measure of Home Rule. This is the triumph of Parnell.
The laws now in force for the benefit of Ireland, which
are the direct result of his efforts, would immortalize
the memory of any statesman, and give him high rank
on the list of patriots.

During O'Connell's time every act proposed for the
relief of the Irish people was killed, but nineteen bills
were passed suspending the writ of habeas corpus, and
twelve to facilitate evictions and enlarge the area of
crimes and punishments. Isaac Butt's brilliant career
presents to the historian years of splendid effort and
barren results. Not a single measure of importance
rewarded his labors. Upon Parnell's monument his
grateful countrymen will inscribe four acts which are a
distinct recognition of tenants' rights, and long strides
toward the redress of tenants' wrongs. (Applause.)

THE LESSON OF HIS LIFE.

The lesson of Parnell's life is the superiority of constitutional over revolutionary methods. He demonstrated that nothing is impossible for Ireland in the
Imperial Parliament if her sons are both united and
wise. His agitation gave a distinct impulse to the
English Democracy, and educated and strengthened the
radical element in British politics. I have often heard
the remark in London that Americans interest themselves about Home Rule in Ireland only because the
Irish form so important a factor in the American
electorate. It is an ignoble reason for a popular sympathy which is universal in the United States. Our
hearts have often been touched by Irish distress, and
our minds and imaginations fired by our Irish fellow-
citizens, but Home Rule appeals to us as an American
principle. It has so superbly stood the strain and been
so elastic to the needs of a century of progress, that
resistance to its beneficent operation in other lands
arouses our interest and excites our amazement.

Parnell appeals to us with peculiar force as the
grandson of Old Ironsides. The victories of the Constitution were the pride and glory of our young Navy
and are the inspiration of our White Squadron. At
every supreme crisis in Parnell's struggles were visible
the qualities inherited from our hero of the seas. At
his hour of greatest danger, when the Pigott conspiracy
was weaving about him a chain which threatened the
destruction of both himself and his cause, his indifference seemed callousness to crime, and when completely
vindicated, and again the acknowledged leader of a
great constitutional reform, and at the moment of his
grandest triumph, Liberals, Radicals and Home-Rulers
were greeting him with cheers such as never before
resounded in the House, "Parnell stood there with his
arms folded, a block of ice amid the general flame."
I saw Wendell Phillips arouse the coldest and most
critical audience in New-England to madness and fury
without making a gesture or raising his voice above a
conversational tone. The superbly controlled passion
of the speaker fired the minds and imaginations of his
hearers. Their leader of iron and ice grew in the
susceptible hearts and brains of Irishmen until he became idealized into a supernatural figure sent by God
for their deliverance. (Applause.)

CLEVELAND AT ANN ARBOR.

THE EX-PRESIDENT'S ADDRESS AT THE UNIVERSITY OF MICHIGAN.

HE TALKS TO THE STUDENTS ABOUT "SENTIMENT IN OUR NATIONAL LIFE"—THE FREEDOM OF THE CITY PRESENTED TO THE SPEAKER.

Ann Arbor, Mich., Feb. 22.—Ex-President Grover Cleveland, accompanied by ex-Governor Campbell, of Ohio; ex-Postmaster-General Don M. Dickinson, of Detroit; W. S. Bissell, of Buffalo, Mr. Cleveland's former law partner, and Richard Watson Gilder, Editor of "The Century," arrived here to-day at 11:45 a. m. from Detroit. The city was gayly decorated in honor of the party. Fully 2,000 students of the University were gathered at the depot and greeted them with the blare of tin horns and with the University yell. Mayor Doty met the party as they alighted from the train and presented Mr. Cleveland with the freedom of the city in a silver casket. The ex-President replied with a few suitable words of thanks, saying that of all the offices which he had held, he had enjoyed none more than that of mayor.

President Angell, of the University, was then presented and a procession was formed of the Ann Arbor and Ypsilanti military companies, students and residents of this and other cities, which marched through the principal streets. After luncheon at President Angell's residence the party proceeded to University Hall where, at 3 o'clock, Mr. Cleveland delivered an address upon the subject of "Sentiment in our National Life." Here is what he said:

Mr. President, Ladies and Gentlemen: Among the few holidays which the rush and hurry of American life concede to us, surely no one of a secular character is so suggestive and impressive as the day we celebrate on this occasion. We not only commemorate the birth of the greatest American who ever lived, but we recall as inseparably connected with his career all the events and incidents which led up to the establishment of free institutions in this land of ours, and culminated in the erection of our wondrous nation.

The University of Michigan, therefore, most appropriately honors herself and does a fitting public service by especially providing for such an observance of the day as is calculated to turn to the contemplation of patriotic duty the thoughts of the young men whom she is soon to send out to take places in the ranks of American citizenship.

I hope it may not be out of place for me to express the gratification it affords me as a member of the legal profession to know that the conduct of these exercises has been committed to the classes of the law department of the university. There seems to be a propriety in this, for I have always thought the influences surrounding the practice and study of the law should especially induce a patriotic feeling. The business of the profession is related to the enforcement and operation of the laws which govern our people; and its members, more often than those engaged in other occupations, are called to a participation in making these laws. Besides, they are constantly brought to the study of the fundamental law of the land and a familiarity with its history. Such study and familiarity should be sufficient of themselves to increase a man's love of country; and they certainly cannot fail to rouse his veneration for the men who laid the foundations of our Nation sure and steadfast in a written Constitution, which has been declared by the greatest living English statesman to be "the most wonderful work ever struck off at a given time by the brain and purpose of man."

Washington had more to do with the formation of the Constitution than our enthusiasm for other phases of the great work he did for his country usually makes prominent. He fought the battle which cleared the way for it. He best knew the need of consolidating under one government the colonies he had made free, and he best knew that without this consolidation a wasting war, the long and severe privation and suffering his countrymen had undergone and his own devoted labor in the cause of freedom were practically in vain. The beginning of anything like a public sentiment looking to the formation of our Nation is traceable to his efforts. The circular letter he sent to the Governors of the States, as early as the close of the War of the Revolution, contained the germ of the Constitution; and all this was recognized by his unanimous choice to preside over the convention that framed it. His spirit was in and through it all.

But whatever may be said of the argument presented in support of the propriety of giving the law classes the management of this celebration, it is entirely clear that the university herself furnishes to all her students a most useful lesson when, by decreeing the observance of this day, she recognizes the fact that the knowledge of books she imparts is not a complete fulfilment of her duty, and concedes that the education with which she so well equips her graduates for individual success in life and for business and professional usefulness may profitably be supplemented by the stimulation of their patriotism, and by the direction of their thoughts to subjects relating to their country's welfare. I do not know how generally such an observance of Washington's birthday as has been here established prevails in our other universities and colleges; but I am convinced that any institution of learning in our land which neglects to provide for the instructive and improving observance of this day within its walls falls short of its attainable measure of usefulness and omits a just and valuable contribution to the general good. There is great need of educated men in our public life, but it is the need of educated men with patriotism. The college graduate may be, and frequently is, more unpatriotic and less useful in public affairs than the man who, with limited education, has spent the years when opinions are formed in improving contact with the world instead of being within college walls and confined to the study of books. If it be true as is often claimed, that the scholar in politics is generally a failure, it may well be due to the fact that during his formative period, when lasting impressions are easily received, his intellect alone has been cultivated at the expense of wholesome and well-regulated sentiment.

I speak to-day in advocacy of this sentiment. If it is not found in extreme and exclusive mental culture, neither is it found in the busy marts of trade, nor in the confusion of bargaining, nor in the mad rush after wealth. Its home is in the soul and memory of man. It has to do with the moral sense. It reverences traditions, it loves ideas, it cherishes the names and the deeds of heroes and it worships at the shrine of patriotism. I plead for it because there is a sentiment which in some features is distinctively American, that we should never allow to languish. When we are told that we are a practical and common-sense people we are apt to receive the statement with approval and applause. We are proud of its truth and naturally proud because its truth is attributable to the hard work we have had to do ever since our birth as a Nation, and because of the stern labor we still see in our way before we reach our determined destiny. There is cause to suspect, however, that another and less creditable reason for our gratification arises from a feeling that there is something heroically American in treating with indifference or derision all those things which in our view do not directly and palpably pertain to what we call with much satisfaction practical affairs, but which, if we were entirely frank, we should confess might be called money-getting and the betterment of individual condition. Growing out of this feeling an increasing disposition is discernible among our people, which begrudges to sentiment any time or attention that might be given to business and which is apt to crowd out of mind any thought not directly related to selfish plans and purposes.

A little reflection ought to convince us that this may be carried much too far. It is a mistake to regard sentiment as merely something which, if indulged, has a tendency to tempt to idle and useless contemplation or retrospection, thus weakening in a people the sturdiness of necessary endeavor and diluting the capacity for National achievement.

The elements which make up the sentiment of people should not be counted as amiable weaknesses, because they are not at all times noisy and turbulent. The gentleness and loveliness of woman do not cause us to forget that she can inspire man to deeds of greatness and heroism; that as wife she often makes man's career noble and grand, and that as mother she builds and fashions in her sons the strong pillars of a State. So the sentiment of a people which in peace and contentment decks with flowers the temple of their rule may, in rage and fury, thunder at its foundations. Sentiment is the cement which keeps in place the granite blocks of governmental power, or the destructive agency whose explosion heaps in ruins their shattered fragments. The monarch who cares only for his sovereignty and safety leads his subjects to forgetfulness of oppression by a pretence of love for their traditions; and the ruler who plans encroachments upon the liberties of his people shrewdly proceeds under the apparent sanction of their sentiment. Appeals to sentiment have led nations to bloody wars which have destroyed dynasties and changed the lines of imperial territory. Such an appeal summoned our fathers to the battlefields where American independence was won, and such an appeal has scattered soldiers' graves all over the land, which mutely give evidence of the power of our Government and the perpetuity of our free institutions.

I have thus far spoken of a people's sentiment as something which may exist and be effective under any form of government and in any national condition. But the thought naturally follows that if this sentiment may be so potent in countries ruled by a power originating outside of popular will, how vital must its existence and regulation be among our countrymen who rule themselves and administer their own laws. In lands less free than ours, the control of the governed may be more easily maintained, if those who are set over them see fit to make concession to their sentiment; yet, with or without such concession, the strong hand of force may still support the power to govern. But sentiment is the very lifeblood of our Nation. Our Government was conceived amid the thunders that echoed "All men are created equal," and it was brought forth while free men shouted "We, the people of the United States." The sentiment of our fathers, made up of their patriotic intentions,

their sincere beliefs, their homely impulses and their noble aspirations, entered into the government they established; and unless it is constantly supported and guarded by a sentiment as pure as theirs, our scheme of popular rule will fail. Another and a different plan may take its place; but this which we hold in sacred trust, as it originated in patriotism, is only fitted for patriotic and honest uses and purposes, and can only be administered in its integrity and intended beneficence by honest and patriotic men. It can no more be saved nor faithfully conducted by a selfish, dishonest and corrupt people than a stream can rise above its source or be better and purer than its fountain head.

None of us can be ignorant of the ideas which constitute the sentiment underlying our National structure. We know they are a reverent belief in God, a sincere recognition of the value and power of moral principle and those qualities of heart which make a noble manhood, devotion to unreserved patriotism, love for man's equality, unquestioning trust in popular rule, the exactions of civic virtue and honesty, faith in the saving quality of universal education, protection of a free and unperverted expression of the popular will, and an insistence upon a strict accountability of public officers as servants of the people.

These are the elements of American sentiment; and all these should be found deeply imbedded in the minds and hearts of our countrymen. When any one of them is displaced, the time has come when a danger signal should be raised. Their absence among the people of other nations—however great and powerful they may be—can afford us no comfort nor reassurance. We must work out our destiny unaided and alone in full view of the truth that nowhere so directly and surely as here does the destruction or degeneracy of the people's sentiment undermine the foundations of governmental rule.

Let us not for a moment suppose that we can outgrow our dependence upon this sentiment, nor that in any stage of national advance and development it will be less important. As the love of family and kindred remains to bless and strengthen a man in all the vicissitudes of his mature and busy life, so must our American sentiment remain with us as a people—a sure hope and reliance in every phase of our country's growth. Nor will it suffice that the factors which compose this sentiment have a sluggish existence in our minds, as articles of an idle faith which we are willing perfunctorily to profess. They must be cultivated as motive principles, stimulating us to effort in the cause of good government and constantly warning us against the danger and dishonor of faithlessness to the sacred cause we have in charge and heedlessness of the blessings vouchsafed to us and future generations, under our free institutions.

These considerations emphasize the value which should be placed upon every opportunity afforded us for the contemplation of the pure lives and patriotic services of those who have been connected with the controlling incidents of our country's history. Such contemplation cannot fail to reinforce and revive the sentiment absolutely essential to useful American citizenship, nor fail to arouse within us a determination that during our stewardship no harm shall come to the political gifts we hold in trust from the Fathers of the Republic.

It is because George Washington completely represented all the elements of American sentiment that every incident of his life from his childhood to his death is worth recalling—whether it impresses the young with the beauty and value of moral traits, or whether it exhibits to the wisest and oldest an example of sublime accomplishment and the highest possible public s rvice. Even the anecdotes told of his boyhood have their value. I have no sympathy with those who in these latter days attempt to shake our faith in the authenticity of these stories, because they are not satisfied with the evidence in their support, or because they do not s em to accord with the conduct of boys in this generation. It may well be that the stories should stand and the boys of the present day be pitied. At any rate these anecdotes have answered an important purpose; and in the present state of the proofs, they should, in my opinion, be believed. The cherry tree and hatchet incident and its companion declaration that the Father of his Country never told a lie have indelibly fixed upon the mind of many a boy the importance of truthfulness. Of all the legends containing words of advice and encouragement which hung upon the walls of the little district school-hous where a large share of my education was gained, I remember but one, which was in these words: "George Washington had only a common school education."

I will not plead guilty to the charge of dwelling upon the little features of a great subject. I hope the day will never come when American boys cannot know of some trait or some condition in which they may feel that they ought to be or are like Washington. I am not afraid to assert that a multitude of men can be found in every part of our land, respected for their probity and worth, and most useful to the country and to their fellow-men, who will confess their indebtedness to the story of Washington and his hatchet; and many a man has won his way to honor and fame, notwithstanding limited school advantages, because he found hope and incentive in the high mission Washington accomplished with only a common-school education. These are not little and trivial things. They guide and influence the forces which make the character and sentiment of a great people.

I should be ashamed of my country if, in further speaking of what Washington has done for the sentiment of his countrymen, it was necessary to make any excuse for a reference to his constant love and fond reverence, as boy and man, for his mother. This filial love is an attribute of American manhood, a badge which invites our trust and confidence, and an indispensable element of American greatness. A man may compass important enterprises, he may become famous, he may win the applause of his fellows, he may even do public service and deserve a measure of popular approval, but he is not right at heart and can never be truly great if he forgets his mother.

In the latest biography of Washington we find the following statement concerning his mother: "That she was affectionate and loving cannot be doubted, for she retained to the last a profound hold upon the reverential devotion of her son; and yet as he rose steadily to the pinnacle of human greatness, she could only say that 'George has been a good boy, and she was sure he would do his duty.'"

I cannot believe that the American people will consider themselves called upon to share the deprecatory feeling of the biographer, when he writes that the mother of Washington could "only" say of her son that she believed he would be faithful to the highest earthly trusts because he had been good; nor that they will regard her words merely as an amiably tolerated expression of a fond mother. If they are true to American sentiment they will recognize in this language the announcement of the important truth that under our institutions and scheme of government goodness such as Washington's is the best guarantee for the faithful discharge of public duty. They will certainly do well for the country and for themselves if

they adopt the standard the intuition of this noble woman suggests as the measure of their trust and confidence. It means the exaction of moral principle and personal honor and honesty and goodness as indispensable credentials to political preferment.

I have referred only incidentally to the immense influence and service of Washington in forming our Constitution. I shall not dwell upon his lofty patriotism, his skill and fortitude as the military commander who gained our independence, his inspired wisdom, patriotism and statesmanship as first President of the Republic, his constant love for his countrymen and his solicitude for their welfare at all times. The story has been often told, and is familiar to all. If I should repeat it, I should only seek to present further and probably unnecessary proof of the fact that Washington embodied in his character and exemplified in his career that American sentiment in which our Government had its origin, and which I believe to be a condition necessary to our healthful national life.

I have not assumed to instruct you. I have merely yielded to the influence of the occasion and attempted to impress upon you the importance of cultivating and maintaining true American sentiment, suggesting that as it has been planted and rooted in the moral faculties of our countrymen, it can only flourish in their love of truth and honesty, and virtue and goodness. I believe that God has so ordained it for the people He has selected for His special favor; and I know that the decrees of God are never obsolete.

I beg you, therefore, to take with you when you go forth to assume the obligations of American citizenship, as one of the best gifts of your alma mater, a strong and abiding faith in the value and potency of a good conscience and a pure heart. Never yield one iota to those who teach that these are weak and childish things, not needed in the struggle of manhood with the stern realities of life. Interest yourselves in public affairs as a duty of citizenship; but do not surrender your faith to those who discredit and debase politics by scoffing at sentiment and principle, and whose political activity consists in attempts to gain popular support by cunning devices and shrewd manipulation. You will find plenty of those who will smile at your profession of faith and tell you that truth and virtue and honesty and goodness were well enough in the old days when Washington lived, but are not suited to the present size and development of our country and the progress we have made in the art of political management. Be steadfast. The strong and sturdy oak still needs the support of its native earth, and as it grows in size and spreading branches, its roots must strike deeper in the soil which warmed and fed its first tender sprout. You will be told that the people have no longer any desire for the things you profess. Be not deceived. The people are not dead, but sleeping. They will awaken in good time, and scourge the money-changers from their sacred temple.

You may be chosen to public office. Do not shrink from it, for holding office is also a duty of citizenship. But do not leave your faith behind you. Every public office, small or great, is held in trust for your fellow-citizens. They differ in importance, in responsibility and in the labor they impose; but the duties of none of them can be well performed if the mentorship of a good conscience and pure heart be discarded. Of course other equipment is necessary, but without this mentorship all else is insufficient. In times of gravest responsibility it will solve your difficulties; in the most trying hour it will lead you out of perplexities, and it will at all times deliver you from temptation.

In conclusion let me remind you that we may all properly learn the lesson appropriate to Washington's Birthday, if we will; and that we shall fortify ourselves against the danger of falling short in the discharge of any duty pertaining to citizenship, if being thoroughly imbued with true American sentiment and the moral ideas which support it, we are honestly true to ourselves.

To thine own self be true,
And it must follow as the night the day;
Thou canst not then be false to any man.

SPEECHES FOR BUSINESS MEN

DINNER OF THE CHAMBER OF COMMERCE.

ADDRESSES BY CHARLES S SMITH, SECRETARY FOSTER, BIHOP POTTER, WILLIAM L. WILSON, DR. BRIGGS, CHAUNCEY M. DEPEW AND OTHERS.

The 123d annual banquet of the Chamber of Commerce was held on Nov. 17, at Delmonico's. The assemblage was a large one, 250 covers being laid At 9 o'clock President Smith arose and said:

Gentlemen: This overflowing gathering of representative business men, limited only by the accommodation of Delmonico's, gives evidence that the members of the Chamber value the social intercourse of the annual banquet, but the chief attraction is the intellectual and educational part of the entertainment, for we always find among our honored guests the leaders of advanced thought and public opinion, and this evening we are unusually favored in this regard. For the first time in the 123 years of its existence the Chamber has now a full complement of 1,000 members, and it is a matter of pardonable pride that the list of membership comprises the most eminent names connected with the financial, commercial and industrial interests of this city, and in this respect the ancient and honorable traditions of the Chamber are well maintained. (Applause.)

If you will look at our roll you will arrive at the conclusion that there is no question affecting the public welfare which can properly claim our attention that might not find an effective and just solution if the power resident in this Chamber were only aroused and put in force. There is not a town or hamlet between Maine and the Golden Gate, and from the Lakes to the Gulf, that does not feel the pulsations of the great heart of New-York.

The present and prospective condition of the silver question has received, as you know, recently, the attention of the Chamber, and it is so important to the commercial interests of the country that it will have our continued thought and attention. (Applause.)

There is no doubt that the people of the United States are honest, and they do not desire 80 cents worth of silver to pass for 100 cents in the payment of debt. Even if the present parity between gold and silver should be maintained permanently, I am of the opinion that legislators, of whatever party, who vote for dishonest money, will in the end be repudiated by the people. (Applause.)

It has been frequently predicted by men on both sides of the Atlantic that the City of New-York will some day become the world's banking depository, as London is to-day. It is historically true, since the times of that great family of merchants, the Medici, who, assisted by the Venetian merchants, made Venice the Bride of the Sea and the Mediterranean an Italian lake, that the European nation which, for the time being, controlled the trade with the Orient, has at the same time assumed the first place in the world's commerce. Geographically the United States is certainly in the best position to command and control the trade with the Oriental world, and our wonderful increase of population and wealth points to the realization of this pleasing vision. (Applause.)

Two things are absolutely necessary before this can be accomplished:

First, we must make the world believe, beyond all possible doubt, that a gold dollar deposited in New-York can be repaid in gold. This is a question of character as well as finance, and it concerns the honor of the American merchant. (Applause.)

And second, we must have steamships sailing under the American flag to all of the world's commercial ports. (Applause.) Commerce regulates exchange, and we cannot do the world's business permanently and profitably unless we can deliver the products of commerce in our own steamers.

The question of the enormous and increasing tide of alien immigrants into this country is one which demands the best thought of our statesmen and of all lovers of our country. The Bureau of Statistics at Washington gives the number of alien immigrants into this country from 1820 to 1855, inclusive, as 4,212,624, and the number of the same from 1856 to 1890, inclusive, was 11,188,566, making a total of 15,567,000.

I do not believe that any man is able to say, at present, just what restrictions, educational or otherwise, should be placed finally upon immigration, but certainly the question is a formidable one, and must have an equitable solution by the law-making power. (Applause.)

I want to say a word or two regarding the government of our city. I believe in a far larger measure of home rule than we now have, and less interference with our municipal government by our Legislature at Albany. And I desire to suggest for your careful consideration the thought that our city charter should be so amended that our Board of Aldermen could be selected, not exclusively from the districts in which they reside, as at present, but that any citizens residing in New-York would be eligible for election to the Board. If this change could be effected, and we could go back to the same character of men, many of whom were members of the Board of Aldermen fifty years ago, it would be desirable to allow all questions which affected the local interest of the city of New-York, such as rapid transit, street railroads, docks and wharves, and the like, to be under the control exclusively of such a Board of Aldermen, extending to the Mayor the right of veto. We might then have reason to expect that the government of the city would be as good or as bad as we chose to have it, and the responsibility for this result would fall directly upon the citizens.

Gentlemen, there is a vacant chair at this table. It has for many years been occupied by a much loved friend and honorary member of this Chamber. A voice which has cheered us with words of patriotic wisdom is still. I ask you, gentlemen, to fill your glasses and drink in silence to the memory of General Sherman.

SECRETARY FOSTER.

The next speaker was Secretary Foster, who was received with loud cheering. He spoke as follows:

Mr. President and Gentlemen of the Chamber of Commerce: To maintain "parity between gold and silver is the fixed policy of the Government," because we all recognize its supreme importance. (Applause.) When we come to the question of what policy is the best to pursue to maintain this desired condition, serious differences of opinion arise.

It is not my purpose, in the short time I shall occupy your attention, to undertake an argument for or against any of the views that may be advanced by members of the Chamber of Commerce, or any official action it may determine to take. I can, however, refer to existing conditions that are, in my opinion, important factors in determining action upon this most delicate as well as supremely important subject. If any body of men in the world ought to be practical in their undertakings, it is the Chamber of Commerce of New-York. They should be able to distinguish the practical things that can be accomplished from the impossible ideal which they would prefer. We are all compelled to admit that we have learned something by the experience of the last sixteen years, even upon the subject of silver. Prior to 1880 we had many sound thinking people, who believed that our financial structure should be based upon gold alone. It is probable that the Chamber of Commerce held this opinion at that time. It is now agreed on all sides that gold alone furnishes too narrow a basis upon which to conduct the money affairs of the world. Fifteen years ago, people of the East who were supposed to understand the question of finance indulged in prophecy as to the evil that would follow the coinage of $2,000,000 of silver per month. I voted for this measure, I confess, with misgivings. I now say frankly that if it had then been proposed to coin 300,000,000 of silver dollars in twelve and a half years, I would have voted "No," and yet I did vote for the coinage of this vast sum of silver dollars. Why would I have voted "No"? Because I did not then believe that the parity of gold and silver could be maintained under such a large coinage of silver dollars. I was of this opinion largely for the reason that all the great financiers of the country—the Chamber of Commerce of New-York and the associated banks—held that the parity could not be maintained even with a smaller coinage of silver dollars. I could not resist such conclusions. Notwithstanding the doleful predictions of eminent authorities, we have coined not only 300,000,000 of silver dollars, but have reached the sum of over 400,000,000. We have besides purchased about $70,000,000 worth of silver bullion at gold value ,and paid for it by the issue of about $70,000,000 of new Treasury notes, and yet the parity is maintained. Is there now living any man who would have been regarded as good authority on the subject who would have predicted that under such conditions the parity of the two metals would be preserved?

So, now, men whose intelligence and patriotism cannot be questioned, and whose purposes are the most exalted, are moved to indulge in gloomy forebodings over the present outlook, and propose, through the Chamber of Commerce and other agencies, to repeal the Act of July 14, 1890 (the present law authorizing the purchase of 4,500,000 ounces of silver per month to be paid in new Treasury notes), hoping thereby to preserve the parity of gold and silver.

ONE EXPERIENCE WITH SILVER.

It is not my purpose to dispute this position; nor do I propose to make myself the special advocate of the law as it stands. I do not propose to indulge in a prophecy as to what is to happen. I remember to have very carefully prepared in 1878 a speech on the silver question. I worked for weeks in digging out authorities from the library. When it was finally completed I was proud of it. (Laughter and applause.) I had obtained the floor for one hour, in which time I expected to astonish the House by my familiarity with so great a subject, and as well with the wisdom of my conclusions. As the time approached for its delivery I began to think that perhaps it was after all the safer course for me not to make a speech. This latter notion prevailed; the speech was not delivered. (Laughter and applause.) Because of the knowledge of its existence I find no fault with "The New-York Times" in its effort to belittle me. If that paper could have the speech to comment upon I think I would feel compelled to resign my office. (Laughter and applause.) This reference to myself is perhaps out of place in the discussion of a very serious subject, but I mention it merely to call to mind the fact that many other gentlemen have not been so prudent as I have. It is not probably true that no man has written or spoken on this subject but who, in the light of our experience, has discovered that he was more or less in error. (Applause.)

There is one very important factor in dealing with this question which has not perhaps been wholly overlooked, but which has not been appreciated to any such extent as it deserves. That is the enormous power given by Congress to those in authority to deal with this question, backed by the almost incalculable resources of the greatest country on earth. The question now is, What policy, that is attainable (remembering all the time that the ideal is impossible) will result in the least strain upon our resources, and will require the least resort to the exercise of the extraordinary powers conferred upon those in authority to do what the law commands, viz., to maintain the parity of gold and silver?

FREE COINAGE WOULD DEBASE SILVER.

In my opinion, with all of our power, natural and conferred by law; with all of our resources employed to their fullest extent; we could not maintain the parity of the two metals if the policy of free coinage of silver prevailed. (Applause.)

I am firmly of the opinion that the parity of the two metals can be maintained under the present policy. We produce in this country about $30,000,000 of gold annually. The present indications are that the balance of trade with foreign nations for the next two years, and for a longer period if the present Tariff laws are maintained, will require gold shipments to us in our favor. Under the present policy we buy 4,500,000 ounces of silver per month, paying for this purchase its value in new Treasury notes. Under such conditions the work of maintaining the parity will not require an extraordinary exercise of power, or be a strain upon the resources of the country. If, however, the balance of trade should turn against us to any great extent, which to me seems quite improbable except in the event of extraordinary contingencies abroad, the strain would come; but even then my faith in our resources is such as to compel me to believe that we would weather the storm and preserve the parity. (Applause.)

The shipment of more than $70,000,000 of our gold to Europe without embarrassment to us is only an illustration of the marvellous financial strength of

this country, to which I have called attention. So, in my opinion, nothing short of an exceptionally large drain of gold is likely to produce a strain upon our resources in the effort to maintain the parity of gold and silver. (Applause.)

But under free coinage silver would take the place of gold in settling balances. If the price of silver were advanced from less than $1 to $1.29 per ounce all the silver for sale in the world would be attracted to this country. We would then have hundreds of millions of silver dollars added to the $408,000,000 we now have, and that, too, as fast as the mints could coin them. To maintain the parity under such conditions would be a task requiring more than our immense resources and the exercise of unusual power to the last degree could supply. But with 4,500,000 ounces of silver only per month, purchased at its gold value, the task would be easy. (Applause.)

THE PRACTICAL QUESTION.

In my opinion, gentlemen, the practical question for you to consider is, which of these two policies will you prefer? I know you have expressed a desire for the repeal of the present law, and, as I understand, you do not propose a substitute of any kind; in other words, if you can have your way, you propose to permit silver to take care of itself. You have doubtless given your proposition the fullest possible consideration. I am sure I do not mistake your wishes when I express the belief that you desire that the parity of the two metals shall be maintained. This being so then, I must also conclude that you have fully considered the effect on price that would follow the stoppage of the purchase of silver bullion by the Government, and if it should result in a large decline, that you have also fully considered the effect this would have toward increasing the burden of maintaining parity. I have not given much thought to this phase of the subject for the reason that I do not believe Congress will indorse your views. But I think I can see clearly that if the Government goes out of the market the price will decline; perhaps it will be a large decline, in which case it seems to me the task of maintaining the parity will be embarrassing and difficult. (Applause.)

Believing that the good sense of the business world must in the near future be brought into harmony with us in the proposition that gold alone is too narrow a base upon which to build the world's financial structure, I have much hope that the best judgment of all concerned will agree to a better and more extended use of silver, to be followed by international agreements by which the parity of the two metals, upon an accepted ratio, may be maintained. (Applause.)

I feel quite safe in saying that one of the hindrances to an early agreement in the direction I have indicated is the belief in Europe that free coinage is to be the policy of this country. If this is to be our policy they know that their silver will come to us, and that our gold will go to them. (Applause.)

Is it not the part of wisdom for us to refrain from doing anything that will impair our ability to preserve the parity? Convince Europe that we will not permit ourselves to fall in this respect, and an obstacle to the agreement so much desired is removed. (Applause.)

In what I have said I express the opinions of myself only; whether they are of any value or not is for you and the country to judge. The position I occupy requires me, for the time being, to give my best thought and attention to this and kindred subjects. I am trying to consider, not the ideal, but the practical only. (Long continued cheers and applause.)

BISHOP POTTER'S WORDS.

This is the way in which the chairman introduced Bishop Potter: "Gentlemen: In these days of war of creeds and confessions, it is a matter of congratulation that we have at the head of a great historic Church in this city a man suited to the times—distinguished in his high profession by conservative views and acts, he has administered the duties of his office in such a manner as to command the respect of all men of all creeds. I have great pleasure in introducing the Rt. Rev. Henry C. Potter, Bishop of New-York, who will speak upon the subject, 'Circulation the Law of Wealth, as it is the Law of Commerce.'" Here is what Bishop Potter said:

Gentlemen of the Chamber of Commerce: In connection with another of our annual fes·ivities—I mean that of the New-England Society—one of those well-worn jests which do duty on such occasions is what may be called the "joke of contras." The eloquent orator whose theme remits him to the Landing of the Pilgrims takes Mr. Delmonico's menu for his text, and discourses with appropriate sarcasm upon the hardships of our New-England forefathers as appropriately celebrated in the prodigal luxury of their descendants.

It is a very instructive contrast, but not more so. I think, in any such connection than in this. The New-York Chamber of Commerce—I do not know how old it is, nor how rich—but if one could exchange this scene for one nearly three hundred years ago, when Hendrick Hudson came to these shores and laid the foundations, in his traffic with the upper Hudson, of your traffic with all the world, if, I say, one could for a few moments exchange this assemblage and this New-York for that New-York, the contrast would certainly be impressive. The first medium of exchange on these shores, the historian tells us, was by means of wampum, or strings of shells; and Professor Sumner would have us believe that the white man soon showed his superiority in the use of this by coun·erfeiting the periwinkles and clam-shells which were the native currency. This simply shows, if it is true—I can only hope that it is not—how early was developed in this country the instinct of debasing the currency by issues which were not really worth their face value. (Laughter.)

But whether our fathers were beguiled by such sophistries in earlier days or not, they would seem to have been tolerably secure from other temptations which are peculiarly the fruit of an age which presents no more impressive and suggestive contrast to the modest simplicity of earlier days than in its enormous accumulations of money. I propose, sir, in connection with the theme which you have assigned to me, to speak of this particular feature of our modern situation, as it concerns especially those whom I address this evening. I fear I shall not be able to be funny, though I shall try not to be dull; and in any case I know that I may count upon your courteous forbearance, even if I am unable to command your cordial sympathy. On the occasion of a very splendid banquet, given last winter by a very distinguished association, I have been told that so soon as the speakers ceased to be comic the guests not only ceased to be attentive, but also to be either silent or civil. Let me say that in an intercourse with this august body, extending now over a period of twenty years, I have myself had a very different and a much more agreeable experience.

EXPECTING OBJECTIONS.

And yet I can anticipate objections to my text. Some one will say that it is a vain repetition. Commerce, or the products of commerce, and wealth are interchangeable terms. "Of course," it may be said, "the end of commerce is circulation—that I may get my neighbor's corn and that he may get my shoes and shirts and steel rails, and as the corn and the cotton must move, so the money must move, too." And this is quite true until we come to the element of profit. No man trades without expecting that beyond a mere barter of commodities there shall be earned increment which shall be left over when the barter is done. What, now, is he to do with that? "Well, he is to maintain himself and his with part of it. He is to enlarge his business, if he can, with another part of it. He is to indulge himself and his in certain luxuries with another part of it. And then—if there is any remainder, he is to put that remainder away."

Yes; I answer within certain limits and for certain legitimate purposes. One may well get ready in fair weather for foul. There wi'l always come a rainy day, and one does not want to be caught out in it without an umbrella. Yes, again: but how many umbrellas does he need? If he hates to lend his umbrella, and knows that the wife of his bosom will incontinently steal his if he does not provide her with one of her own, he will do wisely to get her one, and to see that it has a handsome silver handle. (Laughter.) And as with the wife, so with the children; an umbrel'a is cheaper than rheumatism, pneumonia or influenza, especially when you add in the doctor and the undertaker. In a word, "He that provideth not for his own house," as the Apostle puts it, "is worse than an infidel."

But beyond that due and reasonable provision, what then? Ah, gentlemen, that is the question which confronts Americans to-day. We, in this land, have entered upon a race for wealth to which, I think, the past furnishes no parallel. What is to be the end of it? I do not mean in the wealth accumulated or the number of colossal fortunes which may be reckoned up, that will dazzle our modern world; that is a question of the most infinitesimal consequence—but what will be the end of it in its influence upon personal character, first, and then upon the well-being of the community, the State, the Nation?

I shall not attempt to answer that question in detail, nor need I. There is nothing that I could tell you on this point that you do not know already, as well as or better than I. There cannot be great wealth without great temptations to indolence, to vice, to social and political corruption. There cannot be great wealth in idle hands—the hands of those who have not made or accumulated it—without an accentuation of these dangers. There are some people who are fond of pointing out the failures of great benefactions—bequests, trusts, foundations and the like. Very well. Now I wish somebody would write a history of great accumulations and their posthumous influence on the virtue, usefulness and happiness of those to whom they were passed on. It would be a very instructive, and I apprehend rather a tragic story.

WHERE THERE WAS NO WASTE.

And there is but one way to avoid its indefinite repetition, and that is to avoid the situation that produces it.

The science that, in connection with our vast accumulations of wealth, needs just now to be most diligently studied is the science of redistribution. Do you tell me that there has been a great deal of foolish waste and misapplication in connection with the beneficent redistribution of money? Yes, perhaps it may be so. But the Cooper Union was not a foolish waste. The Astor and Lenox Libraries were not a foolish waste. The Roosevelt and Sloane Hospitals have not been a foolish waste. All over this crowded land you may find the traces of a wise beneficence that in, museums of art and science, in schools and colleges and refuges, has by some wise gift created a never ceasing well-spring of healing and sweetness and light.

But the art of doing such things wisely and effectually does not come by chance. People think that there is nothing easier than to give away money, especially if somebody is to do it! On the contrary, there are few things that are more difficult—that is, to do helpfully and well. And so the science of redistribution is one the study and the practice of which ought to begin with the earliest beginnings of accumulation. It is just here that we have had some of our greatest failures and some of our greatest successes. I may not speak of the failures, but let me speak of one, at least, of the successes. Who that knows the life and work of the Cooper Union, and who that ever knew Peter Cooper, can fail to see that the fruitful ministry of the one was the logical and inevitable result of the sympathetic and painstaking forecast of the other? And what an object lesson the two together may well be to all of us! They say that the poor hate the rich; but nobody ever hated Peter Cooper, or begrudged him even his air-cushion! Men were glad he was rich, and gladder still that he taught other men what to do with wealth. And this, gentlemen, is the lesson for wealth to learn to-day. As one looks at life, its aspect is most of all interesting and prophetic at its beginning and at its end. The fine courage of youth, the noble ambition of achievement—ah! what a chance there for the helping and encouraging hand of opulence. And then, the tragic failures of old age, the broken fortunes, the decaying powers, the disappointed hopes, what a beautiful opportunity there for tenderness, for magnanimity, for generosity. I may not indicate the channels. Here, gentlemen, are the fields through which the channels are to run. Go and make the channels for yourselves. (Long and continued applause.)

WILLIAM L. WILSON SPEAKS.

The president, on introducing William L. Wilson, said: "The gentleman who will now address you is a personal and highly esteemed friend of many of our members, who often enlivens the House of Representatives with his sallies of wit and wisdom. I know you will be glad to listen to the Hon. William L. Wilson, of West Virginia, upon the subject of business men and lawmaking."

Mr. Wilson said in part:

When the Constitution was framed, and the time of the meeting of Congress was to be determined as between May and December, the convention was greatly influenced in the selection of December by the statement of Oliver Ellsworth that as the members of both bodies of Congress would generally be connected with agriculture it would be an unfortunate season to compel them to leave their farms during the summer season. The farmer, however, has not thus far been chief among legislators. Up to the present time the men who have made laws have been generally American lawyers, and they have fulfilled their duty with reasonable fidelity. One of the great political parties through the work of a country lawyer placed on the statute books a law that could go about as far as possible in one direction and another sought to put upon the statute books another law that was intended to go about as far as possible in the opposite direction. We are giving to the development of this great country all that knowledge and science and skill and invention which the world has accumulated in the past can apply. What have a people like this to ask of this Government, especially of the law-making power? Chiefly, from the business point of view, "hands off!" Chiefly that the Government shall not interfere, but shall leave the people to work out their own material welfare.

I do not think that we need a very large amount of law-making in this country. Perhaps I can say from my own observations in the House of Representatives that the country does not get the best that Congress could do because the members are afraid to do the best they know how to do. It was Mr. Hamilton who said that the natural disease of free government was too much legislation. It was Mr. Jefferson who said that under our system a law ought to be proposed a year in advance. We have projected ourselves very far into the principle of paternalism of government when we talk about the Government providing business for the people.

ADDRESS OF DR. BRIGGS.

"Gentlemen," said the president, "I have now the pleasure of calling upon a distinguished professor, whose scholarly acquirements and great fame as a teacher and thinker have lent lustre to one of our foremost educational institutions, the Rev. Dr. Charles A. Briggs, of the Union Theological Seminary, who will speak upon the subject of public education."

Here is what Dr. Briggs had to say:

Mr. President and Gentlemen: The subject upon which I was requested to address you may have several interpretations. Public education may mean education of the public, education by the public, or education for the public. The education of the public is a theme long since worn threadbare. Education by the public, whether at the public expense, or under the supervision of the civil authorities, or in accordance with the average opinion of the community, is a theme which, in some of its aspects, has no attractions. In others is associated with many of the evils which now obstruct the educational advance of our nation. Let me ask you, therefore, to consider rather public education as meaning education for the public, for the public welfare, for the public service.

The excellent Chaplain Sharp, in his proposals to establish a public library, a school, and a chapel in our city, written March 11, 1712, (13,) says:

"There is hardly anything which is more wanted in this country than learning, there being no place I know of in America where it is either less encouraged or regarded. This city is so conveniently situated for trade, and the genius of the people is so inclined for merchandise that they generally seek no other education for their children than writing and arithmetic."

Happily our metropolis has, in many respects, outgrown these defects of its infancy; and yet, relatively speaking, the educational institutions of our city have not received the support that they had a right to expect from our citizens, until quite recent years, and a commercial education has been the prevailing idea among us.

The Rev. James Anderson, the first pastor of the Presbyterian Church in this city, writes to Principal Sterling, of Glasgow, October 29, 1725, that he

could not secure sufficient educational advantages for his children; questioning whether, considering that he was so remote from his native land, his children might not be received as orphans in the Heriot Hospital at Edinburgh.

There is, however, in the proposal of Mr. Sharp, a quaint suggestion of a reason why public education did not thrive in our metropolis. He says, with regard to the citizens of New-York in his day : . . "Letters must be in a manner forced upon them, not only without their seeking, but against their consent.".

To this proposal we must take exception. Public education should be so practical, so adapted to the welfare of the people, so entwined with their life and interwoven with their hopes for themselves and their children, that they would seek it, and rather force their way to it than have it forced upon them.

THE OLD AND THE NEW.

The older education was so theoretical, so speculative, so abstract and apart from human life and welfare, that it did not thrive in commercial cities. It sought the quiet of fields and mountains, where, undisturbed by the bustle and distractions of active busy life, it might muse in the mazes of abstract thought and leisurely unwind the skein of speculation. The older education was essentially monastic, and the birch was the most potent educator.

The newer education does not retire from the world, it rather strives in every way to enter into the world and search out all the avenues in the realm of reality. It is intensely practical. It thrives best, therefore, in the great cities, where the heartbeats of the world's progress are more distinctly felt, and the circumference of knowledge extends with the outreachings of commerce. The greatest universities of our day are in those cosmopolitan cities, Berlin and Vienna. The newer education should be conducted at the great centres of the world—at the heart of all its affairs. (Applause.)

Our Saviour tells us: "If any man willeth to do his will, he shall know of the teaching, whether it be of God, or whether I speak of myself." (John vii, 17.) Knowledge of Christian doctrine cannot advance far beyond Christian practice. Theory and practice should not be divorced. Of them it may be said: "It is not good that they should be alone." They are helpmeets, created by God for one another. Herein is the chief difference between the old and the new theology. The old theology is abstract, speculative, traditional. The new theology is concrete, practical and historical. The old theology regards dogma as more important than life. The new theology does not depreciate dogma, but insists that it is true dogma only so far as it enters into life. All that mass of speculative dogma that has come down to us in the traditional schools is tested by the new theology, in order to ascertain whether it has truth and reality about it. If it has not now and never has had any practical value in the evolution of Christian life, if it has not been an education for the welfare, the prosperity, the increase of Christ's Church, the criticism of the new theology gives it over to the owls and the bats. The new theology is a real theology, it appropriates all that is real and true in the old. It discards all that is mere speculation or mere tradition. Doctrine and life are married, and they look for healthy, vigorous children in a revived church, a reformed society and a transformed world. (Applause.)

So the new education has been obliged to use the fires of criticism upon all that mass of crude, undigested speculation that has come down in the tradition of the schools in order to destroy the illusions and delusions, the conceits and fancies and falsehoods that have so long deceived our fathers. There is no real peril in this house-cleaning, for when the rubbish is cast out into the fire, any grains of the precious gold that may be mingled with it will shine all the brighter in the fire. Truth is indestructible. It is mighty, and it will prevail over every force and every obstacle.

WHAT TRUTH IS LIKE.

The cabalistic book of Sonar gives a parable to illustrate the approach of truth to man. Truth is a beautiful woman, who first gives a gentle hint which none but a true lover can discover; next she whispers through a thick veil that hides her entire form; then she converses through a thin veil which discloses the outlines of her beauty; at last she shows her glorious face and intrusts him with the secrets of her heart.

The modern student is not content to accept truth in abstract propositions, in obscure and indefinite hints; he is not content with truths veiled by thin or thick disgulses. His love for truth is so intense, his quest is so persistent and irresistible, that he reaches after her, grasps her in his arms and clasps her to his heart, as the bride of his home, the companion and inspiration of his daily life. (Applause.)

That ancient book, called the "Instruction of Wisdom," gives us excellent advice in public education:

Wisdom crieth aloud in the street.
She uttereth her voice in the broad places;
She crieth in the chief places of concourse;
At the entering in of the gates,
In the city, she uttereth her words."—(Prov. 1, 20-21.

Public education will never attain its ideal until it becomes so practical, so intensely interested in every department of human life and conduct, that the voice of the educator will be heard in the chief places of public resort, in the great cities, in the cosmopolitan cities, speaking the master words that will be for the public welfare, for the public guidance in all the manifold details of modern life. (Applause.)

If public education should be practical and aimed directly at public welfare, then self-culture is not the most important thing. Public education is for the public. Our Saviour gives us a helpful word here, also. He told His apostles whom He had chosen to educate His church: "Whosoever would save his life shall lose it; and whosoever shall lose his life for My sake shall find it."—(Matthew xvi, 25.) Jesus teaches that the educators of the kingdom of Christ must sacrifice themselves in the public weal of the kingdom; that self-education can only be gained in the kingdom of heaven by seeking, above all, the welfare of the Christian public.

Is this not true of all education? Is not public welfare the aim of it all? No man can be a true teacher in any department who does not give himself freely and fully to his pupils, who does not impart to them of his spirit, of his nervous energy, of his vital powers, as well as the contents of his mind and heart. No institution of learning can fulfil its purpose which aims merely at its own advancement in wealth and external prosperity, in the number of its students or in the extent of its influence. It accomplishes its service to the public only by giving of its wealth of knowledge, of its vital energies, of its invigorating forces to the city in which it is situated, the community of which it forms a part, keeping in view the welfare of the Nation and our common humanity. No institution of learning is entitled to the name of university which does not aim at least at the comprehension of the entire circle of human knowledge in its course of instruction, and keep in mind the welfare of the universe of God. (Applause.)

WHAT IT SHOULD EMBRACE.

A university is a much greater and grander thing than is commonly supposed. It should embrace the classical and the scientific courses of the college, all the professional schools, law, medicine and theology and the training of teachers. It should embrace schools of art and of music, of political science, and of commerce and trade. It should embrace all the circle of human welfare. It needs museums filled with specimens from all departments of nature and art; and great libraries stored with manuscripts, tracts and printed books that will mount up beyond the second million, telling the history of the world and man. Such universities can only be in the great cosmopolitan cities of the world, in those vast centres of population where millions of human beings are assembled from all nations and kindreds and tongues, and whose commercial interests are co-extensive with the globe. What city is there that is more suitable for such a university than New-York? (Applause.)

The citizens of New-York have done nobly in recent years in enlarging our institutions of learning. The Museum of Art and the Museum of Natural History are among the most hopeful parts of public education in this metropolis. The influence of such museums upon public life is incalculable. We need a great conservatory of music. We still need a great public library. Our colleges and professional schools, so excellent under their present management, working together with such general harmony and good spirit, one and all need enlargement in order to enable them to cope with the vast problem of public education. And, in some way, all these institutions should be federated in a university.

No other city in the world has, at the present time, more students pursuing the work of higher education. The difficulty is that these are scattered in a number of institutions, no one of which has sufficient teachers, adequate buildings, or the apparatus needed to do its entire work. It is still necessary for advanced students in most departments to resort to the universities of the Old World for higher education. If the citizens of New-York with one heart and mind would rally about the educational institutions of our city already established, and build them up with the energy and zeal of which they are capable, we might, ere long, anticipate that we would have a university, indeed, one that would come measurably in line with our ideal, one that would train our children for all the varied departments of human life and work; one that would be the pride of our metropolis and the fountain of blessing to the city, the Nation and the world. (Applause.)

WHAT IS NEEDED.

One of the most discouraging features in public education in America is the prevailing opinion that public education is sufficient if it aim to prepare the average citizen for his duties, and that the higher education is only for the few, and can be left to the few. No country has produced more men of native genius than this country, in the brief period of our history. But we have produced very few great scholars, very, very few leaders in human thought. In this respect we have been content to follow the thought of the old world, at a considerable distance in the rear. Our great men have too often lacked that higher education which they needed to do their work as leaders, thoroughly and well. The greatest danger that stares us in the face as a Nation, is the lack of competent leaders. We have an enormous population of men and women who have a common school education, but when we ascend into the higher reaches of thought and ask where are the leaders, the guides, the educators of the masses, we are filled with dismay.

Genius is a gift of God, a native endowment of the few; but these few need training in order that their genius may not be ill-used or wasted, but employed at its best for the welfare of man. How can our great men be trained except in great institutions of learning, where it may be possible to climb to the highest reaches of human thought and undergo that patient, persistent, comprehensive and exact discipline that will enable them to accomplish the greatest work of human skill? (Applause.)

Public education rises like a pyramid, layer upon layer of diminishing extent, until the height is reached in the apex. The foundations and lower course do not make a pyramid. The upper layers and the apex are necessary. Have we not thought too exclusively of training the masses and too little of the public education of the leaders of these masses? There are times in the history of every nation when a master of affairs, a king of men, is more important for the public weal than a million of ordinary citizens; when the lack of competent leaders is disastrous to the whole community. Who, then, will say that it may not be as important to train the leaders as to train the masses? Upon these few will depend the welfare of the great multitude; and their education is as truly public education, education for the public weal, as the education of the multitudes themselves.

The ancient word of Moses's song suits well our times:

"How should one chase a thousand,
And two put a myriad to flight?"—(Dt. xxxii, 30.)

Public education is an education for the welfare of the people, the higher education of the few as well as the primary education of the many, in all those departments of human life and work which constitute the well-being of man; and the metropolis, with its cosmopolitan life and relations, is the place where such education may be carried on in a true university, whose scope should be as extensive as the world of man and the universe of God. (Loud and prolonged applause and cheering.)

MR. DEPEW'S WIT.

Following Dr. Briggs came Chauncey M. Depew who said:

I doubt if the reporters will deem what I say worthy of recording. (Laughter.) It is a rule generally observed by veteran after-dinner speakers not to appear among the volunteers of the toasts. (Laughter.) The place is reserved for ambitious gentlemen who have not yet tested their powers and having tested them there once never try it again. (Renewed laughter.) After the dinner committee have set the pace of the evening and selected all the sentiments which their combined talents could devise there is nothing left for a skirmisher in the rear who is placed where a skirmisher should never be. (Laughter.) There is, however, a certain suggestiveness about the occasion tonight which possibly may allow the opportunity for a remark here and there. I was especially impressed with one of the observations of the Secretary of the Treasury. One of my studies in life has been "What are the processes by which men rise?" Mr. Wilson has alluded to my efforts in that direction (laughter), and it is evident that in his mind my processes were successful. (Renewed laughter.) The Secretary of the Treasury naively confesses that the distinguished position which he has attained in the hearts and in the estimation of his countrymen has been due to the speeches which he never made. (Roars of laughter.) I think it will be admitted by every one here that I cannot be charged with climbing that ladder. (Renewed laughter.) I will say, however, for the benefit of my friend, the representative of the Administration, that the view which he took of the opinion of the Chamber of Commerce in this connection upon silver is not the unanimous opinion of that body. (Laughter and applause.) The President of the Chamber of Commerce in the interesting address which he delivered here last year, or the year before, which I still carry in my memory, said that he had read the records of the body from its beginning down to that period. He is the only man of the body who ever engaged in light literature of that character. (Immense laughter.) He dug out somewhere from there that many years before the adoption of the Federal Constitution this body passed a resolution in favor of maintaining the parity of gold and silver—evidently looking forward to the time when silver should be the needed commodity in the currency and that the genius of American statesmanship would be equal to passing a measure which would preserve its parity.

AN ELOQUENT TRIBUTE.

I want to say that the Secretary of the Treasury said an excellent thing when he said, as a citizen of Ohio, that Ohio would honor herself, do credit to the country, and recognize statesmanship equal to the best we ever had if it returned the author of such a bill to the United States Senate. (Applause.) Agreeing with all that Mr. Wilson has said about American public life and the position which the country lawyer occupies in making our laws, there is no division of sentiment among men of all parties in this country that the man who has done so much for good legislation for honest money, for all that marks distinction in public life to leave the Senate now would be a public calamity. (Applause.)

This dinner to-night marks how the Chamber of Commerce has itself become an illustration of the doctrine of evolution. (Laughter and applause.) I remember long periods of years when dinners of the Chamber of Commerce were held for the purpose of inviting politicians, who knew nothing of commerce (laughter), to enlighten merchants upon their business. (Renewed laughter.) I have been present when a member of the Cabinet from a State which had no shipping delivered an address of an hour and a half's duration upon the methods by which there could be established an immense mercantile marine. (Continued laughter.) The next period was when the Chamber invited controversial political questions, and their eminent advocates and representatives. Then a member of the Cabinet didn't hesitate to state what was the policy of the Administration; nor the gentlemen present on the other side, when they happened to get the floor, hesitate to controvert the position of the member of the Cabinet.

ANOTHER DISCUSSION.

Then we had the discussion of the great industrial questions of the Protective Tariff and of Revenue Reform. And the dinner which was held before the last Presidential election set the pace of the controversy in the battle which went on the following year throughout the country and was brought finally to a close at the polls. (Applause.) Mr. Lamar, who was here then representing the Administration, took occasion in a most eloquent and able address to set forth the view of the Administration to the effect that the policy of this country should be Revenue Reform looking ultimately to Free Trade. An humble citizen in the ranks (laughter) came afterward, and speaking, as I believed, for the party with which I was associated, accepted the issue, and said that if the Administration would only put it forth as their policy in the then approaching campaign it would be as frankly met as it was boldly stated, and an opportunity given to the people to pronounce their opinion. That opinion they pronounced, and I, for one, am satisfied with the result. (Laughter and applause.)

Now that we have passed the controversial period, we come to the higher plane where the Chamber of Commerce invites for its orators and instructors the most distinguished clergymen of the country, for the purpose of enlightening them upon the great questions of how to distribute their money and how to get a proper education. The reason of this is that in the intermediate period the Chamber of Commerce has reached that point where most of its members have retired from business (laughter), and those who have not are not ready to retire. (Renewed laughter.) So they called upon the ablest experts in the United States (roars of laughter) to instruct them what to do with their surplus. We fear the force of Socialism and we dread the power of Anarchy. But, gentlemen, it is well to remember that Socialism does not spring from, nor does anarchy grow and thrive upon the mere ravings of demagogues. (Applause.) A misuse of wealth by men of great riches is often a much greater propagation of Anarchy and Socialism (renewed applause), but a proper and well-directed and unselfish use of wealth by men of great riches is one of the great agencies that prevent the growth of Anarchy and Socialism. (Prolonged applause.)

But I am glad that rising somewhat higher over the mere earthly plane of what you shall do with your money, you came to the great Professor of Theology to know what you shall do with your souls. There is no question that Professor Briggs is competent to speak upon education in that line. He has a certificate from the Presbytery. (Laughter.) In inviting him, instead of the recognized representative of orthodoxy, you have indicated what kind of theology you desire. (Renewed laughter.)

If there ever was a meeting of the Chamber of Commerce when it should feel joyous, when it should feel happy, it is the meeting this year. There has been no time within a decade when this body, representing so much as it does of the commerce, of the finance and of the industrial conditions of this country, should feel as well as it does to-day (applause) at the conditions as they exist, and the prospects as they are. (Renewed applause.) Speaking purely from a transportation standpoint, and without any intention of booming the corporation with which I am connected (laughter), the statement as it comes to me each week of the phenomenal increase over the corresponding week of the last year, and of the week of the year before, tells the story of that which is to come for every business in the country. (Great applause.) For transportation is the barometer of prosperity or of adversity.

There is to be within the next twelve months a famine in this land, but it is to be a famine of the means to carry the vast product of the soil. There is to be a famine of cars, a famine of locomotives, a famine of the methods by which this enormous product which the fields of the country have produced may be conveyed to the sea and so go abroad, where it is needed. (Applause.) There are times when a great surplus of product is thrown upon the market and not consumed, and that is generally a time when there is a general lack of prosperity throughout the country; but this year we have a phenomenal condition of the harvest, unequalled for many a year; of prices greater for our products than have been secured for them in the last ten years; of the railways receiving whole and remunerative rates for what they carry, and having more than they can do, and a demand from the other side of the water, owing to the horrible conditions there, which will take the whole of our surplus; and it will probably be unequal to the demand.

These conditions are going to make railways more than usually prosperous in their net earnings; are going to give an unusual business to every house, no matter what the particular article in which it deals; are going to put an amount in the hands of the farmer such as he has not had in a long time before; are going to lead to the construction of new lines of railway; are going to make a demand for iron, coal and coke; are going to pour back into this country in the next fiscal year twice the surplus of imports of money over the amount we expend abroad. (Applause.)

This banquet is as it was the year of the Presidential election. My friend Mr. Mills says that the way to preserve this prosperity is to have free trade and an income tax to carry on the Government. My friend Mr. Cleveland says the way to preserve this prosperity is to have revenue reform and honest money. My friends of the South and of the West say the way to preserve prosperity is to have free trade and the unlimited coinage of silver.

My friends with whom I am associated say the way to preserve this prosperity is to have the protective principle applied in such a way that it will protect wherever another mill can be built and another man can be given employment who hasn't it now (cheers), and the reciprocity project so pushed that treaties by this country shall be made with every country that has a surplus of the things we cannot profitably produce, and needs the things of the factory or the farm of which we have a surplus; and that parity of silver and gold shall be maintained in such a way that both metals will be used to the utmost extent that the product of our mines shall afford, but that in the Treasury there shall be always enough of both to keep the silver equal to the gold and the promise of the Government upon its paper equal to gold. (Prolonged applause.)

A WELCOME TO MR. REID.

WARM WORDS OF FRIENDSHIP, RESPECT AND ADMIRATION.

MEN OF BOTH PARTIES AND MANY PROFESSIONS GIVE HIM A CHARMING DINNER—ELOQUENT AND WITTY SPEECHES BY CHAUNCEY M. DEPEW, SECRETARIES FOSTER AND ELKINS, COL. M'CLURE, ST. CLAIR M'KELWAY, MR. REID AND OTHERS.

The Ohio Society of New-York entertained Whitelaw Reid, United States Minister to France, at a dinner at Delmonico's on April 9. It was a welcome home on the part of natives of Mr. Reid's own State, who, like himself, have gravitated eastward and made New-York City their permanent abode. It was a thoroughly representative gathering, and the greeting extended to their principal guest was of the most cordial character. There were more than 250 covers laid, and the tables were set in the big dining hall. The table of honor extended on one side of the room, north and south, and there were six other tables arranged at right angles to it and designated by the first six letters of the alphabet. The room was simply decorated, the principal feature being the coat-of-arms of Ohio, with the French colors on one side and the United States flag on the other, the group entirely covering the front of the orchestra gallery.

The Lotos Club contributed for the occasion the bronze bust of Mr. Reid presented to that organization by Norman W. Kingsley, and this occupied a place against the wall opposite the table at which their delegation was seated. These consisted of Frank R. Lawrence, president; John Elderkin, secretary; S. S. Packard, Dr. E. F. Hoyt, E. F. Phelps, Dr. Louis L. Seaman, Robert E. Bonner, G. W. Monroe, E. B. Harper, W. P. Phillips, Uriah Welch, Chester S. Lord, E. C. James, James M. Ashley, jr., Stanley N. Cohen, George H. Jones, F. P. Morris, F. A. Burnham, John W. Vrooman, N. W. Kingsley, William Lloyd and Carson Lake. The Lotos Club had made special application to the Ohio Society to be represented in this tribute to Mr. Reid, who had been for years president of their own organization, and the request was promptly and courteously granted.

It was shortly after 7 o'clock when the guests entered the dining hall. Previously, Mr. Reid had been closely occupied in one of the parlors shaking hands and receiving the greetings of those who had not met him since

his return. Colonel W. L. Strong, the president of the society, was not there, owing to the enfeebled and precarious condition of his venerable mother, though a seat had been reserved for him at the table of honor until the last moment, in the hope that he might be able to come. General Wager Swayne, formerly president of the society, was chosen to act in Colonel Strong's official capacity and as such he escorted Mr. Reid to his seat, and they were followed by the other invited guests, with escorts. At the right of General Swayne sat Mr. Reid, and by his side Secretary Elkins, and at the left of the presiding officer sat Secretary Foster, with Chauncey M. Depew at his side. Others at this table were Thomas Ewing, Charles A. Dana, George W. Childs, Colonel A. K. McClure, D. O. Mills, Viscount Paul d'Abzac, French Consul-General at New-York; Murat Halstead, St. Clair McKelway, Ballard Smith, Warner Miller and Frank R. Lawrence, president of the Lotos Club.

BEGINNING THE SPEECHMAKING.

Promptly at 9 o'clock General Swayne rapped for order. Addressing those assembled, he said:

Gentlemen, there once was a time, as you remember, when Horace Greeley signalized himself by forcibly saying to a young man from Ohio, "Come East, young man; come East." (Laughter.) And thereupon our distinguished and most welcome guest moved from Cincinnati to New-York, as more or less of you have since enjoyed the privilege of doing. (Laughter.) In due time his beneficent activities led him to be one of the founders of this Society, which, with such singular pleasure, this evening welcomes him home from a distinguished and valuable career in the foreign service of his country. (Applause.)

If it be true, and it may be so, that this night the great soul of Horace Greeley contemplates our meeting here, we may be sure his benediction mingles with our own. (Applause.) This is not the place, gentlemen, to recount our guest's achievements abroad. It is rather the place where we should cherish him at home. It is enough to say that his going abroad at the time of the great Exposition in France was provident, in that he went as the ambassador and the forerunner of his countrymen abroad. His coming home is provident in the same sense, for no man could be so truly the forerunner of those Frenchmen whom we expect to welcome here, and at no man's hands would they so thoroughly enjoy the welcome which we know they would receive. (Applause.)

It is Auld Lang Syne peculiarly for this company, as you know. It is a long time now since the educational interests of Ohio began to recognize the graduate of Miami, and afterward rejoiced when he became the Regent for life of the university system of New-York. (Applause.) But oh, how much deeper and stronger the feeling that grew when the patriotic impulse and anxiety of Ohio, during the war, learned to rely upon the man who could be fearless without anger, candid without accusation, and always fearless and yet truthful. (Applause.)

When the capillary power of a great city brought him here to voice its great opinion, the people of Ohio knew that a great city had justified itself, and great sentiments were after this to be part of the power of the press in the city of New-York. (Applause.) Beyond that I shall follow him into his public history no further. It reminds one of what Webster said of Massachusetts and its history, the world knows it by heart. (Applause.)

Only one single defect. I was reading to-night the speech at Paris, in which he said that he went abroad for recreation. (Laughter.) One could have told he was no prophet, from the honor he enjoys at home. (Laughter and applause.) He said in that speech also, gentlemen, that not having found recreation abroad, he was now coming home for recreation. (Applause.) Do you think that that is a fresh illustration of his prophetic powers? (Laughter.) Gentlemen, to dwell further upon Mr. Reid or his achievements would be simply keeping you from him. I invite you, gentlemen, one and all, from your hearts, to drink to the Hon. Whitelaw Reid. (Applause and cries of "Ohio to the front!") Gentlemen, Mr. Reid.

WHAT MR. REID SAID.

When General Swayne finished, all assembled arose and drank the health of Mr. Reid with enthusiastic cheers, which were continued while he stood upon his feet before beginning to speak.

Throughout his remarks the more serious allusions were applauded and merriment followed the livelier portions of his address. This is what he said:

Mr. Chairman: No greeting could touch me more profoundly than this. No words could go straighter to my heart than yours; and when I remember what honor your father brought our State, and at what a price you yourself have served her and the Nation, I am doubly glad that, in the regretted absence of its President, it is by your voice the Ohio Society receives me back.

This is indeed an ideal welcome. It gives the first hand-grasp from the Metropolis which is our home and our pride; and at the same time it carries me really home—to that fairest of lands that lies between the lakes and the beautiful river—to the dear, gracious mother of us all. When she stretches out her hand, the joy of return is complete.

No other applause can ever be so sweet to a man as that which comes from those who have known him earliest and longest. Better, to many a tired man of the world, the cheer of his native village than more stately honors from the most powerful of communities. Believe me, Mr. Chairman, in retiring from public office there can be no compliment more grateful than an assurance like this with which you honor me to-night, that your old friends and neighbors have not been ashamed of you.

And next, it is pleasant to be made to feel once more that those to whom you were sent were not tired of you. Two weeks ago, at a banquet like this, I had the honor to say good-bye to the high members of the French Government, and to representative Frenchmen who were kind enough to say they were sorry to have me go. To-night I find my friend, the Viscount d'Abzac, representing the same Government here, to add another grace to the warmth of this most charming of greetings to a returning townsman. In the large banqueting hall of the Continental, in trying to express to the great American colony and to the Frenchmen about me the conflicting emotions by which I was possessed, I told the simple truth in saying that while I was eager, even to home-sickness, in my desire to get back to New-York, I did not in the least want to leave Paris. Who that has ever passed under the spell of the City of Light—the one city of the world—can fail to understand or to sympathize with the truly Irish perplexity? Who that has ever known France or the French will not join with me in urging the duty, not merely of perpetual friendship, but of the warmest appreciation for that fascinating and chivalric people

who have for many centuries commanded the admiration or the wonder of the world, and who are now well entered on the second century of an unbroken and most helpful friendship for us. I never met a Frenchman, from the Elysée or the Faubourg St. Germain to the forests of Auvergne, who did not, as soon as he found I was an American, receive me without question as a friend. We shall see more of them here during the next year; and I hope every American to whom the opportunity may come will exert himself to make them feel as much at home among us as we have always made ourselves and been made at home among them.

NOT UNALLOYED PLEASURE.

Those of us who have entered the fifties have learned that there is no great happiness in this world without attendant pain. To-night the joy of coming back is marred by finding such gaps in your ranks. The numbers, to be sure, are not diminished; but, ah! what faces we miss. I cannot speak in the Ohio Society after a three years' absence without one word of tender and reverential regard for the memory of your greatest member. Rough on the surface, sometimes, as a chestnut burr, but always sweet and tender inside as the nut; that is the man as one loves to recall him. We had occasionally the sharpest differences of opinion, and yet, from my early manhood till he said good-bye to me on sailing, he had honored me with his friendship. Not a syllable do I care to utter to-night of his public career. The world has long known that by heart. I only wish, as I recall the kind parting and the kinder messages and letters sent over seas, and as I now note the vacant place, to pause before it for a moment, and salute the mighty shade. What glories the future may have in store for the Ohio Society we know not, but the past, at least, is secure. We have had William Tecumseh Sherman.

We have had another, too, whose absence strikes sadly on a returning son of the State. He had guided the finances of the country through a most critical period—Ohio has had a specialty of great finance ministers, from Ewing and Chase and Sherman to Foster. He had achieved a brilliant success. Mr. Windom stood to the financial world as the champion of sound measures and as the pledge of National solvency and faith and honor; and in that moment, in a supreme effort, he fell. When in a foreign land I read the story, grief for the great loss was almost swallowed up in pride for the splendid end this son of Ohio had made.

There is no occasion to-night to call the roll of our Ohio worthies. We have never been charged, even by our worst enemies, with ever neglecting the duty to celebrate ourselves. But perhaps you will permit me a single reminiscence. On one of the last occasions when I had the opportunity to act in the office with which you honored me as Vice-President of the Ohio Society, I found an occasion, in presenting to you a gentleman who had been recently dropped from the Senate, and had thereupon described himself as a "dead statesman," to point out that, nevertheless, he had in him the material for an uncommonly live President. Well, gentlemen, I haven't yet seen the necessity of apologizing for any mistake made in that prediction as to the future of that particular member of this Society.

Now it is said that the other party is looking about for a candidate. But why should it have the slightest difficulty? Here is the first President of the Ohio Society ready to its hand, statesman himself, and the son of a statesman; and although he has the proverbial shyness of both the politician and the lawyer, I will undertake to be responsible that he will answer quite soon after his name is called. And if, for any reason, that name of Ewing is not called, then in the language of my friend, Mr. Bennett, I would like to know, "Why not Calvin S. Brice?" Two States claim him; and he is bright enough for the whole forty-four.

THE SON OF ALL AMERICA.

It has been sometimes said that there are two kinds of men in this country; those who were born in Ohio, and those who wish they had been. A brilliant example of the latter class is with us to-night; and very pleasant it is for tired eyes to rest on the familiar features of this prince of orators and of good fellows. His genius and versatility have accomplished wonders in the way of acquiring nationalities; but this is a shining height he has not reached. He has, on a hundred occasions and to the entire satisfaction of thousands of auditors, announced himself as a Dutchman, a Puritan, a Huguenot, a Scotchman, a native of Peekskill, and a bit of an Irishman. But he has missed the crown. He was never born in Ohio—and now I am afraid he never will be.

Nevertheless, the Ohio man continues to be prevalent. In the present Cabinet, for example, out of the eight members, four of them are from Ohio—and two of them are here to-night to explain the circumstance. When these four Cabinet officers vote together, and the President joins with them, the rest of the concern must feel lonely !

Mr. President, I forbear. The trend of feeling seems to be toward levity. And yet nothing could be further from my purpose. I am most happy to find myself so thoroughly at home—so completely surrounded by those I know the best and prize the highest. I am most grateful for the care which has assembled here so many whom it is a pride and a pleasure for me to meet again—Howells, almost the oldest and certainly one of the dearest of my friends, with whom I lived in the same house nearly a third of a century ago, when he paid his board out of a salary of $15 a week, and I out of one a good deal less; Ward, who made statues in those days, while we made newspaper articles, and whose early wares have lasted better; the gentlemen of my own profession; Mr. Childs, who is the friend of all of us; I see beside him in most amicable conversation a man whose name is identified with the history of journalism in the United States and peculiarly identified with two newspapers, one of which I have the honor to control and the other of which is one of my most dangerous rivals. (Applause and laughter.)   Colonel McClure and Mr. McKelway, who lend to the wrong side such potent and persuasive pens; my old master in the newspaper business, Mr. Richard Smith, and my old opponent, Mr. Murat Halstead; Mr. Gilder, who has made one of the most successful magazines in the world; the delegates of the club which for fourteen years endured me as its president; these representatives of the Government, National, State and city; and this whole brilliant and imposing assemblage. I am touched beyond words that you should have shown me this kindness—I am happy to have escaped in apparent safety from public service and to be received among you again; and I close as I began, with a heartfelt expression of my profoundest and most grateful thanks.

As Mr. Reid resumed his seat, the entire assemblage again arose and cheered him lustily for several minutes.

Mr. Reid's pleasantries directed toward Mr. Ewing caused that gentleman to blush, but without embarrassment.   His allusions to President Harrison were heartily cheered, as were also those of Mr. Elkins, in the course of that gentleman's address. His reference to Mr. Blaine,

who it was hoped to the last moment would be present, excited great applause.

Then General Swayne said:

Gentlemen—Mr. Reid's description of brilliant Paris will enable us to understand the saying, now long prevalent, that good Americans do go there when they die. (Laughter.) The peculiarity of Mr. Reid's experience is that his inherent excellence has secured for him a brief translation in advance. (Laughter.) It is the triumph of his human sympathies, thank God, surviving, that has brought him home again. In presenting Mr. Reid to you, I was not unmindful of the fact that he had been our country's Minister to France. I shrank from entering (until he introduced it) on that long-time connection with which you are familiar, between the early history of Ohio and the sympathies of France. . . . But this is no place for history. It is rather a place for memory. The distinguished gentleman has reminded us of Sherman, and he has reminded us of Windom; and perhaps what he has said reminds you that both those names are memories of this room. Only three days ago, and here in this room, that other great Sherman told us the wonderful history of his brother who has departed; and it was in this room that Mr. Windom fell. And so, one might go on through all those incidents. It is no wonder that they bring up Presidential suggestions. The names of Sherman and of Ewing bring up that story, which we all know, of how when General Sherman was urged to accept a nomination for the Presidency, he replied: "No; I am a soldier; take my brother John. If you don't want my brother John, there is my brother-in-law, Tom." (Applause.) I remember, too, those days, for I was in Columbus then, when Quincy Ward, Whitelaw Reid and William Dean Howells were living in one house. The most historic incident, perhaps, that Mr. Reid spoke of, was the fact that by a happy accident, or by the fitness of things, as you may prefer to call it, it was in this room that the first mention was made, or the first suggestion, that Benjamin Harrison ought to be President of the United States. (Great applause.) His sympathies are with us now. I wish we had him here. (Applause.) We have him not, but we have here a ranking member of the Cabinet to represent him, the Hon. Charles Foster, the Secretary of the Treasury, who will now address you. (Great applause.)

MR. FOSTER FOR THE CABINET.

Secretary Foster had a hearty reception, and showed evident signs of improved health since he last spoke in the same hall at the dinner of the St. Patrick's Society. He said:

Mr. Chairman and Gentlemen of the Ohio Society of New-York: If I have paid my dues I am a member of this society, and I am not quite certain about that. (Laughter.) I have been a member from the beginning, but it has never been my pleasure to attend one of your banquets before. I am here to-night the ranking officer of President Harrison's Cabinet, to testify to you of the great success of Minister Reid in the discharge of his duties at the Court of France. (Applause.) Minister Reid has had considerable to say about Ohio. We never forget to glorify ourselves; but while I was Governor, that was for four years, I was called upon many times to respond to the toast of the State of Ohio. It began to be irksome; I found myself repeating, and I went into a study of the reasons why Ohio people had so singularly and beyond all other States of the Union distinguished themselves. (Laughter.)

Upon examination of the State I found a peculiar

condition of things, conditions that exist in no other State. Our manufacturing, our agriculture, our mercantile and mining interests exist there in about equal proportions, while in no other State do these conditions exist in any such proportions. New-York and New-England are largely financial and manufacturing; Pennsylvania manufacturing; the South and West agricultural. Now all these great forces operating upon the minds of the people of Ohio so equally produce a level-headed set (applause and laughter); while in New-York and New-England, these forces not operating equally produce a lopsided faculty. (Laughter.) Our institutions are peculiar. We believe them to be the best of any country on earth; certainly here every man, be he rich or poor, has an equal chance in the race of life. We believe in rotation in office. (Applause.)

Mr. Reid—But not now. (Laughter.)

Mr. Foster—No, not just now. (Laughter.) We have no class of people, perhaps we may get some in the Civil Service, who hold office for life. In other countries, especially in the diplomatic service, the diplomats and the people who perform that duty are trained from boyhood and remain in that service all their life. In this country we pick up our diplomats from our lawyers, from our merchants, from our newspaper men, and we send them abroad to discharge this duty. Now, I undertake to say that from Benjamin Franklin down to the present time our diplomats have been as able, have been as successful, and I think more so, in the discharge of these duties than the trained men of other countries. (Applause.) And I think, my friends, that one of the finest illustrations that we have of the success of the newspaper fraternity exists in that of Mr. Reid. (Enthusiastic applause.)

There was much applause at the close of Secretary Foster's remarks, and the enthusiasm continued for some time after he had taken his seat. Then General Swayne introduced Secretary Elkins in the following remarks:

Gentlemen: It may be necessary to suggest to some of you who did not come from Ohio—it may be as well to call your attention just here to Mr. Reid's extreme veracity and carefulness of truth in this, that when he was attempting to explain how it was that the bronzes of Mr. Ward had outlasted the correspondence of Mr. Reid himself and the sonnets of Mr. Howells, he said that it was because the bronzes were drier than the other two, and not because they had more brass. (Laughter and applause.) The distinguished Secretary of the Treasury reminded me this evening that his business was with figures and facts, and not with speaking. I cannot say that there came in to my mind then the celebrated adage which prevails among lawyers, that there is nothing so misleading on earth in figures as facts (laughter); but I was very sure that when he came to speak what we should have would be the truth of facts with the exactness of figures; and we all agree precisely and unqualifiedly with him in the estimate of the foreign services of Mr. Reid which he tells us are entertained by the Administration. (Applause.) But he has not sung the whole praise of Mr. Reid, nor are we tired of hearing from the Administration about Mr. Reid, and I therefore have renewed pleasure in calling up before you the Secretary of War, the Honorable Stephen B. Elkins.

SECRETARY ELKINS ALSO.

Mr. Elkins spoke as follows:

Mr. Chairman and Members of the Ohio Society: I am glad the honor has come to me, as a member of the Ohio Society, to take part in this splendid reception and expression of respect and regard for a fellow-member, who, by his ability in the untried field of diplomacy, has gained new laurels and added to his fame and distinction in this and other lands. (Applause.)

I am not permitted, in what I have to say, to dwell on the story of the life of our distinguished guest, nor to speak of the unhindered succession of triumphs which has marked his career in everything he has undertaken. All this has, happily, been intrusted to safer hands. I am allowed, however, on behalf of the Administration, of which I am a humble member, and which our guest has done so much to make popular and respected at home and abroad (applause), to perform the most pleasing duty, I am sure, that will fall to me while in office, of saying to you, Mr. Minister Reid, in this presence, that the Chief Executive and those associated with him in administering the affairs of this great Republic send you words of cordial greeting and a warm welcome on your return home. (Hearty applause.)

You went abroad, taking with you the esteem and affection of many of the leading men of your country. You had already risen to distinction and your name, your ability and your varied accomplishments were widely known and appreciated. You return decorated with the confidence and approbation of the two leading Republics of the world by reason of your great services to both. (Applause.)

There is a fitness in what we are doing here this evening. Our guest aided in organizing this Society, which honors itself in honoring him. Here he is at home, surrounded by the loyal sons of Ohio, among whom are many of his truest and best friends, proud of him and proud of his achievements.

It will be remembered by many here that at the first annual society of this Society the distinguished gentleman, now President of the United States, was an invited guest. (Applause.) General Ewing was then the worthy head of the Society. Our guest, then vice-president, in fitting and graceful terms called on General Harrison to respond to a sentiment, and in his remarks ventured to suggest that it was among the possibilities that another Harrison might some day fill the Presidential chair. From this happy allusion, some members of the Ohio Society claim they saw in the speaker as he responded, with that clearness, power and strength which always characterize his graceful oratory, what his countrymen later on discovered, that he was fitted for the high office of President, and to which by their choice he was soon after elevated. (Applause.)

A TRIBUTE TO THE PRESIDENT.

As Ohio men, we are proud of our Ohio President. (Cheers for President Harrison.) He enjoys the confidence of his countrymen everywhere. He has shown to the country and the world, in point of integrity, intellectual force, power of administration and ability to deal with large and difficult questions, that he will stand among the first of the great Presidents of the Republic. (Loud applause.)

It may be a matter of historic interest to some, surely to this Society it is a source of pride, that the State of Ohio has given to this Administration the President and four members of his Cabinet, an event not likely to occur again in the history of any State in the Union. (Cheers for Ohio.)

In the long future history will busy itself with our guest's name. It will attempt to tell us what he did and what manner of man he was. Among other things, I am sure it will set down that his home was always open to his friends, and the strong men of his time gathered there. Oftentimes might be seen in his library the leading men of his party, meeting to discuss its policy, among them the mightiest names that adorn the history of our country. There have been seen at these gatherings James G. Blaine (great and enthusiastic applause), Chauncey M. Depew (applause), William M. Evarts (applause), Warner Miller, (applause), Frank Hiscock (applause), and many others that I might name.

At another time, under his hospitable roof might be seen the representative journalists of the country, and at another the great business men of the metropolis, and at another the leading people in literature and art. All welcome, all at home, and the host easy and at home with all. (Applause.)

The Administration rejoices in Minister Reid's success. His services to his country in his high office are among its best assets. The great Secretary under whom he served (applause) regrets that he is detained at Washington and prevented from joining in this reception. He could and would tell you, were he here, with what ability, zeal and satisfaction to him Minister Reid always discharged his duties, and the beneficial results he secured for his country. (Applause.)

May I not hope that it is within the permission of good taste to add, in all the good things said of our guest to-night, that the Ohio Society has not forgotten, and can never forget, his gifted, cultured and charming wife, known to so many of us, who has done so much to make his home one of the most attractive in all this land, and who has aided him largely in his progress toward success and preferment here and abroad; and to her, returning to us again, the sons of Ohio gathered here to-night extend a most hearty welcome and greeting. (Prolonged applause and cheering.)

MR. DEPEW'S ELOQUENCE.

General Swayne then introduced Chauncey M. Depew in the following happy style:

It is part of the singular good-fortune of Ohio, and particularly of Ohioans in New-York, that if ever those results which seem traceable to the mingling on one soil of many people in Ohio, and the development thereby of many-sided excellencies of individual character, if ever those influences or those results threaten to impinge upon the braces of diffidence and the virtue of Ohio modesty (laughter), they encounter a check at once in the more manifold brilliance of the character of Depew; just as it behooves us, after what has been said, to remember that the crowning achievement of our distinguished friend and the crowning blessing of his career, quite irrespective of honors that the future has in store, has been the acquisition in New-York of that most gracious lady who became his wife. (Continued applause.)

Mr. Reid's return is from Paris to New-York. Like the rest of us, it is in New-York that Mr. Reid has found his fitting and most satisfactory home. And like the rest of us, his dwelling here, like the existence of this society, is but a tribute to the generosity of the great city and commonwealth of New-York. (Applause.) We have our little fun; we endure the little jests that come; we take the fun that is made of us quite easily, because the jest is hushed by the reality of the achievement, as the criticism is stilled because the emulation has been generous.

We should do ill in welcoming Mr. Reid home to New-York without a welcome from New-York. (Applause.) We welcome him to our recollection and to our society, of which he is one. New-York welcomes him. We welcome him as belonging in a sense to him. New-York welcomes him mainly because he is hers. Who can so well welcome him home to New-York as Mr. Depew? (Cheers and applause.) There was a man asked not long since, in examining him as to his qualifications to sit as a juror, if ever he had heard of Mr. Depew, and he said no. (Prolonged laughter.) I heard the Mayor of Philadelphia say soon afterward that if there was found such a fellow in a court in Pennsylvania, he would be at once ejected as too slow to live in Philadelphia. (Laughter and applause.) It is, therefore, probably an unnecessary precaution for me to point Mr. Depew out to you, yet I think I am peculiarly qualified in that respect, if need be, for my memory of him goes back to days at Yale College, when there came there one day a bright youth with a shrewd face and a kindly eye, who soon became the great master of our college politics. The shrewd face and the kindly eye are still here, but those marks happily are not uncommon; they are universal in this company. Therefore, perhaps I might suggest to you that in those days, and you may recognize him, the distinguishing characteristic of his appearance was the abundant and excellent quality of his long, light hair.

(Laughter and applause.) Let me present to you the Honorable Chauncey M. Depew. (Cheers and applause.)

Mr. Depew said:

Mr. Chairman and Gentlemen: It is not only a pleasure, but a distinction to be here to-night as the jumping-place for these Ohio orators. (Laughter.) Lieutenant Totten has predicted that we may look for the millennium about this time (Laughter.) As I glance up and down this table I think it has come. (laughter)—and Reid seems to be our Gabriel. (Renewed laughter.)

But it is not only in journalism that we have these the millennium advantages, because to-night our guest is welcomed by two worlds, this and the next—in Elkins and Warner Miller. (Prolonged laughter.) I have frequently heard my friend Reid complimented upon the qualities which he exhibits, derived from his Scotch descent, but he never exhibited them more kindly than when he offered to give a bond to-night with any penalty that any Ohio man who might be nominated for President would accept. (Laughter.) That is the cheapest risk I ever knew. (Laughter.)

The Secretary of the Treasury has reminded us that the equal industries of Ohio lead to a level-headedness that is not evidenced in other States, but it is a level-headedness that is characterized by a single ambition (laughter), and the praises of an Ohio man in office for rotation in office are the Pickwickian utterances of an after-dinner speech. (Laughter.)

But New-York is delighted to welcome Mr. Reid here to-night because she created him. (Laughter.) She always prefers that her creation should be born elsewhere, in order to show what she can do with raw material. (Laughter.) It has been my lot every year for the last ten to deliver a eulogy upon some eminent son of Ohio. He has always been dead. (Laughter.) It has created an impression in my mind that there was some mysterious relation between eminence in Ohio and the grave. But it is delightful; it is atonic; it revives my spirits, and brings me into harmonious relations with level-headedness, to be able to speak about an Ohio man who is very much alive. If any person here present, or not here, doubts that he is alive, they will find it out through the columns of the New-York Tribune during the coming months of the Presidential canvass. (Applause.) They will discover there that this brilliant journalist will occasionally—and on rare occasions, because on only those occasions do they merit it—criticise his party friends; and on all occasions—because on all occasions they merit it—criticise his party enemies. (Prolonged applause.)

One of the severest criticisms uttered against President Harrison was the fact that he selected journalists for diplomatic places. I confess that as a lawyer I felt in full harmony with that criticism. (Laughter.) It was enough to have these newspapers trench upon our prerogatives in the Legislature and in Congress, but the diplomatic services we had claimed for ourselves, except when for ornamental purposes it becomes necessary to appoint a literary man. (Laughter.) The critics said: "What can a journalist whose mind, whose training, whose thought, whose efforts are in discussions of theoretical politics and practical religion (laughter), of sociological questions and party candidates, whose distinguishing and almost only public service is at innumerable banquets to respond to The Press (laughter)—what can he know about international law and the delicate intricacies of the diplomatic service?"

Only twice in the history of the relations between France and the United States as Nations has France been prominently and interestingly in the eye and mind of the American people. First, when she gave us the assistance which secured our independence, and second, when there was negotiated with her a treaty which will be of incalculable advantage to the people of this country. In the first instance our Minister was Benjamin Franklin and in the second Whitelaw Reid, both journalists. (Applause.)

THE SISTER REPUBLICS.

By sentiment and service we are more closely bound to France than any other European nations, and yet in the rapidity of our own development and the crowding events which have brought us in commercial communion or collision with other nations, we have taken little account of and given little thought to France during the last hundred years. Her fleet, her army and her credit enabled us to bring our revolution to a triumphant conclusion; and the ideas of liberty absorbed here by the French soldiers and carried back to France revolutionized the continent of Europe. (Applause.) Upon the lines of civil and religious freedom and of the ideas and the measures which tend to the promotion of the happiness of mankind, France and the United States have developed together. Their friendly relations have been enormously strengthened by the moral support which we gave the young Republic in its struggle for the permanence of its free institutions; by the vigorous, wise and enlightened course of the American Minister who is our guest to-night. (Applause.)

Our poets, our orators and our great writers, in celebrating the glories of our Western Empire, have all failed to recognize in epic verse and fitting phrase that principal and perennial source of our prosperity, the American hog. (Laughter.) He, more than any other agency, has solved the problem of the farm and the market. When the Western farmer would be compelled to burn his corn because the price at the seaboard would not enable him to bear the cost of transportation, this intelligent animal consumes the corn, chemically works it up in his own person into profitable pork, and then transports himself to market to clear the mortgage from the farm and add to the wealth of his country. (Laughter.)

The Governments of the Old World have always been jealous of our growth and prosperity, and fearful of the penetrating and propagating power of American ideas. They could not keep out Yankees, for they go everywhere. They could not keep out Yankee inventions, for their adoption was necessary if they would keep pace in industrial competitions. They could not keep out American wheat, because their fields were insufficient to raise their own supply. But in self-preservation and with marvellous unanimity, and backing up the effort with the whole force of their great armaments, they banished and then prohibited the re-entrance of the American hog. For eleven years this great staple of our country has been denied admission. The popular sentiment was so strong in favor of the prohibition that any attempt to remove it threatened to hurl the Government of the day from power. It was to this most difficult task that Mr. Reid applied his ability and his energy. His success has moved the torpid pulse of the Chamber of Commerce to enthusiastic gratitude, and has done more for the commerce and wealth of our country than any single diplomatic transaction of the last decade. (Applause.)

It is an old saw that every good American goes to Paris before he dies. It is generally admitted that the visit hastens that desired or lamented event. (Laughter.) Paris is known to our countrymen as the metropolis where their women are gowned and their men bankrupted. (Laughter.) For the last three years we, which means virtually the majority of the American people who travel, have found in Paris a model American home, whose perfect appointments made us proud of our country and whose generous hospitality made us feel at home. (Applause.)

The position of an American Minister among the ironclad customs and inflexible traditions of the diplomatic service in the older countries is not a happy one. According to immemorial usage the Ambassador, in the absence of his sovereign, is the sovereign in person, or if his State is not monarchical he represents the sovereignty of the commonwealth. Immemorial usage assigns to the Minister only the dignity of a diplomatic agent. At the great capitals like Paris all the Powers of Europe and Asia send Ambassadors, the republics of South America and the Isthmus send Ambassadors, and Hayti is represented by an Ambassador. Whenever the representatives of these Governments call upon the Foreign Minister of France the obsequious attendant throws open both doors of the Foreign Office to the Ambassador; he opens one door to admit the American Minister. At state receptions, official functions, Presidential dinners, the American Minister decorates the rear of the diplomatic procession and sits next to Hayti at the foot of the table. (Laughter.)

DIGNITY WITHOUT ARROGANCE.

Our adherence as a Nation to this Spartan simplicity decorates the rhetoric of the Fourth-of-July orator as to the prestige and power of the great Republic, and degrades among his official associates the representatives of the great Republic. The American Minister, who is thus officially handicapped and who has a proper patriotic appreciation of the dignity and position which his Government rightfully holds among the nations of the earth, has a most difficult and delicate task. But it can be truthfully said by every one who was on the spot to observe that with tact which was never at fault, and dignity which compelled recognition, and assertiveness which was never offensive, and a pride which was never arrogant, the grandeur and glory of the Republic of the United States so pervaded all official assemblages when the Minister was present that for the last three years wherever the American Minister has sat has been next to the head of the table. (Enthusiastic applause.)

New-York stands to the people in all parts of our country as does a great university to its young men. The student who has won academic honors in Ohio or California, in Idaho or Indiana, comes to Yale or Harvard. Thereafter for the rest of his life he is known as an alumnus of Yale or of Harvard. So the man who has grown too large for his neighborhood or his State in the West, the South, the East or the North comes to New-York. Here he is welcomed without ardor and given such equal chance that in due time he may stand in social rank among the Knickerbockers, or find himself crystallized among the "four hundred." (Laughter.)

It is this cosmopolitan spirit which gives New-York an Ohio Society larger than any to be found in any city in Ohio, and a Southern Society stronger than any organized in any city in the South. It is in this spirit that we have more Germans than in any German city, save Berlin, and more Irish than in any city in the Emerald Isle. It was this attraction which brought to us Ohio's great son, General Grant, and caused him to request that he might be buried upon our island, a request which I trust will soon be honored by a monument erected over his grave worthy the great captain and the great metropolis. (Loud applause.) It was the multiplied charms of New-York which drew here the most attractive soldier of our time and made him

loved by us as he loved us, another of Ohio's grand
contributions to the glory of the Republic, General
Sherman. (Applause.) New-York welcomes the children of her adoption, when they are worthy of her
recognition, with the same unstinted and generous
gratitude or honor as she does her children to the
manor born.

I speak for her best impulses, for her vigorous manhood, for her broad and catholic judgment, when I
say on her behalf to Whitelaw Reid, "Welcome!
thrice welcome, back to New-York!" (Applause loud
and long-continued.)

COLONEL McCLURE FOR THE PRESS.

The next speaker was Colonel McClure, who
said :

This is to me a most pleasant occasion. I have
known the distinguished guest of the evening for thirty
years as a journalist; remember him well as one of
the most brilliant of the remarkable galaxy of war
correspondents developed during the Rebellion, and
have noted his rapid advancement to the very front
rank of his profession, not only with the pride that I
have always felt in those who dignify the newspaper
calling, but also with the gratification that ever comes
to us all when cherished friends attain exceptional
success. There is eminent fitness in this gathering of
distinguished sons of Ohio to do honor to Whitelaw
Reid, who is now a leading figure in American progress
as journalist and diplomat, but whose name will be
cherished chiefly, not only in this but in other lands,
as one who has shed the richest lustre upon American
journalism. (Applause.)

What is journalism in this great Republic? In
England it has been called the fourth estate; in the
free institutions of America, where the people are
sovereign, and where the newspapers are the chief educators of those who govern the land, the Press is the
first estate. Like all great elements of power, it has
its shadowed aspects. It has many teachers of its
own creation who are discreditable to the great calling
and a reproach to the most intelligent people of the
earth; but, discounted by all its imperfections, the
Press of the United States is the best the world has
ever known, and is the most potent of all the varied
factors in our free government. I regard the editorial
chair as the highest public trust of our free institutions. Presidents, Cabinets, Senators, representative
bodies come and play their brief parts and pass away,
many of them into forgetfulness; and great parties
rise and fall in the swift mutations of the political
efforts of a free people. Journalism not only survives
all the varied changes of our political system, but
its duties and responsibilities multiply with each year
as it becomes more and more the great teacher of the
people in their homes. (Applause.)

When President Harrison came into power he honored himself by nominating to three of the four first-
class missions of the Government distinguished representatives of American journals—Whitelaw Reid to
France, Charles Emory Smith to Russia and Murat
Halstead to Germany. High as was the compliment
paid to journalism by the President, the highest compliment of all was paid to Mr. Halstead when he was
rejected by a Senate of his own political faith; and
an exceptional compliment was paid to Mr. Reid, the
honored guest of the evening, by his narrow
escape from rejection by the same body. (Laughter.)
There was not an objection urged against the confirmation of either of these eminent journalists that
was not inspired by resentment for the best journalistic efforts of their lives. It was the manly, fearless criticism of public men and public measures:
the exposure of the infirmities and perfidy of those
who pose as representative statesmen of the Republic,
that honored Mr. Halstead by refusing him the mission
for which he had been nominated, and that paid a
rare tribute to Mr. Reid by grudgingly assenting to
his appointment. The cowardly, submissive journalist
is innocent of antagonisms; the aggressive, fearless,
faithful journalist commands the highest distinction
of malignant hostility from all who make politics a
trade and prostitute statesmanship to mean ambition
and jobbery. (Applause.) I recall also with great
pleasure the fact that the two great editors who were
confirmed to fill first-class missions have both voluntarily resigned to resume their newspaper duties.
We are here to-night to welcome Mr. Reid back to
his high public trust of journalism, and in Philadelphia we shall soon be able to welcome Mr. Smith,
who has resigned his mission and will resume the

great calling of his life. These leaders of our profession have learned the littleness of official trust
when compared with the highest of all public trusts—
the direction of a great newspaper. (Applause.)

EDITORS IN PUBLIC OFFICE.

Need I remind this intelligent assembly of Horace
Greeley, confessedly the ablest of all the many able
journalists our country has produced? He was often
more potent even than the President, and no man
ever accomplished so much in the education of
the people in all that was beneficent and just. He
cared not for the honors or emoluments of public
office, but he had fought the battles of the people,
for he had braved obloquy in his tireless efforts for
the oppressed and lowly, and his great sympathetic
heart that ever beat responsive to the cries of the
oppression craved the grateful recognition of the
people to whose cause he so sincerely dedicated his
life. (Applause.) A brief term in Congress proved to
all, as it must have proved to himself, that while the
great editor was a master in criticising the imperfections of public men, the Congressman who had
criticised his fellows through his own newspaper
columns was a dismal failure. At last the great
dream of his life gave promise of fulfilment as he was
nominated for the Presidency; but the clouds came,
his hopes perished; and, smitten in all that he loved or
dreamed of, his death was welcomed by his friends
as ending the fitful life that had settled in a starless
midnight of mental darkness. And Raymond,
whose name is spoken with reverence by every
American journalist; the only man whose lance was
never shivered in his many conflicts with his great
master, is now hardly remembered as Legislator,
Speaker, Lieutenant-Governor and member of Congress.
He was a leader of leaders in politics. He was at
the baptismal font of Republicanism, and he penned
the platform of Pittsburg in 1856, that crystallized
the greatest party of American history and made the
most heroic achievements of any civilization of the
world. I have seen him calm a turbulent National
Convention, call it to order and method, and guide
it to the great results of its mission; but who re-
members him as Congressman save as the target
of the matchless invective of Stevens, or as having
recorded failure after failure in statesmanship?

Dana, the Nestor of American journalism, dated his
great success and power as a newspaper man from the
time when he indignantly declined a second place in
the Customs of your city, tendered to him by a President whose election he had favored. (Applause.)
Thenceforth he was free from the thongs of political
expectation, and no one has more pointedly illustrated
the difference in distinction and achievement between the editor who puts journalism before party
and party honors and the editor who struggles
for party success to share party spoils. (Applause.) The elder Bennett has grandly illustrated the true theory of journalism by the assump-
tion that a great editor could never be an acceptable
popular candidate for any party, and I have reason
to know that he regarded it as the crowning distinction of his life that he had the opportunity to decline,
as incompatible with his journalistic duties, the same
mission from which our honored guest of to-night
has just returned.

NONE MAY DECLINE THE CALL.

All respected newspapers teach that it is the duty
of the citizen to accept public trust when called upon
by the sovereign power of our free government, and
none will dispute the correctness of the theory: but
where in all the land is there a higher public trust than
that accepted by the editor of a widely read newspaper?
In our free government there is no official position
that can reasonably be accepted as promotion from the
editorial chair; and the fact that political place is only
attainable by a greater or less amount of dependence
upon the favor of political partisanship emphasizes
the necessity of maintaining the absolute independence
of journalism by the absolute refusal of the public
places for which the jostling of mean ambition is ever
in struggle. The time was when journalism was confined to party organs and when newspapers were a
luxury. Public office was then measurably com-
patible with the public trust of journalism; but that
age has passed away never to return. To-day the
newspaper is the educator of the home and is read in
almost every family in the land. It is the daily lesson
to our children; the daily monitor to those who exercise the sovereignty of our government. It is constant

in its duties and its achievements. On great occasions it arouses public sentiment to aggressive action; in common times it is ceaselessly fulfilling its mission as gently as the dews which jewel the flowers of the early morning, and it is the one calling of our free land that cannot be dependent upon the whims of party leaders or the resentments of those who control official positions. It must be "unawed by influence, unbribed by gain." Such is the true mission of the journalist where journalism is so inseparably interwoven with the sovereignty of the Republic, and it is to this high trust and duty that we welcome back the honored guest of the evening. (Loud applause.)

FOR THE PRESS OF NEW-YORK.

The next speaker was St. Clair McKelway, who responded for the press of New-York. He said:

Mr. President and Gentlemen of the Ohio Society: I am asked to speak for the press of New-York at this dinner to Whitelaw Reid. A lifelong relationship to that press enables me to know what it is and how it feels toward the guest of the evening. My active labors on the press of this State began about when Whitelaw Reid swung from the West to the East, and became entitled to membership in an Ohio Society in the City of New-York. I have watched with interest the effect of him on the press of the State and the effect of the press of the State upon him. (Laughter and applause.) He began by preferring news to everything else. He preferred the best news, as he regarded it, to any other kind. (Of course the very best in his opinion was such as told of Republican victories. (Laughter.) In that sense he tried to make his news as he went along, like the lecturer on history of whom Froude said that he made his facts as he went along. (Laughter.) Mr. Reid, however, could not always publish that kind of news. Happily that kind does not always occur, although it does occur with depressing frequency about every fourth year. (Laughter and applause.) He, therefore, carefully discriminated among the news which can always be depended on to occur, and of that he preferred the best to the worst. The best, in his opinion, was that which told of good things done or incited to the doing of things that were good. (Applause.) I do not mean good in a namby-pamby sense, but in the broad and liberal sense of the word. It would take too long to give you a disquisition on news, or to tell the story of Whitelaw Reid's relation to it. Only large, luminous, typical and representative statements need to be made on this head.

Whitelaw Reid early magnified the news of education and the educational power of news. He set the fashion of having colleges completely reported on the occasion of their great events. He caused the social science congresses of the United States, Great Britain and other countries to be carefully written up. The best thought which science, teaching or religion uttered found room in The Tribune. The paper was made desirable to those who know much and necessary to those who would know more. The work of agitation committed to the lyceum had ended in the achievement of union, freedom and manhood suffrage. (Applause.) As the agitator stepped down and as the reformer retired to a well-earned rest, the teacher, the instructor, the educator, the men of exact knowledge and careful investigation, the scientists, as we call them, came to the front. Permanent institutes of knowledge took the place of scattered lecture bureaus. The specialists of the country organized on the lines of their learning in the world. The Tribune became their organ by becoming their chronicle. Other metropolitan papers now share that honor and that responsibility. The Tribune, under Whitelaw Reid, was the pioneer in that work. (Applause.)

THE PAPER OF EDUCATORS.

It still does it better than any of its contemporaries, for it has learned how to do it well, and the men and women who formulate the educational thought of the country, while admitting the claims and desiring the good offices of the entire press, regard The Tribune as the preferred medium between the public and themselves. No newspaper man would recognize in what I have to say that conformity to the facts which honor his calling if I left out of view the service which The Tribune, under Whitelaw Reid, has done in journalism, by raising the standard of news from Washington, London, Paris, Albany, Boston, Chicago, San Francisco and other points of importance and interest in the affairs of the world. I do not acquit his correspondents at those points of expressing wrong opinions, for they do not always

express my own. (Laughter.) I do, however, claim for them that they have raised the standard of the expression of opinion to a high plane. They have written as gentlemen and as ladies for persons of like culture. They have had the confidence and the support of the home office in every instance. (Applause.) Otherwise they could never have done so well as they have done. Their views are always their own, whether they are the views of the reader or not, and in notably trusted cases, whether they are the views of The Tribune itself or not. If they dissent from their paper and if their paper dissents from them, two expressions of value on the subject are thereby certainly secured. The impersonality of The Tribune, under Whitelaw Reid, in the sense in which the paper is collectively regarded as the product of many minds controlled by one, has not been more observable and commendable than the consideration shown to the individualities of the important workers at important points in the various fields where they exercise their practised functions. This fact has received a complete illustration during Mr. Reid's absence. While he was abroad he took his hands off the paper, and he kept them off. The paper went on, and none but experts or those behind the scenes could very well have told that the chief editorship was in abeyance, or, if you please, in commission. I predict that when he puts his hands on again, only a little difference, inseparable from the new importance which his personality has taken on in the service of his country, will be observable at the first, and that pretty soon it will not be observable at all. The renewed force will revitalize the whole paper, or the paper as a whole will absorb and dominate the renewed force and make it over again into its likeness.

There is another thing I want to say about this man. He brought to a stop, so far as he was concerned and his paper was concerned, the business of making personal attacks on other newspaper editors, or of replying to such attacks made upon himself. (Applause.) The wars between Greeley and Raymond, and Raymond and Bennett, and James Watson Webb and all the rest of them, which were a feature of New-York journalism for years, were very exciting, very suggestive, of their kind, very able, but while "magnificent," they were not journalism. (Laughter.) Readers would not be interested and editors would not be helped or hurt by a renewal of such personal controversies now. The presumption is that readers were not interested by them so much as editors thought they were in the past, and the certainty is that editors were not helped or hurt by them so much as readers thought they were in the past. (Laughter and applause.) When those strong men died, that which they believed was right was remembered and honored. Their anger and their epithets toward one another, if not forgotten, were regretted, and had long before been discounted. Whitelaw Reid's new policy for The Tribune raised journalism to the parlimentry plane of courtesy. It did not weaken controversy. It only civilized it. (Applause.) For quite awhile he was the only scholar in his own school. The other fighters, trained on lines of old-time war, turned their batteries or him, but got tired when they found that he was not wounded and that they had not drawn his fire. (Applause.)

The exchange of personalities between journalists has not ceased, but it is so infrequent now as to show that the example of The Tribune is receiving general adoption. Certainly all the younger journalists of the country are adopting that example. They do not treat a difference of opinion in a contemporary as a form of moral obliquity. They do not think that because somebody else is trying to draw wages in the same town by the same sort of work which they are doing they should therefore regard him as an enemy, to be hunted down and killed, or written up inversely and made unhappy. (Laughter and applause.) Personal controversies are now left to the lower order of politicians and to the shadier set of lawyers, the proverbial disagreements of doctors, of course, being excepted. (Laughter.) I cannot say that journalism has become gentle (laughter), for it is a calling in which there are blows to give and blows to take, but the fighting in it is fair, and when we want to say a peculiarly mean thing about somebody else in our calling, we charge it on his newspaper and not on himself. (Laughter and applause.) I may have to, out of a sense of duty, or because of an attack of indigestion, call The Tribune next week a conspicuous evader of veracity (laughter), but I shall never asperse the truthfulness of Whitelaw Reid. (Laughter and applause.)

JUST BIG ENOUGH FOR NEW-YORK.

I have indicated the effect of Mr. Reid upon the State press. The effect of the State press upon him has also been notable. When a man outgrows Ohio he reaches just about the size of New-York. (Great laughter and applause.) When he outgrows New-York he attains the altitude of Brooklyn. (Renewed laughter.) Mr. Reid has not yet outgrown New-York. (Laughter.) He has, however, wonderfully broadened and brightened in the metropolis. (Laughter.) He knows that the press of the State, from Dunkirk to Sag Harbor, and from Flushing to Ogdensburg, thinks well of him. (Applause.) He knows that his contemporaries have felt proud of his ability to take a journal stamped with the personality of a remarkable man and strengthen it under impersonal administration into an institution more remarkable than any man ever concerned in the making of it. (Applause.) He knows that the best minds on the press of the State, no matter what the drawbacks are of the instrumentalities with which they work, are at one with him, not on protection, but for real ballot-reform; not on protection, but for high license; not on protection, but for an assimilated and intelligent suffrage; not on protection, but for pure politics, for equal laws, for an untainted judiciary for the strong and true Governorships, for honorable Presidencies of principle and genuine Americanism, and for the victory of the best and the beating down of the worst in the influences entering into all political parties. (Applause.) Mr. Reid in France has worthily honored an office in which Franklin, Washburne, Dayton, McLean and Bigelow and John A. Dix won for themselves a lustre as bright as the day and as long as time. He brings back the gratitude of all Americans abroad, with whom he has been in contact, and he meets here not only the greetings of his friends around these tables, and not only the congratulations of his fellow-laborers in all the newspaper offices of the English-speaking world, but the salutations of his countrymen and their best wishes for his happiness and prosperity, either on the lines of his resumed profession or on the paths of any higher duties that events in their unfolding may solicit or require him to tread. (Applause loud and long continued.)

WARNER MILLER'S REMARKS.

General Swayne next introduced Warner Miller in these words:

The distinguished gentleman took occasion to remark that his senses had been cheated this evening by the spirit of self-laudation. It is gratifying to know that at the close of a late dinner his senses were not cheated by any spirit less elusive. (Laughter.) I am happy to supplement his remarks by a fresh illustration of the power of the press. There was picked up this evening in the ante-room, before we took our seats at these tables a carefully, thoroughly, accurately and brilliantly written account of all that has taken place here to this date, and of some things that are yet to come. At first I supposed, when it was handed to me, that it was the remarks of some gentleman who was to speak: but Mr. Depew's discerning eyes perceived the fact and brought it to my knowledge that it was a newspaper account intended for publication to-morrow morning. Out of a consideration, which I hope you will appreciate, I have not inquired as to the handwriting. (Laughter.) And now, gentlemen, Mr. Reid's great services to international commerce remind us that the facilities for international commerce are becoming so extensive and so far-reaching in their ramifications that they compel the uniting and the co-operation of governments by the necessities which they create, and which are common to the whole family of nations. We have with us this evening a very distinguished gentleman of New-York and a former member of the United States Senate from this State, who is now engaged in doing for the American people at the southern end of North America what unfortunately our French confreres have been unable to do for us—the perfecting of a great international canal. The evening would be incomplete if we did not hear from the Hon. Warner Miller. (Applause.)

Warner Miller said:

Mr. Chairman and gentlemen of the Ohio Society: Until this evening I had supposed that this organization was a secret society, and that no one was permitted to come into these meetings unless he could furnish a certificate of his Ohio origin. We have been told here to-night that four members of the present Cabinet were born in Ohio. Just how much that is to the credit of this Administration I will not under-

take to say. (Laughter.) Certainly it is true that only one of those four was ever able to arrive at that distinction by remaining in Ohio. They had to come out and get training in New-York and in other great and broad States to fit them for the places which they now hold. (Applause.) It was my good fortune, three years ago, to be present at the parting banquet given to our guest of to-night upon the eve of his departure to his great mission; and I took occasion that evening to give him some wholesome advice. Last September, when I was in Paris, I took occasion to find out whether he had followed that advice or not. I am happy to be able to report to-night that I learned there that he had followed strictly the advice that I had given him. That advice was simply this: That in his career in Paris he should not follow too closely in some of the footsteps of his most distinguished predecessor, Benjamin Franklin. (Applause and laughter.)

I am glad to be here to-night to welcome back Mr. Reid from the mission which he has filled with so much credit to himself and to his country. But I am not here to praise him for having thoroughly and honestly, and with all his ability, discharged the duties which devolved upon him. Any American citizen, any citizen of our Republic, who in his public office would do less than his full duty, is unworthy of that place. While praise may not be due to any man in this republic for thus discharging his public duties, certainly condemnation would be heaped upon him if he had not properly fulfilled them.

Mr. Reid, I welcome you back to your old place, and I welcome you for many reasons. You have been missed by your former associates, and for the last two or three years your party associates would have been glad to have had you here for consultation and for guidance and direction. All matters connected with our party during the last few years, have not gone on quite as well as we could have wished, or as well as we believe they would have gone if your guiding hand had been with us. One of the distinguished journalists at the table remarked to me that Mr. Reid had come home to put The Tribune back into political journalism. I said that I hoped so, for we should need it badly during the next six months. And so I am happy that the great journal which has done so much not only for its party, but for every good cause in this country, will again have your guiding hand upon it; for I know that the results which will flow from that guidance will be for the interest not only of your party, but of your city and of your country.

I am also glad that you have come home to us in order that you may exercise your powerful influence upon some of your old comrades and associates. I see that your former close friend, Mr. Depew, has already left the table. It would have been of very great service to him if you could have been here during the last three years; for he has not gotten on quite so well in some respects as he did when he had your daily association. You may have heard, sir, that the great misfortune has fallen upon him to be struck off the list of born millionaires, and to be cast outside of the immaculate 400. (Loud laughter.) I trust you will be able to offer him consolation; and that we may be able to welcome him back to his early associates (laughter), to the men with whom he was always jovial and cordial before he was trained to that high distinction.

If you had been here also you might have prevented the making of some of the mistakes which were made with regard to the last election. (Laughter.) But be that as it may, I simply want to say in conclusion—for I do not propose to touch at all upon the great subject which the chairman was kind enough to mention as having been set down for me; I do not propose at this late hour, and upon this festive occasion, to ride any such hobby as that—I will only say in conclusion that in your career during the last three years you have done more to broaden the channels of American commerce than anything I have yet accomplished, no matter how high my ambitions may be in the future. (Laughter and applause.) In conclusion, Mr. Reid, allow me to say, with all of your old associates—and I am speaking of those outside of the press—that we have heard here to-night of the great dignity and high character of the press. As a theory, not as a condition, we approve those sentiments. (Laughter.) We only hope that they may be fully carried into effect, and that my good friend on my left (Secretary Elkins) and some others, perhaps, would think then that certain things which come to them every day in their lives would be spared to them; and that life would be happier than it is now.

Mr. Elkins—If they kept up to their theories.

Mr. Miller—Yes; if they kept up to their theories. I was surprised to hear Mr. Depew bemoan the fact that he was not a journalist, and that he was only a lawyer; that therefore he could not hope for promotion in the future. I think in the country at large he is ranked as a journalist and not as a lawyer. If any one takes up a newspaper nowadays and doesn't find from one to four columns of Mr. Depew's beautiful work in it he throws it down in disgust, and wants to know what has become of the editor of the paper. (Laughter). Mr. Depew told us that journalists had been promoted by the present Administration, and that Mr. Reid had been sent to Paris because he was a journalist. It is the fact that journalism in the Republic of France has been one of the chief stepping stones to promotion in political life; and that there they are not only the controller of public opinion through their journals, but they are the holders of the great offices and the directors of the Administration. I do not know whether Mr. Reid has "caught on" in Paris with the capability of the French journalists for securing the high offices and places, or not; but I imagine that he was enough of a Yankee, even if he was born in Ohio, to find out how the French journalists do it. And therefore I want to say to those gentlemen here to-night who are ambitious and who are not entirely outside of politics, that they had better beware of the journalists who are coming back to us—Mr. Reid, Mr. Smith and scores of others—who have been away on important missions. I am afraid, Mr. Secretary (Mr. Elkins) that even your place will be in danger, and that other high offices will be sought and taken perhaps by them. Permit me simply to say, and most sincerely, on behalf of your old associates in politics (among whom I may count myself), that we have been delighted with the record which you have made for your country and for your party; but we are a thousand times more delighted and rejoiced that you have returned to us to take up the old work, as we know that we shall find in you the counsellor and guide we knew you to be before you left us. (Applause.)

MR. LAWRENCE FOR THE LOTOS CLUB.

General Swayne then introduced Mr. Lawrence, saying:

A great naturalist and biographer once wrote that in his judgment the difference between man and animals lay chiefly in the broader exercise by man of what he called the faculty of selective attention.

The consciousness of that power commends itself to the readers of Franklin's biography and finds with them a certain response. Perhaps if our distinguished friend will look closely at that book again he will find that the peccadilloes of which Franklin treats with such entire frankness were not a feature of his life as United States Minister to France, but pertain to the days of wild oats, to the earlier days when he was a working man in London. Certain it is, however, that we have the autobiography of our friend written in our hearts, and we are as confident of his future as we are proud of his past.

And now, gentlemen, comes that which the good housewife always saves for the last dish at a feast like this, that which is known as the dessert. There is an organization in the city of New-York whose ties of membership with Mr. Reid are closer than his ties with this society. (Applause.) Not only are they closer, but they are of longer existence, and of a higher grade of personal identification. Busy man as he is, worthy man as he is, busy men as they are, and worthy men as they are, they have had this common tie that they have sought from time to time that sweet, refreshing recreation of mutual intercourse whose fittest emblem is the flower of forgetfulness, the Lotos Club. At some cost to myself, of self-denial, at some tax upon your patience, I have felt, nevertheless, that we should keep that which is best to the last; and now we are to have a final greeting to Mr. Whitelaw Reid, so long the president of the Lotos Club, from his successor, Mr. Frank R. Lawrence.

Mr. Lawrence then said:

It was but last evening that I received your gracious invitation, and I confess myself at a loss for adequate terms in which to address this distinguished assemblage; yet it needs neither preparation nor skill to utter the words of greeting which rise spontaneously upon so happy an occasion as this.

It is indeed a distinction to be permitted to take part in this festivity, and upon behalf of the Lotos Club, whose sentiment it is my privilege to speak to-night, I most heartily thank the Ohio Society of New-York for the courtesy which prompted it to invite the members of the club to be represented in this evening's proceedings.

Perhaps no organization may claim closer affiliation with your illustrious guest than the Lotos Club. He was one of its earliest members. His name stands high upon the list in the charter of its incorporation. For many years he was its president. Upon his departure for Europe his fellow-members bade him the heartiest "God-speed." During his absence they have watched his career with constantly increasing pride, and you may judge with what supreme satisfaction those of them who are here present take part in this, the first public demonstration in honor of Mr. Whitelaw Reid upon his return to his native land.

Aside from all personal association or endearment, the career of Mr. Reid in the public service has been such as should arouse feelings of gratification and pride in the mind of every American citizen. The place of Minister to France is, perhaps, the most honorable foreign station within the gift of our Government, for the American Minister to France is accredited to no king or potentate. He goes as the representative of the one to the other of the two great nations who have thrown off every vestige of obedience to royalty, and who proudly vindicate the right of man to govern himself. (Applause.) The largest field for genius exists in connection with the peaceful solution of the vast and complicated questions which grow out of the commercial relations between these two great peoples, and what higher tribute could be paid to the genius of Mr. Reid than lies in the verdict of all his countrymen, that he has proved equal to every requirement, and has discharged every duty with consummate skill and distinguished success? European nations train men to diplomacy as to a separate profession. America does not, perhaps upon the theory that every American is a born diplomatist. Whatever the theory, the wisdom of our practice is certainly proved by the success of Mr. Reid. (Applause.)

THE POWER OF A GENIAL NATURE.

Speaking only to voice the welcome of an association of friends, I shall not attempt to add to what has been said in the way of description or eulogy of the services of Mr. Reid to our country, but I may say that in my judgment his efforts in the direction of cultivating a closer relation and more cordial feeling between the people of the two nations have been almost equally valuable with his achievements in the negotiation of new treaties; and I may add that in my belief a principal cause of all his success, whether diplomatic or social, has been that kind and genial personality which so greatly endears him to his friends, and which his old associates of the Lotos Club know almost better than any. (Applause.)

We can scarcely think of the office held by your guest of to-night without associating with it the name of that great American who was the first to hold it; and when we view the devotion, the labors and the success of its latest incumbent, we feel that the office first held by Benjamin Franklin has gained new lustre and usefulness through having been held by Whitelaw Reid. (Applause.) The friendship between the two nations which Franklin did so much to establish, his latest successor has striven by every means to cement and make closer, and his efforts have been attended with the most complete success that the people of this country could have desired. (Applause.)

It is a happy fortune that has linked inseparably with the administration of the Government of our country the names of so many of our great scholars, journalists and men of letters. Speaking for a club which makes some claim to literary association, I am proud to recall that wherever men of literary and scholarly attainments have entered public life, they have distinguished and ennobled it, and one of the most creditable facts in the history of our Government during this and the last generation is that its diplomatic service has been enriched by such men as John Lothrop Motley, Bayard Taylor, James Russell Lowell and Whitelaw Reid. (Applause.)

You and he will pardon us of the Lotos Club if to-night we do not try to express all the satisfaction we feel in greeting Mr. Reid again, for we look forward in the near future to the same privilege which the Ohio Society to-night enjoys, and are hoping that when the public ovations shall have somewhat abated, your guest may glide back for a little into the old Bohemian land and receive a Lotos welcome under the roof-tree that for so many years has been his own. (Applause.)

To-night the Lotos Club joins the Ohio Society of New-York in greeting and honoring this gentleman, whose career reflects so much credit both upon the State of his birth and the city of his adoption. His friends of the Lotos Club rejoice at the large part which he has had in linking together two great nations more closely, both in commerce and in kindliness; and in welcoming him home, we pledge for the future a continuance of the same warm ties of friendship which have already existed full a score of years. (Applause loud and long continued.)

At the close of the speech-making General Swayne said: " I am quite sure you will commend the housewifery which kept that viand for the last, and now, gentlemen, to our friend long life and happiness, from each and all of us the best wish of our hearts. (Here the company arose and

drank Mr. Reid's health.) From each to all, from all to everyone, good-night. "

The banquet committee, to whom great credit is due, was composed of General Wager Swayne, chairman, Colonel William L. Strong, Senator Calvin S. Brice, Colonel W. L. Brown, General Henry L. Burnett, Leander H. Crall, Thomas Ewing, Andrew J. C. Foye, Henry A. Glassford, Curtis G. Harraman, Warren Higley, Homer Lee, S. S. Packard, Samuel Thomas and William Ford Upson.

FROM THOSE WHO COULD NOT COME.

The following letters of regret were received :

THE LETTER OF THE FRENCH MINISTER.

The Legation of the French Republic,
Washington, D. C., March, 1892.

General: You have done me the honor to invite me to take part in the banquet that your society has tendered to Mr. Whitelaw Reid after his arrival in New-York on the 9th of April.

I hasten to thank you for your courtesy, and regret that it will not be possible for me to accept, as I already have another engagement for that day.

I regret this all the more because during my stay in Paris I had occasion to appreciate the extreme courtesy of the honorable representative from the United States, and because I should have been very happy to associate myself with this occasion of expression of esteem which is given to Mr. Reid by his compatriots.

Accept, General, the assurances of my most distinguished consideration.　　PATENOTRE.
To General Henry L. Burnett, No. 45 Cedar-st., New-York.

FROM VICE-PRESIDENT MORTON.

Vice-President's Chamber,
Washington, March 31, 1892.

My Dear General : I very much regret that previous engagements deprive me of the pleasure of accepting the invitation of the Ohio Society to be present at the banquet to be given the Hon. Whitelaw Reid on the 9th of April.

Mr. Reid has discharged his duties as the representative of his country to our sister republic of the Old World with conspicuous ability, in a manner alike honorable to his country and himself, and it would be a source of great gratification if I could join the members of the Society of his native State, and present in person my cordial congratulations, a hearty greeting and a warm welcome to your distinguished guest on his return to his native land.

Thanking the Society for the courtesy extended, I am, with renewed regrets, very faithfully and truly yours.　　LEVI P. MORTON.
General Wager Swayne, New-York.

SENATOR HISCOCK'S REGRETS.

Washington, D. C., March 31, 1892.

General Henry L. Burnett, No. 45 Cedar-st., New-York.

Dear Sir : I acknowledge the honor of an invitation from the Ohio Society of New-York, to be present at a banquet to be given the Hon. Whitelaw Reid, at Delmonico's on the 9th proximo.

Nothing would give me greater pleasure than to unite with you in this expression of friendship for and admiration of our distinguished fellow-citizen, Mr. Reid. As our Minister to France, he has conferred great honor upon our Government and added to his distinction as a great American journalist that of an able diplomat. Entertaining for him great personal friendship, I regret exceedingly that I cannot join you at the banquet; but I have an engagement here for the same evening, of an official character, that I could not disregard without great personal inconvenience to others, and therefore, I am compelled to decline the invitation. With great respect,　　FRANK HISCOCK.

A TRIBUTE FROM SENATOR HAWLEY.

Senate Chamber, Washington, April 6, 1892.

My Dear Sir : I intended and sincerely desire to

attend the dinner in honor of Mr. Reid, but engagements and imperative duties are crowding upon me beyond my power or time, and I must deny myself some of the pleasures and luxuries, and stay in Washington next Saturday.

Mr. Reid was congratulated by all his brethren of the Press when he was appointed. He has been congratulated upon his eminent success in his honorable mission—his social, diplomatic, political success—and we congratulate ourselves upon his return. Please convey to him my warmest wishes for his health and happiness and my regret. Sincerely yours,
JOSEPH R. HAWLEY.
General Wager Swayne, New-York City.

FROM EX-MINISTER PHELPS.
New-Haven, Conn., April 6, 1892.

My Dear Sir: I have had the honor to receive the invitation of the Ohio Society to the dinner to be given to Mr. Reid on the 9th inst. I had hoped for the pleasure of attendance, but regret to find that in a great pressure of engagement and very probable absence at that time it will be impossible.

It would have given me special satisfaction to have joined the Society in the expression of the sense we all entertain, I think, of his distinguished and valuable services as Minister of the United States at Paris. His whole residence there has, in my judgment, been not only honorable to himself, but has reflected great credit upon the diplomacy of our country, and has materially strengthened American relations with the Nation to which he was accredited. The compliment you offer him is most appropriate, and the occasion will doubtless be in all respects gratifying.

Will you, in expressing to the Society my thanks for their invitation and my regret at being unable to accept it, make known to them the contents of this note, and ask for me the privilege of joining with them, though in this imperfect manner, in the congratulations they will extend to Mr. Reid?

I am, dear sir, very sincerely yours,
E. J. PHELPS.
Wager Swayne, esq., President.

MR. PULITZER'S ILL HEALTH.
New-York, April 5.

Gentlemen: Mr. Joseph Pulitzer regrets extremely that he is compelled to decline the polite invitation of the Ohio Society. He sympathizes with the proposition to do honor to Mr. Reid, whose distinction as a journalist and success as a Minister he is pleased to see recognized. But the state of his health makes it impossible for him to take part in the proposed banquet.
To General Wager Swayne and others of committee.

GEORGE WILLIAM CURTIS'S LETTER.
West New-Brighton, Staten Island, N. Y.,
March 26, 1892.

Dear Sir: I am exceedingly sorry that an important engagement for the evening of April 9 deprives me of the pleasure of accepting your invitation and of paying my respects personally to your distinguished guest. But I join with you in the hearty welcome home wish which you will receive him. The applause of France will be still ringing in his ears as he begins to hear that of his native land, and he returns crowned with the highest reward of a Minister, the consciousness that he was most honored in the country to which he was most because of his fidelity to the country which sent him. Very faithfully yours,
GEORGE WILLIAM CURTIS.
General Wager Swayne, Chairman.

SECRETARY RUSK DETAINED AT WASHINGTON.
Department of Agriculture,
Office of the Secretary,
Washington, D. C., April 5, 1892.
General Henry L. Burnett, No. 45 Cedar-st., New-York.

Dear Sir: I beg to thank you and the officers and members of the Ohio Society of New-York for their kind invitation to me to be present at the banquet to be given to the Hon. Whitelaw Reid Saturday evening, April 9.

It would, I assure you, afford me the greatest gratification to participate in an occasion designed to do honor to the distinguished gentleman who has so well represented his country and maintained its dignity and honor at the capital of France, but I am sorry to say that I find it will be impossible for me to leave Washington on the day mentioned to attend the banquet, and I must therefore ask you to accept my regrets. Very respectfully,
J. M. RUSK.

PRAISE FROM COLONEL JOHN HAY.
No. 800 Sixteenth-st., Lafayette Square,
Washington, March 27, 1892.
General H. L. Burnett, New-York.

Dear Sir: I regret extremely that I shall not be able to join you on the 9th of April, as I have engagements for that day from which I cannot free myself. Mr. Reid has richly merited all the honors that can be conferred upon him. His services in Paris have been especially valuable and brilliant. Without lowering for a moment the standard of independence and aggressive Americanism, he has been for three years one of the most popular as well as one of the most distinguished personalities of Paris and has gained in the truest sense the citizenship of the world. He has deserved well of his country in his absence and is entitled to the heartiest welcome on his return. Yours respectfully,
JOHN HAY.

FRANK HATTON UNABLE TO BE PRESENT.
"The Washington Post," April 6, 1892.

My Dear Sir: I have the honor to acknowledge the receipt of an invitation to be present at a banquet to be given to the Hon. Whitelaw Reid at Delmonico's on the 9th inst.

I regret exceedingly that it will be impossible for me to be present and join you in honoring the distinguished gentleman who was our Minister to France and who has done such credit to himself and the country he so ably represented.

Please convey my thanks and regrets to the committee of which you are the secretary. Very truly yours,
FRANK HATTON.
Mr. William Ford Upson, secretary, etc., New-York.

HONORS FOR MR. REID.

NEW-YORK MERCHANTS GIVE HIM A BRILLIANT DINNER.

SPEECHES BY PRESIDENT C. S. SMITH, OF THE CHAMBER OF COMMERCE, F. R. COUDERT, MR. REID, C. A. DANA, GENERAL HORACE PORTER, PRESIDENT LOW AND MURAT HALSTEAD.

Rarely if ever in its many years of association with the most brilliant social gatherings of the metropolis has the large dinner hall of Delmonico's presented so beautiful a scene as that on the evening of April 16, on the occasion of the dinner given by the Chamber of Commerce of this city to Whitelaw Reid, United States Minister to France. Mr. Reid had arrived in New-York from France a fortnight before. The following Thursday the Chamber of Commerce held its monthly meeting, when not only was Mr. Reid elected an honorary member of that organization, but it was unanimously voted to entertain him at dinner at an early day. The arrangements were in the charge of a special committee, consisting of Cornelius N. Bliss, Chauncey M. Depew, Samuel D. Babcock, General Horace Porter and Alexander E. Orr.

Cornelius N. Bliss, as chairman of the Committee of Arrangements, called at the home of Mr. Reid at 6 o'clock, and the two drove to Delmonico's, reaching there at half-past 6, the hour for assembling. With business-like promptness many of those who were to enjoy the dinner had already arrived. Mr. Reid was escorted to the parlors on the second floor, where he was received by President Smith, by whose side he stood and responded to the greetings of those who pressed forward to shake his hand.

At 7 o'clock the procession moved into the dining-room. The guests at the table of honor entered first, the others remaining in the corridor until President Smith, Mr. Reid and those accompanying them all stood at their places on the dais. Soon the 200 gentlemen were ranged by the sides of the tables, and at the request of President Smith, the Rev. Dr. John W. Brown asked a blessing.

AT THE TABLE OF HONOR.

Mr. Reid sat at the right of President Smith, with Senator Frank Hiscock in the seat adjoining. George W. Childs, who was expected, sent a letter at the last moment, expressing his regret at his inability to be present. The seat assigned to Vicount Paul d'Abzac, Consul-General of France at New-York, was also vacant, and his place was filled by Governor Merriam, of Minnesota, at whose side sat President Seth Low. His neighbor was the Rev. Dr. James H. McIlvaine, and the other seats at that end of the table were occupied by David M. Stone, D. O. Mills and the Rev. Dr. John W. Brown, in the order named. Immediately on the left of President Smith sat Charles A. Dana, with Frederic R. Coudert at his side. The others were Carl Schurz, Abram S. Hewitt, Murat Halstead, Isaac H. Bromley and Senator Calvin S. Brice.

The arrangements provided that at each of the five lower tables one of the five members of the special committee having charge of the details should preside. Thus Horace Porter was assigned to table A, Chauncey M. Depew to table B, Cornelius N. Bliss to table C, Samuel D. Babcock to table D, and Alexander E. Orr to table E. Mr. Depew, however, was not present at the dinner.

PRESIDENT SMITH'S OPENING ADDRESS.

When the hour of 9 o'clock arrived President Smith brought his gavel sharply down upon the table in front of him, and conversation instantly ceased. Then he said:

Gentlemen: As I look into the faces of the men who surround this table, it seems to me that it must be a matter of great gratification to you and a source of pardonable pride to our guest to find here so many of his warm personal friends, whose respect, admiration and affection he has so worthily won. While the charms of social ties always have special attraction, and contribute much to lighten and sweeten the burdens of life, still it is not the possession of these admirable qualities alone on the part of our guest which has brought together this distinguished company of representative citizens in honor of the United States Minister to our sister Republic of France.

During the century and a quarter of the existence of the Chamber of Commerce, its honorary membership has been conferred but twenty-four times; it is the American merchant's patent of nobility (applause)—"The Iron Cross" of American commerce. This marked expression of the obligation of the Chamber to Mr. Reid was conferred upon him because he has conducted his high office with conspicuous ability and fidelity to the interests of American commerce, and with a view to the promotion of American ideas and traditions. (Applause.)

Mr. Reid has enlarged and strengthened the historic friendship of France for this country. (Applause.) He has cemented the relations which are consecrated in our memories by the illustrious names of Washington and Lafayette, of Mirabeau and Franklin.

It is within the bounds of truth to say that at no time in our history has the genuine good will and mutual esteem of the two great countries been so intimate and reciprocal as at this moment. (Applause.) I know from personal observation something of the difficulties which Mr. Reid has had to encounter, and which, by patient industry and diplomatic tact, he surmounted, and which (to paraphrase a witty saying of Mr. Phelps at Berlin) lead to the triumphant entry of the American pig, under the shadow of the Arc de Triomphe, into the markets of France. (Laughter and applause.) Let us hope that the products of Chicago and Cincinnati will nourish the stomachs of the Frenchman and enlarge the pockets of the American, and so illustrate true commercial reciprocity. (Laughter and applause.)

Our guest is still young, and to him fame came early with her laurel wreath of power. Perhaps one of the secrets of that power was in his early experience and training under that great master of journalism, Horace Greeley. (Applause.) It has been in the line of the profession of Mr. Reid to give and receive public criticism, and, at times, to exchange severe blows; he possesses the enviable ability to perform this duty with such courtesy as to command the respect and retain the friendship of all good men and of all parties. (Applause.) Now, gentlemen, please fill your glasses and drink to the first regular toast.

Then President Smith announced as the first toast, "The President of the United States," and all arose while the orchestra played "The Star Spangled Banner."

FOR THE PRESIDENT OF FRANCE.

The next toast was, "The President of the Republic of France." The Marseillaise hymn was played, while the assemblage remained standing. Then President Smith said:

"There is no man in the United States, in the absence of the French Minister, better fitted to respond to this sentiment than our distinguished fellow-citizen, Frederic R. Coudert. Although by birth an American, he inherits the grace and wit so characteristic of the country to which he owes his name."

BRINGING THE GUEST TO THE FEAST.

Mr. Coudert was most cordially welcomed, and his speech was pronounced one of unusual interest and beauty of expression. He said:

It was once said, with little exaggeration, that when France had a cold in her head, the rest of Europe sneezed. An epigrammatic tribute, I take it, to her genius, her power and perhaps her restlessness; or rather to that overflowing activity of life that would not be restrained by narrow geographical or political limitations, but must look abroad for moral and sometimes physical conquests to satisfy the cravings of exuberant health. No disease could touch her that did not move the world to ready and sympathetic unrest. How could it be else? Was she not the mother of civilization, the queen of the arts, the champion of every great and generous cause? The tramp of her victorious armies had been heard with almost wearisome monotony on every battlefield of Europe from Charlemagne to Saint Louis; from Saint Louis to Louis XIV; from Louis XIV to Napoleon. What a record of heroism; what a catalogue of heroes. (Applause.) And as she pursued her career of moral and physical triumphs she effaced the traces of war with the same hand that smote; for she sowed the seed of a glorious democracy while her philosophers, scientists and literary men prepared the way for the brotherhood of Nations. Who can gainsay her title to the gratitude of mankind? I need not rehearse her claims nor produce her witnesses before an American tribunal. Her blood, her treasure, her sympathy; she spent all that she had to make American liberty her debtor. Your honored guest will tell you that the tenderness that she once lavished on America she has never taken back. (Applause.) Whether or not that love has been fully or constantly requited, whether in the dark hours of desolation, when she wept in sackcloth and ashes and refused to be comforted because her children were not, whether in the hour of humiliation her brethren of America heard her voice and wiped her tears, why should we ask? She never did. Her trust and affection were always as of old. Whatever else she might question she could not doubt that those who honored Washington would mourn with the bereaved countrymen of Lafayette. She comforted her bruised heart, in sore defeat, by remembering the trials and sufferings that culminated in the common glory of Yorktown. So long as fortune could not obliterate the records of the past, the jewel of American love and sympathy must be hers forever. And then while still weak from loss of blood and soiled with the dust of defeat, she raised the torch of Liberty, and waving it that the world might be gladdened by its rays, she called America to witness that there was a new bond between the two nations. (Applause.) Thus did she consecrate the old allegiance by a gift embodying the glories and triumphs of the past, the union of the present and the aspirations of the future.

A GREAT TITLE AND A GREAT OPPORTUNITY.

The President of the French Republic! What a title, what an opportunity, what a burden! To direct the destinies of the nation that knew Richelieu and Henry IV, Louis XIV, and Napoleon, to be the foremost man in a nation of thirty-six million gallant people, to represent before the world her rights, to be responsible for the performance of her duties, to see that no detriment shall befall the young Republic that has fallen heir to such priceless treasures! This is no light task. He must remain faithful to sacred memories and march to the music of a brilliant future. He must be the pioneer of the people in the emancipation of thought and the development of freedom. He will, if faithful to his trust and equal to its performance, justify great expectations and fulfil great prophecies. A heavy task this, to fall on one man's shoulders! The Republican President who lives in Paris and the Republican President who lives in Washington with 100,000,000 people behind them are the real representatives of the new civilization. To them is committed the standard of all that is best in modern progress.

The President of the French Republic bears a name well fitted to commend him to his people's affections. In the battle for freedom that began a century ago, the great Carnot was at his post and faithful to his duty. History reports his unflinching fidelity to Republican principles as one of his claims to the gratitude of posterity, but history clothes him with a far stronger title to posthumous veneration. He was a Republican, it is true, but, first and always, he was a patriot. The love of country was stronger than the love of party or the scruple of consistency. We, who

have heard the echo of Washington's voice warning us against the destructive potency of party spirit, as the danger most likely to disrupt our union, may uncover in reverent homage to the Carnot of the French Republic, the organizer of victory. It was the same Carnot who dropped and brushed aside his personal preferences to join hands in patriotic forgetfulness of self with the tottering Napoleon of 1814. For that Napoleon, whatever the blemishes upon his matchless genius, then incarnated in his person, though his star was on the wane, the traditions, the honor, the patriotism of France. It was no time for ponderous Senates to discuss nice questions of constitutional law, nor to dilate in sonorous periods upon the abstract blessings of civil liberty. The enemy were thundering at the gates, the soil was trodden and polluted by the invader, the grim warriors of Marengo, Austerlitz and Moscow were doing their heroic duty, but melting away before the swarms of their united enemies. Then the patriot Carnot hastened to the side of the lion at bay, and urged his countrymen to forget all things except the insulted land of their fathers. "Ah, Carnot!" said the Emperor, "I have known you too late!" And yet, when he was the manufacturer of Royalty and the master of a continent, he had said to this same Carnot: "You may have all that you want, as you want, and when you want." But the stern Republican was not then bound to yield allegiance to the man who had brushed aside the Republic. The hour came with the nation's humiliation and he only proffered his service when it could not be rewarded. Well might the German Neibuhr, glowing with admiration at this heroic and patriotic citizen's deeds, declare: "If all that I had in the world were a crust of bread, I should be proud to share it with Carnot."

HE HAS PROVED HIS WORTHINESS.

And now the grandson is the chief magistrate of the nation that Napoleon ruled and covered with renown. (Applause.) Is he worthy of this conspicuous honor and may we hope that his hands will hold up the dignity and prosperity of his people? The years of his probation have answered the question. It has been the rare good fortune of the Republic to find among her citizens a man who knew how to fill this exalted part. (Applause.) Happy the people who possess the man required for their emergency; happier still the people who esteem him at his worth and honor him accordingly. Party differences are subdued and silent when he challenges judgment. The people know him and repel partisan criticism of their faithful servant. For such he is, and such they know him to be. No craving for a wider sphere of uncontrolled action, no selfish hope of personal aggrandizement, have ever marred his conduct or dimmed his fame. He has learned, perhaps from the traditions of his household, that the first citizen of France is simply the most honored servant of the people; that the duty of a President is to execute the laws, not to make them; that the function of his office is to enlighten the nation, not to endanger its peace or to destroy the liberties of his people. The President of the French Republic is the pedagogue of Europe. His chair is a pulpit whence he is to teach that liberty means light, that she carries the book and the pen where she may, the sword only where she must; that his first duty is to teach obedience to the law, by practising it; to accept, not to dictate, to be vigilant and true and honest and brave in his allegiance to the Sovereign, for the law is his master, even when he reviews one hundred thousand men.

Truisms, these things seem to us. A successor of President Washington who would dream of usurping the power confided to his hands and of placing himself above the laws, could hardly hope for anything more serious from an American audience than to be Hissed off the stage. More probably a continent would shake with laughter and a performance intended to be dramatic would end in burlesque. The American people are not without a sense of humor, though it is often Inadequately expressed. There are springs in their intellectual makeup that may be touched with effect and they would rise to all the requirements of a mirth provoking situation, if any citizen whether in the White House or out of it should act upon the theory that he was indispensable to the welfare of the nation. The Savior of Society has no place here. He is not classed among our vertebrated animals and the popular diagnosis would at once recognize the presence of mental disease. Hellebore was the reputed cure in the old Roman days; the straitjacket or mild confinement is the more modern method. But we have not ten millions of armed men in our close proximity, most of whom may in the chances of diplomacy or accident be our enemies to-morrow. The waves and fogs and storms of the Atlantic are the steady and inexpensive bulwarks of our main frontier, and as to other possible foes—but we have none. (Applause.)

THE LEADERSHIP WHICH FRANCE NEEDS.

Not so, however, in the old land of France. The man on horseback still lives in legend and tradition. He has done great things in days gone by and may perhaps forget that he is no longer a factor in the peaceful destinies of the country. One thousand years of unremitting activity have surely earned the right to repose. Glory may have its uses, but glory palls in time upon the taste, and its music loses all charm for modern ears. France wants a leader who will tap the boundless resources of her genius for the pursuits of peace. He must insist that she shall freely extend the new domain that she has chosen for herself. True, a shadow is still on the wall, and the day may come when her children shall be summoned again to try the cruel chances of war. But, should the fated day come, which may heaven avert, she will remember that of her fathers, the Gauls, it was said by their Roman foes that they did not fear funerals. This is a sombre theme, and we all prefer to watch her growth in the field of her own selection, the arts and sciences and literature that adorn and delight and bless our race.

Honor then to this, her chief magistrate. May he succeed in his mission of peace. The experiment of free government is being made by a nation under whose soil lie sleeping fifty generations of men; they were born and bred under a system that made one man better, by accident of birth, than all other men; what wonder if she has not, at one bound, mastered the excellencies of a wholly different scheme. The habits of a nation may not be shaken off in a day. Nor, on the other hand, must we forget that democracy and republicanism are not convertible terms. France has been for a century the most democratic of nations. As one of our own great leaders of thought once said: True democracy does not consist in saying, I am as good as you, but rather in saying, you are as good as I. She knows this lesson by heart. True republicanism consists in obeying equal laws with ready and cheerful alacrity. Why should not the young republic live up to this simple canon of republican conduct? Adversity has bowed the head of her people in humiliation and sorrow. It were idle to deny that old wounds are not quite healed or that retrospection is unmixed with bitterness. But the nation has turned its face to the light of a new dawn. Another generation is coming forward that will be slow to abandon the fruits of

their fathers' trials, and will readily be taught that liberty is better than servitude; that it is better to be a citizen than to be a subject; that to serve one's country is better than to serve a king. We of America may be pardoned if we rejoice in that belief and exult in our possession. May we not hope that the old nation, who was our friend when we sorely needed friends, may join hands with us, not for selfish purposes and selfish aggrandizement, but for the benefit of the human race? (Applause.) Made up as we are of so composite a texture, representing every nation of the world, because each one contributed from its best citizens to our prosperity, we may truly say that nothing that interests mankind is foreign to us.

And in drinking the health of the honored President of the French Republic, we will with grateful recollections and renewed affection, pledge the fair land that still lives in undiminished brilliancy to instruct and charm the world. (Loud and continued applause.)

MR. REID'S SPEECH.

When Mr. Coudert had resumed his seat amid much cheering, President Smith introduced "The Guest of the Chamber," by saying: "Gentlemen, let us now drink to the continued health and prosperity of the guest of the evening, the Hon. Whitelaw Reid." All arose, and the orchestra played "And He's a Jolly Good Fellow," many of those present joining in the words. On the conclusion of the music Mr. Reid said:

Mr. President: I accept your words. The approval of the New-York Chamber of Commerce, given to a townsman returning from the service of his country abroad, is a decoration. Your electing him to the little group of your honorary members confers more than ribbons and crosses and jewelled orders. No man knows better than your guest what and how much it means; and if in a fortnight at home, renewed and persistent kindnesses had not made him a very beggar for words, no man could more sincerely or more gratefully thank you. Outside of politics and religion, to a New-Yorker little is left unsaid, when the Chamber of Commerce has spoken.

In a letter of remarkable candor, which appeared the other day in the morning journals, a distinguished citizen, who has held the highest office in the gift of his countrymen, wrote with honest simplicity that he often feared he did not deserve all the kind things said of him. Under favor of that example, I may venture to say that I have often experienced the same feeling. I wish I could believe that I deserve what you say; but the net result of it all is, a sense, not of increased importance, but of the increasing necessity for more than my natural modesty.

And yet there is one point, Mr. President, on which I accept very frankly and very honestly all your eulogium. I have tried to do my full duty, to this great city, and to the great country behind it, which I had the honor to represent near the Government of our earliest European friend.

My difficulties there were largely lessened and my power for any useful service increased from my having had the good fortune to be supported by my countrymen without distinction of party. It is his high incentive to duty, and indeed the inspiration of his office, that the American Minister represents no party, however glorious its record, or however devoted his attachment to it; but that like Richelieu in the elder Bulwer's play, with the receipt of his commission there has entered his official veins the power, the dignity, the honor of the whole sixty-five millions of people of the magnificent continent they inhabit and the matchless history they inherit.

AT HOME AMONG HIS OWN COUNTRYMEN.

It has been another comfort for your Minister in Paris during the past three years to find myself still among his own countrymen. Naturally a Minister from New-York is likely to see more friends and acquaintances in Paris than a representative of any other locality. But the truth is that American friends so surrounded and supported the Paris Legation, from the first day of my incumbency to the last, that I was scarcely ever left reason to realize that I was far from City Hall Square or Fifth Avenue or Pennsylvania Avenue.

And now, Mr. President, I wish, if not to discharge, at least to acknowledge, my heaviest obligation. I wish to tender my best thanks to my own profession, the Press, for the uniform and considerate kindness with which it has treated me without distinction of parties and without exception. This was as it ought to be, for a Minister in a foreign nation representing his whole country is entitled to its whole support, or to immediate recall. But in my case there has been a spontaneity about it and a generosity alike from old friends and old enemies which touched me to the heart's core. There has been in it too a species of comradeship most grateful to a man who has held every place in the ranks, from the lowest, and who prizes, above all other honors, the distinction conferred by the good-will and the esteem of his colleagues and rivals in his own calling.

HONOR TO WHOM HONOR IS DUE.

If there has been any success at the Paris Legation in the past three years, to warrant this great kindness of the press, and this distinguished honor your Chamber now bestows, it is due first of all to Benjamin Harrison and James G. Blaine. They determined their policy and stuck to it. They gave me their instructions, and then gave me unquestioning confidence and support, and left me a free hand. The man who, under those circumstances, cannot do good work, has no good work in him.

But with reference to any diplomatic success, I am reminded of what seemed to me a very sagacious remark, made not long ago, by Lord Salisbury, to the effect that, while it was desirable to carry your points in diplomacy as far as possible, it was equally desirable not to brag about it afterwards. The other nation might thus be led to think it had conceded too much; and so, in the end, the brag might undo the diplomacy. The counsel is good for us now and always; though in the present case there can be no such danger, since most of the agreements have been confessedly in the common interest—as all of them were, in our opinion—and since the only ones about which a difference of judgment as to actual interest could exist were in the furtherance of an absolute justice, to our demand, for which no adequate reason for refusal ever had been or ever could be given.

JULES SIMON'S FAREWELL WORDS.

May I be pardoned for reading, as appropriate to this view of our diplomacy, the charming words in which the great French orator, Senator and Academician, as well as newspaper writer, M. Jules Simon, closed his good-bye to me, three weeks ago, at a banquet in Paris:

(The following is the text of M. Simon's concluding sentences. Mr. Reid held the Paris paper in his hand, but turned it into English as below:)

"Vous allez partir, Monsieur Reid, mais vous laissez ici des amis qui ne vous oublieront pas. Lorsque le paquebot qui vous emportera vers le Nouveau Monde quittera les cotes de France, je voudrais etre sur le promontoire le plus avance de ces cotes, et je vous crierai dans un dernier echo, Repandons la liberte avec la lumiere; repandons la justice avec la liberte.")

"When the vessel which carries you toward the New World shall quit the coasts of France, I should like to be on the promontory of the most advanced of these coasts, and would cry to you then in a last echo, from our land to yours, Let us spread liberty with the light; let us spread justice with liberty."

Well, gentlemen, your president has referred to what my friend, Mr. Phelps, has grotesquely styled the passage of the American pig under the Arc de Triomphe. He didn't get in very quickly, and he didn't get in very easily; but in the language which the West has made classic, he got there. The absolute prohibition of American pork in France lasted eleven years. It was an invidious discrimination, since it touched only the United States, and it was defended and screened from the charge of distinct unfriendliness only on the ground that the American product was dangerous to the public health. At the same time, importations were permitted from other countries, in at least one of which trichinosis was notoriously abundant and fatal. It must not be forgotten that, from the long time prohibition had lasted, as well as from the charges on which it had been ordered, the great mass of the French people honestly believed it to be needful; while there were three powerful classes absolutely sure of it—the French pork-growers, the French pork-packers, and the Protectionists; and they had overwhelming majorities in Parliament. Let me say at once that the diplomatic contest was ended as soon as the case had been fully presented. When the judgment of the French Government was convinced it was instantly ready to do right. What remained was a question of convincing the Chambers also, and of adjusting duties on the general scale then about to be adopted in their new tariff. On that point, as you know, legislators on both sides of the water are apt to have views of their own.

I had the pleasure of bringing home an extradition treaty completed in the last week of my stay and signed on the day of my departure. It will be of some interest to the merchants of New-York, for it more than doubles the number of extraditable crimes with France. And if the Senate should now kindly take the same benevolent view of it with its authors and confirm it promptly, it may have the effect of making the crimes which peculiarly harass the merchant more rare among you, and Paris less attractive to any Americans except the good ones.

TRADE RELATIONS WITH FRANCE.

A limited commercial agreement which I had the pleasure of closing just before my return, and in which the Chamber will take some interest, has not yet been proclaimed by the President, since it needs first the assent of the French Chambers. The Tariff Commission has reported, however, unanimously in its favor, and the French Ministers seemed to have no doubt about its approval. Here, coming under Section 3 of the new Tariff bill, it requires no ratification by the Senate. It gives us the French minimum tariff and the treatment of the most favored nation, on an amount of our products equal to their exportations to us of hides, skins, sugar and molasses. Unfortunately for us, neither France nor her Colonies have sent us a great deal of these articles. Still, we are able to secure in exchange reduced rates for some nine or ten millions of our exports; and for this we took care to select articles in which we already have some trade established, and in which a duty discriminating in our favor should develop. We have for France, and for Guadeloupe, Martinique and her other colonies, the whole range of common woods, lumber, clapboards and staves; canned meats; fresh, dried and pressed fruits, and hops. These articles have been chosen, as you will see, with a view of affecting large classes of small producers and large sections of the country. We had some other beautiful selections made, but, unfortunately, the trade in them was already so large that it more than filled the bill.

There is another matter on which we have had some talk, and on which I hope for something definite by an early steamer. It is possible that this may lead to a little more reciprocity that shall be mutually beneficial. I betray no confidence, indeed, in saying that the thoughts of French statesmen, in and out of the Government, are turning in the present economical condition of their country more and more toward some general reciprocal arrangement with the United States. Some suggestions that came to me on this subject could not, perhaps, be properly detailed here; but there can be no harm, I think, in quoting a remark made to me more than once by the President of the last Chamber and the President now of the Chamber's Tariff Commission, M. Meline, who is, more than any one other, the author of the new tariff—the Major McKinley, in fact, of France. Said he: "One of the first things I should favor, after the workings of our tariff are known, would be a complete commercial treaty with the United States."

This is a matter, however, in which the assent of the Legislative bodies on both sides the water would be required; and when I recall the trials of pork, and the entirely unsentimental view both countries take of trade problems, I am not sure that the lot of the Minister who is fortunate enough to negotiate that treaty will be an altogether happy one.

A GREAT INCREASE IN DUTIES.

In any case, the trade situation of France for the next few years is sure to be peculiar and most interesting. She is just entering upon an untried economical regime. She has become overwhelmingly Protectionist—no doubt in part because of our example—and in one respect she is bettering our instructions with vengeance. We have generally reached our present high duties by successive steps, often extending throughout a century. France has suddenly, on dozens of important products, doubled, or trebled, even quadrupled, her late duties, at a single blow. What is to be the effect upon her trade relations? That is a problem on which it is not wise to dogmatize beforehand; but one or two of its elements seem clear. In this sharp and sudden advance on her old duties, France has gone on our road faster if not farther than ourselves, while she must remain under the influence of radically different conditions. Practically speaking, the United States has no neighbors and no frontiers, while it preserves within its own borders from side to side of the continent, and from the lakes to the Gulf, the largest and most beneficent example of absolute Free Trade the world can yet show. France has no continent for such a commerce, no room for four or five times her present population, no such undeveloped opportunities for mining, manufacturing and trade. Now, hemmed in as she is by Spain, Italy, Switzerland, Germany and Belgium, and with but a strip of water like Long Island Sound (though some travellers say a trifle more turbulent) between her and Great Britain—whether thus situated France can successfully adapt our practice to her conditions is a question which her statesmen are not sure of, and to which the leading journals of her capital would generally at the present reply in the negative.

EVERY REASON FOR A GROWING COMMERCE.

In any case, we shall have plenty of trade with her, and I hope a growing trade. There is every reason for it. Each country produces at the best what the other wants. France must buy our raw materials and certain of our manufactures. We must buy the finest and most artistic things in the world, whatever they cost, and it is France that makes them. Who supposes that you could stop American women from buying French gowns, fine silks, ribbons and articles de Paris; or American men from buying French pictures and bronzes and tapestries, Bordeaux and champagnes, even if a dozen McKinleys stood in the way? We'll grumble about the price, of course; why shouldn't we; but we'll buy all the same.

And all the time till France loses her secret—the secret of doing the finest things just a little better than anybody else in the world can do them. We know the commercial value of it now; some day, perhaps, we may learn the secret for ourselves, but it will not be till we have learned another lesson—to wit, that the diffusion of art is not merely a luxury but a commercial necessity, that free art is as vital as free air, and that the country which burdens or which even doesn't protect and encourage and diffuse art is hopelessly doomed to remain second-class all its years.

We all believe that within this generation New-York is to be the financial and possibly the commercial centre of the world. With all my heart, I hope so. But we must never make the stupid mistake of underrating our rivals; and it is perhaps needful also to guard against the natural tendency of a young and prosperous community to overrate themselves. Whatever our natural endowments, or whatever the genius of our people, we are always in danger whenever we shut our eyes to the experience of the world.

THE MOST PROSPEROUS NATION IN EUROPE.

Our friends, the French, are at this moment enormously prosperous—probably the most prosperous nation in Europe; and with their prosperity the most widely diffused. And yet, when I contrast the French condition with ours, when I recall our own popular grievances—as to railroads, for example—and remember that there is not in all France a train to be compared to those on which you daily travel to Washington or to Chicago—that no money can there purchase equal luxury, and that what you can purchase costs you double as much per mile—or when I recall another of our grievances as to the cost of living, and referring to my cash-book am reminded that Paris, to a foreign Minister, at any rate, and I think to Americans generally, is as dear as New-York, if not dearer, I wonder if occasionally our national complaints may not spring less from the acuteness of our sufferings than from the acuteness of our politics.

We shall be on exhibition next year in Chicago, and here too. It may not be a mistake to assume that among the other things the merchants of New-York will wish to show their foreign guests will be a dollar which, following the thought of the President, is as good as any other dollar the country has issued, clean streets, a Navy no longer ridiculous, and a Judiciary for which we have no occasion to apologize.

IN HER SPHERE FRANCE LEADS THE WORLD.

The French are coming, not exactly in squadrons, perhaps, but in larger numbers than they have ever travelled before. They are coming to a land in which they believe their welcome is ready, and I am sure you will make it so. They will teach this generation of Americans how in her sphere France still leads the world. She will come to the Nation she helped to create as our old ally; better still, she will come as the great sister Republic. She will come, as I ventured to predict in Paris, even before the action of the Chambers on the appropriation, as France ought to come to America—on the front line, and with all her banners flying. She will show what higher development the country has reached under the Republic, and in the stirring language of her own Ministers, she will carry to this new Western centre, in which the progress of civilization now asserts itself, the shining proofs of the activity and the genius of her children.

Our hearts will go out to her, I am sure, as to none else. We hold in high honor that upright and most successful statesman and that model citizen, the President of the Republic, M. Carnot. We know how faithfully and how ably the country is served under him by Ribot and De Freycinet, by Jules Roche, by Tirard and Spuller, by Royer and Floquet, and their colleagues in the Ministry and in the Chambers; and the earnest desire of our people, without distinction of parties and without dissent—I have said it as your Minister in France, and I wish to say it as the guest of the Chamber of Commerce in New-York—the desire of our whole people is that under their wise guidance and that of their successors, the Republic which has now become the strongest as it is the oldest government France has had for a century, may endure throughout the generations of men, and that it may mean always, as it means now, order and prosperity for the French, and peace for Europe.

The speech of Mr Reid was listened to attentively. He spoke in a serious manner, and there were frequent outbursts of applause during the delivery of his remarks.

MR. DANA SPEAKS FOR THE PRESS.

The next regular toast was "The Press," which was responded to by Charles A. Dana, in introducing whom Mr. Smith said: "It is eminently fitting and proper that this powerful exponent of public opinion should be represented upon this occasion by the learned and eloquent Nestor of New-York journalism. I now have the peculiar pleasure of calling on the Hon. Charles A. Dana to respond for his profession."

Here is what Mr. Dana said:

Mr. Chairman and Gentlemen: I cannot imagine that there is any occasion for any representative of the press to arise here, after Mr. Reid has taken his seat. Who can speak for the press so well as he? Who has had an experience so wide, so varied, so creditable, so successful as he? There was in the earlier history of this Republic a school of thinkers who held that diplomacy was comparatively unnecessary, that we should have no foreign ministers except upon special occasions when they might be sent out to settle some pressing controversy and then come home, leaving the country without any representative except its consuls in foreign lands. That school was never very extensive. So far as I am aware, its principal members were two men of different parties and most distinguished genius, one of them, Thomas H. Benton, a great and broad-minded statesman of the earlier days of our political life; and the other was another man of genius, Horace Greeley. (Laughter and applause.)

They both taught this doctrine, and taught it with such ability and such success that they made at least one convert, and at an early age I entered their school myself. (Laughter.) I also know of one other newspaper man who belonged to the school, but it never was a successful party; it never got any standing in the world; the American people never adopted the idea, and why? Well, in the first place, there is a kind of politeness and good society among nations which requires that every power, every nation of any consequence, should have its regular representatives near the governments of other nations. That is a kind of international honor which the world has never been willing to resign.

We all agree,—I have joined the other side, I have gone over to the majority, (applause,)—we all agree that diplomatic representatives and ministers maintained permanently abroad are indispensable for the good conduct of international affairs. Another con-

sideration also bears upon this question. There are certain offices, certain political and public functions which are indispensable to the conduct of society. There must be governors, there must be legislators, there must be judges, there must be tax collectors—all those functions are absolutely necessary, and they are maintained as a matter of necessity. But the catalogue of public offices is not complete with those indispensable functionaries. It has to go further.

THE ORNAMENT HAS ITS USES.

We must have officers who under certain circumstances and to a certain extent are ornamental. There must be places of importance for public men of distinction. They cannot all be elected judges, or lieutenant-governors, or members of Congress, or Senators; there must be other places to which, when a new President comes into power, he can send distinguished men of his party, and he ought not to send any other to foreign lands as the representatives of the Government and of the power and dignity of the United States.

For a great part of the time these foreign representatives of ours may have very little to do; but it is indispensable, I think, to have them there, and when the occasion arises, when there is a need, when there is some important question to be settled, then we must have them there; and unless they are there with some antecedents, and some experience, and some knowledge of the medium in which they have to labor, and of the men with whom they have to deal, their efforts would be comparatively ineffectual and useless. So we have for all these reasons come over to the doctrine that there must be a diplomatic establishment maintained by the United States.

Now, we do not maintain it as other countries do. The old Governments make diplomacy a profession; men are educated to it; they make their careers in it; they follow that business all their lives through. Here we do not do it that way for the reason that this is a Government of change; that it is a Government in which men pass from one sphere of life to another, in which they are promoted according to their deserts; so that we, instead of educating our diplomats to be diplomats, put them early in life in newspaper offices, and when they graduate it is something brilliant and admirable. (Laughter and applause.)

The honors which you are paying to our distinguished fellow-citizen, Mr. Reid, this evening, are not only well deserved, but, as has been remarked, they are paid in substance by all parties in this country. (Applause.) When you can get, not merely a Republican like my friend Mr. Smith, and a celebrated Mugwump, like my friend, Mr. Coudert (laughter), and modest and unpretentious Democrats, like Senator Brice and myself (laughter), to come here and join in the honor; and when General Schurz, the worst Mugwump of them all, comes (laughter), and when they all combine in paying this well-deserved tribute to a distinguished and successful public servant, we may be sure that the honor is perfectly deserved; and that greater services hereafter may be expected from the gentleman who has rendered them. (Applause.)

THE PAST INDICATES THE FUTURE.

The fact is that there is not any important public service that a successful newspaper man is not perfectly well able to render on the shortest notice. (Laughter and applause.) The foundation of success such as Mr. Reid has achieved is considerably made up of good fortune. It is not merely talent, it is not merely devotion to the duty undertaken, it is not merely the concentration of every faculty, but after all, good luck comes into it very considerably. This good luck I look to see further illlustrated in the case of our distinguished guest of this evening. (Applause.) The past at least is secure. (Applause.) That is a common saying, but the past is always a pointer to the future, and these distinctions, outside of those strictly belonging to the newspaper press, may be placed upon Mr. Reid hereafter, as the laurel is placed upon the head of a great and successful soldier. We shall feel, we who belong to the newspaper press, whether in the capacity of retired members like General Schurz, or active members like my friend Mr. Halstead, or occasional contributors like my friend Mr. Coudert (laughter), we shall all feel that a part of the honor and a part of the renown belongs to the profession of which Mr. Reid is so distinguished a member. (Applause.)

GENERAL PORTER'S WITTY REMARKS.

There was no lack of good feeling manifested at Mr. Dana's kindly words for the guest, and his speech throughout was an entertaining feature of the evening. When he had ended, Mr. Smith announced the last regular toast, "Modern Diplomacy, the Ally of Commerce," and simply said: "Our friend and fellow-member, General Horace Porter, needs no introduction to this assembly." General Porter arose with his customary air of seriousness and apparent embarrassment, but his own embarrassment was as nothing compared to that of his audience when the speaker opened his remarks in a foreign tongue with many shrugs of the shoulders and gesticulations, which in their quality gave assurance that he was indulging in an attempt at speaking French. He soon dropped into English and humor, but preserved the seriousness of his demeanor throughout. This is what he said:

Monsieur le President et Messieurs: Si je m'addresse a vous ce soir dans une langue que je ne parle pas et que personne ici ne comprend, j'en impute la faute entierement a mon ami, l'ex-ministre, car on me dit que depuis son retour il a oublie tout son Francais et il ne peut pas parler Anglais, et c'e.t tres embarrassant. (Laughter and applause.)

A friend by my side tells me that, notwithstanding the short time which has elapsed since our Minister's return, he has succeeded in catching up with enough English to understand me fairly well if I speak in that language. (Laughter.) And yet I always like to speak in a foreign language where there are no foreigners present. (Renewed laughter.) It invariably calls down less adverse criticism on one's accent. (Laughter.)

I am exceedingly glad to participate in a dinner given to a gentleman upon his return home. We have usually been engaged in giving dinners to gentlemen upon the eve of their departure from home, in which it seemed to be an implied condition that they should leave the country within twenty-four hours thereafter. (Laughter.) Less than two years ago I started to Europe to visit Mr. Reid, in the hope that I might get from him a straight tip in diplomacy. I found a great many public men going over to Europe about the same time. Our public men seem to think that it will add greatly to their public reputations in crossing the water, particularly when they think of how much it added to the reputation of George Washington even crossing the Delaware River. (Great laughter.) On my arrival abroad I immediately began the study of the difference between the French race and our English race. The real difference did not strike me until I crossed the English Channel. The last man I saw in England was a soldier with his red coat and his blue trousers. The first man I saw on my landing in France was a soldier with his blue coat and red trousers, and I said to myself, "That settles it; when you turn a Frenchman upside down he becomes an Englishman." (Roars of laughter.)

AN INVITATION TO FIVE O'CLOCK TEA.

On my arrival in Paris I found that the people had adopted many of our customs, and our English phrases descriptive of them. A French friend, wanting to invite me to take tea with him in the afternoon, said: "Voulez-vous 5 o'clocket, avec moi?" and I replied: "Yes, with a great deal of pleasure; at what hour?" He said to me: "You seem to understand everything I say except my English." (Laughter.)

Then I visited the Chamber of Deputies. I found

that body vociferous. A deputy made a motion, and immediately all the other deputies arose, howled, upset piles of books, yelled and jerked benches loose from the floor, I supposed they were mutinying, but I was mistaken; they were only coinciding in the motion. (Laughter.) Then I saw on the opposite bank of the river from the Chamber of Deputies that most beautiful of all street scenes, the Place de la Concorde, and a gentleman of a philosophic turn of mind said: "Here we have the Place de la Concorde opposite the place de la discord. (Renewed laughter.)

Everybody in France was excited on the subject of the tariff; and I was somewhat surprised to find the familiarity with which they continually spoke of our Ohio statesman. They were constantly alluding to "Ze Bill McKinley." I told them that it was only a matter of taste; that in this country we usually spoke of him as William. (Great laughter.)

The American hog was in every Frenchman's mind, but that did not suit the grasping disposition of our exporters ;they wanted to have it in everybody's stomach. (Renewed laughter.) They were attacking the American hog in all directions and I saw that he was not having a fair show. Every disease, from cerebro spinal meningitis to interstertial nephritis was attributed to a lack of health in the American hog. They had an exaggerated idea of the hog in America. They believed that the people in Chicago found lard oil light cheaper than daylight and that the merchants closed their stores in the daytime and burned lard oil lamps for the sake of economy. (Laughter.) Whenever they heard of a man in Paris who was from Chicago they went to testing the matter by feeling for the bristles on his back. (Renewed laughter.)

DEFENDING THE AMERICAN HOG.

Now I do not like to see the American hog abused. He had been a friend of ours in the army. I have many a time helped to slaughter him and eat him in all his various phases of health. (Laughter.) They did not seem to appreciate how many different kinds of breeds of hogs we had until I told them the experience of the Berks County hog-raiser in Pennsylvania. He had a breed of hogs so fat that they could not walk—they only waddled. They looked as if their skins had been stood up and they had been poured into them in a liquid state. (Great laughter.) He took some of these hogs to a fair in North Carolina to compete for a prize. He was warned to guard them, as the colored population were laying hands on everything after nightfall, from a chicken up to a hog. The Pennsylvanian was a good deal astonished when he saw the North Carolina hogs on exhibition. They were built like greyhounds, and the nose looked as if it had been caught in the crack of a door; and the architectural construction of their backs was patterned after the razor-blade clam. The Pennsylvanian said: "It don't pay to raise hogs like them; you want to get some of my breed of hogs down here." The North Carolina man replied: "Ef you lived yer you'd find it's no use to try to raise pork, unless it can run faster than a nigger." (Great laughter.)

Mr. Reid was eminently successful in securing France as the first nation to ratify our international copyright act, and the first nation to reduce the prohibitory duty on pork. In both instances he was successful in securing justice for the products of the pen. (Laughter.) Of course a large slaughtering of hogs has resulted from his successful efforts. (More laughter.)

I enjoyed a number of very elaborate dinners at Mr. Reid's house, and I have a lively recollection that the list of courses was longer than Leporello's list of all of Don Giovanni's sweethearts. I read some time after of a man who died from a foreign growth in the stomach, and I said, "That man has been eating one of Reid's dinners." (Laughter.)

HEARTSEASE PLANTED IN THEIR GARDENS.

And now, in behalf of Americans who have sojourned abroad, I wish to make the most graceful acknowledgments for the attention, courtesy and hospitality which they invariably received from Mr. Reid while they tarried in that foreign land. He does not fully realize how much heartsease he planted in their gardens. (Applause.) As Americans we have all had reason to feel justly proud of his triumphant career as an American diplomatist. Scarcely had he reached France when the most complicated, intricate and difficult problems in diplomacy were presented to him for solution; and it is a great gratification for us to be able to say that in bringing order out of chaos, in regard to American exhibits at the Paris Exposition, in securing France as the first nation to ratify our International Copyright act, the first nation to accept our invitation to the Columbus Exposition, in negotiating an admirable extradition treaty, in carrying through a most important plan for reciprocity and in the inestimable benefit he conferred upon American industries by his complete success in securing the removal of the prohibition duties upon American pork, he has never once lowered the dignity of his Government; he has maintained throughout the entire period the confidence of his Government, and by his firmness, tact and sense of justice has commanded the cordial sympathy and respect of the Government to which he was accredited. It was exceedingly gratifying to have us represented by such a man in France: to have his efforts successful in increasing the cordial relations which existed between the oldest Republic of the New World and the youngest republic of the Old World. (Prolonged applause and cheers.)

CALLING ON PRESIDENT LOW.

This closed the regular toasts. Mr. Smith then said: " Gentlemen, the Chair finds himself at this moment surrounded by an embarrassment of riches. We have got through with the regular order, and volunteer toasts are now in order. I find on my right a distinguished president of a great college, and also a distinguished clergyman of a great church. We have in our company an ex-Mayor of New-York, and also a distinguished ex-member of Congress. Now, I have refrained from calling any of these gentlemen by name, but I am sure you will select one or other of them to speak to you." (Cries of " Low.")

President Low responded as follows:

Mr. Chairman and Gentlemen: General Porter, I am sure, will not consider it any discredit to the Latin with which he began his recent eloquent speech if I say that it reminded me of a recent conversation between a sophomore and a freshman at Columbia College. The freshman appealed to his elder brother with this query: " What is the French for eau de vie?" and the sophomore replied that he was not quite sure, but he thought it was eau sucre. (Laughter.) A few evenings ago it became my duty in the capacity of a man at the head of an educational institution, to try and explain this phenomenon of nature. I found myself at a dinner given to the great Sir Edwin Arnold, and the question naturally arose, how could it be that the poet and the editor could exist in the same person? The explanation suggested was that it was because the editor and, poet alike live upon their imagination. (Laughter.) To-night I am obliged to hazard a conjecture as to how it is that an editor and a diplomatist can exist in the same person.

I think far too highly of the press to intimate that that could be the explanation which Talleyrand suggested that the art of using language by a diplomatist was to use words so as to conceal your thoughts. (Laughter.) I rather think the historian hit upon the correct explanation when he said of a certain historical character of the Middle Ages that he discomfited all the diplomatists of his time by telling the truth. (Laughter.) What is more natural and characteristic of the newspaper than that? And yet for the explanation of the particular phenomenon which concerns and interests us to-night, Mr. Chairman, of why it is that our distinguished

guest and fellow-countryman has been so great a success as a diplomatist, I can contribute one item of information.

ONE REASON FOR SUCCESS.

You heard him say, we all heard him this evening say, how in that position the greatness of the country entered into his veins, and all the dignity and the power of this great people stirred and animated his heart; but they did not make him great beyond sympathy with the small and the unknown. (Applause.) It came to me to send a couple of our younger students to his care, asking that he would give to them access to the great libraries of France. He not only did that, he not only placed his official services at their disposition, but he treated them with a personal courtesy that won their hearts and the admiration of the university to which they belonged. (Applause.) And, because of this consciousness of the greatness of the country, he remembered its attitude of honoring the small and the inconspicuous therein, and I think that is one way in which Mr. Reid distinguished himself as an American Minister at the Court of France. (Applause.)

Mr. Chairman, in the days when it was my pleasure to begin business life, I had many dealings with France, and particularly in connection with the manufacture and importation of silks, or rather with the importation of raw silk for manufacture here; and I used to think that no one feature, no one element, had contributed more to the progress of manufacturers in this country than the teachableness that was characteristic of our men. They would learn from Lyons and from Zurich with equal open-mindedness. They imitated the patterns, they dissected the cloth, and so the manufacture has made wonderful progress.

ARTISTS IN THE WORKSHOP.

But Mr. Reid has pointed out one thing that we have still to learn, that is, perhaps, of more importance than any material lesson which France can teach us. I asked how many men one of these manufacturers in Paterson employed, on one occasion, and he told me that there were in his employ so many hundred hands. When I reached Lyons I found that they called those hands " artists." (Applause.) That is the reason why France leads the world to-day in everything that is beautiful and that appeals to the universal taste. But I want to point out simply one other thing with regard to her attitude. She throws her art schools open to all the world. (Applause.) She recognizes that there are no artificial boundaries in the domain of art, that truth and beauty are not only eternal, but that they are to be found all the world over. (Applause.) I think we want to show the same hospitality to art that France displays, before we shall be worthy to stand as a republic in the world of art, side by side with the great Republic of France. (Applause.) I thank the American Minister for taking this occasion of saying to our people what I hope he will repeat in season and out of season—that he who would be truly great must be willing to meet the world on even terms. (Applause.)

MR. HALSTEAD ENDS THE SPEAKING.

At the close of President Low's speech, the chairman said: " Gentlemen, I will ask my friend from Brooklyn to make the valedictory speech, if he has not gone. General Woodford. Has the gentleman left the room? (Cries of "Halstead!") Mr. Halstead, will you say a word to those present?"

Mr. Halstead responded as follows:

Mr. Chairman: The embarrassment of riches that is upon you makes this to me an entirely unexpected pleasure and honor, the time is so short. It was Thomas Jefferson, I believe, who said of the Americans that they were fortunate in having two countries, one their own and the other France. The guest whom we honor to-night was fortunate in the time of his Ministry to France in finding her restored to her place among the nations of the world and giving to European countries their equilibrium. And one of the things which aided France more than anything else to prove that, was her magnificent Exposition which she gave to the world a short time ago. It has not been long since it was my privilege to be in Europe and to meet there the American Ministers in several of the great countries of Europe, and more charming and delightful American homes are not to be found anywhere upon our continent than those of the Ministers of the United States representing us in those great countries.

Now I have had very often much sympathy with our guest of this evening. We were born in the same State and in the same country, and have known each other long and well, and there is one thing and one only, that I will undertake to say here and now touching his relation abroad, one thing that has been in some degree neglected, and yet that seems to me the most important and most distinguished of all his honorable distinctions, and that was that he recognized from the first in France the fact that he was the representative of a Republican Government, and that France was a republic, and his constant sympathy, as I know, was the republicanism of that great Nation, in which all Europe is interested, and in which we ourselves take just and laudable pride. (Applause.)

I have, gentlemen of the Chamber of Commerce of New-York, for forty years known much of this great city, and, as I have become better acquainted with it, there is one institution in this city of New-York that is not lost with close acquaintance, with familiarity with its methods, with a knowledge of the influence that it exerts, with the information of the power it wields, and the interest that it commands, and the resources with which it distinguishes itself throughout the globe—there is one institution from which the enchantment has not gone—and that is the great Chamber of Commerce of the City of New-York. I congratulate you, my old friend upon the distinguished honor of this reception at your hands—one that I am sure he, as no one else would, with his experience in affairs of the world, prize most highly and esteem as the crowning honor of his career in diplomacy so happily terminated and his entrance upon new duties at home which are so promising in regard to the future. (Applause.)

THE LETTERS OF REGRET.

Many letters of regret were received. Among others was one from ex-President Cleveland, received late, announcing his regrets at not being able to accept the invitation. The letter of President Harrison was read, and the mention of his name was greeted with loud applause. These were the letters received:

EX-PRESIDENT RUTHERFORD B. HAYES.

Fifth Avenue Hotel, Madison Square,
New-York, April 14, 1892.

Gentlemen: In full sympathy with your purpose to recognize the services of Mr. Reid in France, I am, with regret, compelled by my engagements to deny myself the pleasure of accepting your invitation for Saturday evening. Sincerely,
RUTHERFORD B. HAYES.
Messrs. Depew, Porter, Bliss, Babcock, Orr, Committee.

FROM PRESIDENT HARRISON.

Executive Mansion,
Washington, April 11, 1892.
Hon. Chauncey M. Depew and others, Committee, etc.

Gentlemen: I am very sorry that I cannot accept the invitation of the Chamber of Commerce of the State of New-York to attend the banquet to be given to the Hon. Whitelaw Reid on the evening of Saturday, the 16th inst. There are controlling reasons of a public and private character that will prevent my leaving Washington at the time indicated. I am glad to notice that New-York so gracefully and fully recognizes the important services which Mr. Reid has been able to render to this country during his residence in Paris as United States Minister, and would be glad to participate with the members of the Chamber of Commerce in the expression of this feeling if it were possible. Very truly yours, BENJAMIN HARRISON.

SECRETARY JOHN W. NOBLE.

Department of the Interior,
Washington, April 11, 1892.
My Dear Sir: On the afternoon of Saturday, the 16th inst. I have an engagement at the Fifth Avenue Hotel to meet my brethren of the fraternity of the Beta Theta Pi, and thereby am prevented from accepting your very kind invitation to the banquet to the Hon. Whitelaw Reid, Minister of the United States to France, given by the Chamber of Commerce of the State of New-York, at Delmonico's, on the same evening.

Nothing would give me greater pleasure than to bear my tribute of respect to our eminent fellow-citizen, who has so faithfully and successfully performed the duties of the office entrusted to him.

American commerce has been greatly promoted and our friendly relations have been signally advanced, not only with France, but with other countries, by his labors.

It gives me pleasure to add that, from the testimony of many who have met Mr. Reid abroad, though engaged in the onerous duties devolved upon him, he has at all times shown the utmost consideration for our fellow-citizens abroad, and proved himself in private affairs as well as in public a patriotic American.

With the best wishes for the success of your entertainment, I remain, most respectfully,
JOHN W. NOBLE.
Mr. Cornelius N. Bliss, Chairman Banquet Committee, Chamber of Commerce, New-York.

CHIEF JUSTICE FULLER.

The Chief Justice begs to acknowledge the invitation of the Chamber of Commerce of the State of New-York to be present at the banquet to the Hon. Whitelaw Reid, Minister of the United States to France, at Delmonico's, on Saturday evening, April 16, at half-past 6 o'clock, and to express his regret that official duties here will prevent his participating in this manifestation of the appreciation of the service rendered by Mr. Reid to his country in promoting its commercial interests while discharging the duties of that high position.
Washington, April 8, 1892.

SENATOR JOHN SHERMAN.

Senate Chamber, Washington, April 8, 1892.
Cornelius N. Bliss, esq., Chairman.

My Dear Sir: I have the honor to acknowledge receipt of the invitation of the Chamber of Commerce to attend their banquet to the Hon. Whitelaw Reid, Minister of the United States to France. It would give me great pleasure to evince in this way my appreciation of the service rendered by Mr. Reid, and the great benefit he has conferred upon his countrymen by his wise, sagacious and liberal course during his important mission in promoting the commercial interests of the United States, but my public duties here will not permit me to do so. Very respectfully yours, JOHN SHERMAN.

CHARLES F. CRISP, SPEAKER OF THE HOUSE.

Speaker's Room, House of Representatives,
Washington, D. C., April 8, 1892.
The Hon. Cornelius N. Bliss, Chairman Banquet Committee, Chamber of Commerce, New-York.

My Dear Sir: I beg to acknowledge the receipt of your kind invitation to the banquet to be given to the Hon. Whitelaw Reid, Minister to France, on the 16th inst., and regret very much that my engagements here are such that it will be impossible for me to accept it. Yours very respectfully, CHARLES F. CRISP.

EX-SECRETARY THOMAS F. BAYARD.

Mr. Bayard has the honor to acknowledge the invitation of the Chamber of Commerce of the State of New-York to the banquet to be given to the Hon. Whitelaw Reid on April 16, at Delmonico's, and regrets that a previous engagement prevents his acceptance.
Wilmington, Del., April 8, 1892.

CONGRESSMAN ROBERT R. HITT.

House of Representatives,
Washington, April 12, 1892.
Hon. Cornelius N. Bliss, Chairman, etc.

Dear Sir: I have been trying to so arrange that I might accept your bidding for Saturday to meet you at dinner and join the Chamber of Commerce in greeting Whitelaw Reid. But it is impossible—engagements and duties prevent it.

He did much for America and Americans. He pressed wider open the doors for our commerce in everything, as coming years and increasing returns will show, for which the Chamber of Commerce of New-

York may well testify appreciation; but the West has a special and grateful satisfaction in his success in securing the readmission, after a long taboo, of "the short and simple annual of the poor." This is a great, substantial fact, with solid results already felt. The immense difficulties and powerful resistance overcome I can well appreciate, knowing the strong interest of the great agricultural proprietors and their compact organization and political power in the Chamber of Deputies, which, during the first Administration of President Grevy, when we thought we were on the eve of success and had already obtained a decree from the Executive, thwarted all our efforts by the action of the Chamber. The skill, the untiring patience and discreet activity with which his triumph was won mark him as one of the worthiest in the long line of illustrious men who have filled the French Mission, and prove again that America can, without the training of a diplomatic career, produce one whose abilities, tried by the severest test of success, place him in the very front rank of diplomatists. Very truly yours,
ROBERT R. HITT.

THE FRENCH MINISTER.

Legation de France, aux Etats Unis,
Washington, April 6, 1892.

Sir: I hasten to thank you for the very great kindness of your invitation to the banquet, on the 16th of April, to the Hon. Whitelaw Reid. Unhappily it will be impossible for me to accept it, as I am unavoidably occupied at that date by other engagements. I regret all the more not to be able to accept your very gracious hospitality, because the personal relations between myself and your Minister at Paris have always been most agreeable, and I am very much pained not to be able to be present at New-York upon the interesting occasion.

Accept, sir, the assurance of my distinguished consideration.
PATENOTRE.
To Mr. Charles S. Smith, President of the Chamber of Commerce.

EX-SENATOR WILLIAM M. EVARTS.

231 Second-ave.

Gentlemen: I have had the honor to receive the invitation of the Chamber of Commerce to attend a public banquet to be given in honor of Minister Whitelaw Reid on Saturday, the 16th inst.

I most heartily appreciate the eminent services to the country rendered by Mr. Reid, in the commercial and other great interests, in his conduct of his important mission during the last three years as our diplomatic representative in France. It is but a just tribute to these great public services which the Chamber of Commerce proposes to pay to our distinguished citizen, and in which the cordial sentiments of all our people will find their just expression.

I regret, however, to feel that the impaired condition of my eyesight precludes me from taking part in public assemblages, and with my sincere wishes for the prosperity of this noteworthy celebration, and with my thanks for the attention shown me by the invitation of the Chamber. I am, gentlemen, very respectfully, your obedient servant,
WILLIAM M. EVARTS.
Cornelius N. Bliss, esq., Chairman of Committee.

GEORGE WILLIAM CURTIS.

West New-Brighton,
Staten Island, N. Y. April 11, 1892.

My Dear Sir: I beg to acknowledge the invitation of the Chamber of Commerce to the banquet in honor of Mr. Whitelaw Reid, and I regret sincerely my inability to accept it. It is most fitting that the ancient and honorable institution which has so long represented with the highest character and dignity the commercial interest of New-York should pay a tribute of respect to the distinguished citizen who as Minister to France has served with such eminent ability the interests both of New-York and of the country. As a fellow-craftsman of Mr. Reid in the press, I share its pride in the distinction of so eminent an associate, and join heartily in welcoming his return "to drink delight of battle" with the eager host he knows so well. Very respectfully yours, GEORGE WILLIAM CURTIS.
Mr. Charles S. Smith, President.

FREDERICK W. SEWARD.

Montrose, N. Y., April 11, 1892.

Gentlemen: More than a dozen years ago, when a high diplomatic place was offered to Mr. Reid, he declined it—wisely, I thought, because his great journalistic enterprise then needed his personal presence and attention. When, during the present Administra-

tion, the Government again sought his aid in affairs abroad, The Tribune had become so thoroughly organized and assured of success that he could accept the proffered honor. So, in fact, he has been serving his country on both sides of the Atlantic at once—as journalist and diplomatist. How well and faithfully his diplomatic labors have been performed is now a matter of historic record. He has rendered eminent service in promoting the interests of American commerce in Europe, as well as in strengthening the traditional friendship between France and the United States, which dates back to the very beginning of our Republic, and I trust may continue to its end.

Your welcome to him on his return is a deserved recognition and tribute. I regret that other engagements will deprive me of the pleasure of sharing in it. Very respectfully yours,
FREDERICK W. SEWARD.
Messrs. Cornelius N. Bliss, etc.

EX-SECRETARY HAMILTON FISH.

New-York, April 8, 1892, No. 251 East Seventeenth-st.
To the Chamber of Commerce of the State of New-York.

Gentlemen: I have the honor to acknowledge the invitation to the Banquet to the Hon. Whitelaw Reid, to be given on April 16. It would afford me much pleasure to join in this well-merited tribute to Mr. Reid's valuable services to the country, but the condition of my health compels me to deny myself the pleasure. I am, very respectfully,
HAMILTON FISH.

GEORGE W. CHILDS.

Philadelphia, April 15, 1892.

My Dear Mr. Babcock:

I suppose I am indebted to your kind thoughtfulness for the invitation to the Chamber of Commerce dinner to Mr. Reid. I promptly accepted, and expected much pleasure in being among so many of my old friends, but I find now it will be impossible to be present. Will you please notify the secretary, so my seat may be filled, perhaps by a be.ter man.

None who will be present to-morrow night can possibly have a greater regard or greater appreciation of Mr. Whitelaw Reid than your old friend,
GEORGE W. CHILDS.
Samuel D. Babcock, esq.

HENRY WATTERSON.

Everett House, New-York, April 15, 1892.

My Dear Sir: I deeply regret that I am unexpectedly called away, and that I shall not be able to be present to do honor among his neighbors to my old and beloved friend, Whitelaw Reid. No man appreciates his private worth more than I do, or has a higher appreciation of his public services. I share to the fullest the spirit of the occasion, and am truly sorry that I cannot personally join in its celebration. With many thanks, dear sir, to you and the Chamber of Commerce for your hospitable and kind invitation, I am, sincerely, HENRY WATTERSON.
The Hon. Cornelius N. Bliss, etc., etc.

VISCOUNT PAUL D'ABZAC, CONSUL-GENERAL OF FRANCE.

Consulate-General de France, a New-York,
April 16, 1892, 4 Bowling Green.
To the Honorable President of the Chamber of Commerce of the State of New-York,
New-York City, N. Y.

Sir: I regret deeply that the condition of my health prevents me from enjoying the courteous invitation the Chamber of Commerce of the State of New-York has extended to me to be one of its guests at the banquet tendered to the Hon. Whitelaw Reid, Minister Plenipotentiary of the United States to France.

I respectfully request you to express to the Chamber of Commerce and to your distinguished guest my sincere regrets at not being among those who will welcome the Hon. Whitelaw Reid on his return to his native land after the successful and brilliant achievements of his diplomatic mission, which will be long remembered in France as well as in the United States. I remain, sir, respectfully yours,
PAUL D'ABZAC, Consul-General.

THE REV. DR. R. S. STORRS.

80 Pierrepont-st., Brooklyn, N. Y., April 11, 1892.

Gentlemen: It would give me very great pleasure to accept your kind invitation, and be present at the banquet proposed to be given by the Chamber of Commerce to the Honorable Whitelaw Reid, in recognition of the recent distinguished services rendered by him as Minister of the United States to France.

I yield to no one in my admiring estimate of the ability and shining success with which he has discharged the sometimes critical and difficult duties of that high office—laying both nations under almost equal obligation; and if it were possible I should be most happy to join with you, and with those for whom you are acting, in expressing to him in person my special esteem and honor But the evening selected for the banquet is one on which I cannot be away from home, and I must hope for some other opportunity to say more fully what in this hurried note can be only briefly and imperfectly suggested.

With great personal regard, and with thanks for your pleasant remembrance of me in connection with an occasion so signal and delightful, I am, gentlemen, ever faithfully yours,   R. S. STORRS.

Messrs. Cornelius N. Bliss, Samuel D. Babcock, Chauncey M. Depew, Horace Porter, Alexander E. Orr.

BISHOP WILLIAM ALEXANDER.

Episcopal Theological School,
Cambridge, Mass.. April 9, 1892.

The Bishop of Derry and Raphoe desires to thank the gentlemen of the Chamber of Commerce for the invitation with which he has been favored to the banquet to be given to the Hon. Whitelaw Reid on Saturday, April 16.

The Bishop esteems it as the highest honor to have been invited to such a gathering in commemoration of the services of so conspicuous an American citizen, whose name stands high in the ranks of contemporary diplomatists.

But he finds that it will be impossible for him to have the gratification of being present at the banquet, owing to his engagements.

THE REV. DR. JOHN HALL.

April 8, 1892, 712 Fifth-ave.
Cornelius N. Bliss, esq., Chairman, etc.

My Dear Sir: I am sorry that a fixed duty and a meeting (on each Saturday night) will prevent my sharing in the well-deserved honor you propose to our late Minister in Paris. He has done good service in a difficult place, and deserves National recognition. I am, dear sir, with respect, yours most truly,
                                    J. HALL.

DINNER OF THE LOTOS CLUB

HAPPY MEMORIES RECALLED AND PROPHECIES MADE.

WHITELAW REID THE GUEST OF HONOR—REMARKS BY FRANK R. LAWRENCE, COLONEL THOMAS W. KNOX, ST. CLAIR M'KELWAY, WILLIAM H. M'ELROY, JAMES W. ALEXANDER, MURAT HALSTEAD AND OTHERS.

Everything which appertained to affectionate regard and good-fellowship was embodied in the dinner given Saturday evening by the Lotos Club to Whitelaw Reid, a former president of that organization. It was a home-greeting, a heart and soul welcome, to an associate. and it was evident that Mr. Reid appreciated the cordiality of the offerings of good-fellowship, by a body of men between whom and himself there are many ties of friendship, some of which are too sacred to be made commonplace in stereotyped print. The dinner was given in the clubhouse, but many members of the club consented to occupy seats at tables on the second floor, rather than forego an opportunity to join in the festivities.

Frank R. Lawrence, president of the club, presided at the centre table on the first floor and W. H. White, vice-president, ruled the fifty gentlemen who sat at the tables on the second floor. At the main table down stairs, by the side of Mr. Lawrence, sat the guest of the evening, Mr. Reid, and at his right was ex-Mayor Abram S. Hewitt, whose presence was greatly appreciated. Charles Stewart Smith, president of the Chamber of Commerce, sat at the left of Mr. Lawrence. Others at the same table were Murat Halstead, D. O. Mills, St. Clair McKelway, J. W. Alexander, William Winter, General Wager Swayne, W. H. McElroy, Thomas W. Knox, Paul Dana, Robert E. Bonner, Arthur F. Bowers, Collin Armstrong, Viscount Paul d'Abzac and F. B. Thurber.

The decorations consisted of an oil painting of Mr. Reid, full length, on one side of which was the flag of the United States and on the other that of the Republic of France. On the opposite side of the room was a painting of the steamer La Champagne, on which Mr. Reid returned from France, and above it was the inscription: "She brought our guest over the sea from honors abroad to greater honors at home."

BEGINNING THE SPEECHMAKING.

It was after 10 o'clock when Dr. Lawrence called the assemblage to order. In rising to introduce the guest of the evening he said:

The gentleman in whose honor we assemble to-night requires less than any man an introduction to the members of the Lotos Club. The charter of the club, by the Legislature of the State, was granted some twenty years ago to Whitelaw Reid and other gentlemen, Mr. Reid's name being the first upon the list. From then until now he has been actively identified with the club, and has always held a foremost place in the regard of its members.

When, some three years ago, Mr. Reid was chosen by the President of the United States to fill the honorable office of Minister to the great sister republic of France, the members of the Lotos Club were among the first to express their sense of the fitness of the selection; for they, better than almost any, knew the man, and knew how rarely he was qualified to dignify and adorn the station to which he was called. We parted from him with highest expectations of what he would achieve, and now that he has returned, with every anticipation realized, who should rejoice more heartily than his old friends and companions of the Lotos Club?

We knew he must succeed, for what could so adequately prepare a man for a diplomatic career as fourteen years in the presidency of this organization? Such a course of treatment is perhaps severe, but the survivor is qualified to cope with any nation whatsoever. (Laughter.)

Since his return from abroad, Mr. Reid has been publicly entertained, first by the society composed of the sons of his native State, and then by that greatest association of merchants, the Chamber of Commerce of the City of New-York; and upon those occasions much, though by no means all that might be said, has been uttered in his praise.

NO FORMAL WELCOME NEEDED.

To-night he has come home. He would no more expect a formal greeting here than at his own fireside!

Yet even here, where we are not always serious, some serious words should be uttered to show that not merely as friends, but as citizens who partake in all that adds to the glory of our country, we honor and rejoice over the great public services of Mr. Whitelaw Reid. (Applause.)

To his services to commerce the merchants of the country have already given testimony. Of his earnest and arduous labors the treaties between this country and France stand as monuments. Yet what he has done in the direction of bringing more closely together the people of the two countries is perhaps as great a service as any; and there are many gentlemen present to-night who can tell from personal experience how delightful was the relation established and maintained by Mr. Reid among the people of the great, brave and talented nation in whose country he has lately resided.

It is occasionally suggested by those who favor extreme simplicity in our government that diplomatic establishments abroad are useless to a country like ours, and should not be maintained. That suggestion finds its complete and perfect answer in the diplomatic career of Mr. Reid. (Applause.)

We hear it said, upon the other hand, that the United States should dignify its diplomatic service by bestowing more sounding titles upon those who represent it in foreign countries, in order that the Minister of the United States at a foreign court may no longer be outranked by the Ambassador of every foreign Power. To us this seems of little moment: for it is a happy circumstance in the history of our Government that in a great number of instances those who have represented it in foreign countries have been men who rise superior to rank or title; our greatest and our best. We recall with pride that the Ministry to France, which Mr. Reid has just laid down, was earliest held by Franklin and Jefferson, while almost contemporaneously in diplomatic service with our guest of to-night was the lamented James Russell Lowell.

A HINT AT SOMETHING HIGHER.

Mr. Reid has resigned his Ministry to France and returned among us, the same genial, kindly, unaffected gentleman as in years gone by, and he would have us think that he has laid down public office for good and all. Yet, whatever may be his belief or desire, I ask you, without attempting to cast an augury, might it not prove another instance of the happy destiny which so long has ruled our country if, in the future, so typical an American citizen, possessed of character so pure and ability so splendid, should be called to serve his country at home in a station more exalted than that which he has lately occupied abroad? (Applause.)

But, gentlemen, you are eager to hear our guest. As citizens, companions, friends, we greet him: the Lotos Club welcomes him home. He will find some changes here, but there can be no change in the affection of the members of the Lotos Club for Whitelaw Reid. (Loud and prolonged applause.)

MR. REID'S REPLY.

The remarks of Mr. Lawrence were frequently interrupted by applause. When Mr. Reid arose he was most heartily cheered, all rising to drink his health at the suggestion of President Lawrence. He spoke as follows:

It is evident that the traditions of the Lotos Club are preserved. We always praised our guests—sometimes too much!

It seems to me that, in days gone by, I have sometimes heard the Lotos spoken of also as the club where they always entertain foreigners. I wish it distinctly understood that this is no occasion of that sort. You are entertaining no foreigner to-night.

Furthermore, you are entertaining a man who feels uncommonly at home. Several things have happened to inspire such a feeling. I have ridden uptown hanging to a strap in a Sixth-ave. elevated with the market basket of the woman behind poking me in the ribs and the heels of the man in front reposing on my toes. I have been invited to deliver a lecture, and I have had an opportunity to make a political speech. My friend the reporter has interviewed me, once or twice, I think; and I have even been asked to write for the newspapers. I hadn't landed twenty-four hours till a subscription paper was presented, inviting me to join my neighbors in raising a fund to hire a man to sweep our street; and in looking over my tax receipts I found that our paternal city government had discharged its duty in presenting its own little bills for not doing the same work. I have likewise

enjoyed the privilege of saving from the horrible torture of a lingering death by thirst several gentlemen who had had nothing to eat for the past forty-eight hours, and had no place to sleep that night. Their faces were familiar, but it struck me that they had fattened a little on their misery during the past three years, and that their fine complexions had an even ruddier glow than ever.

All these, you will admit, are circumstances that ought to make almost any old New-Yorker feel at home again, no matter how long his absence.

And then there are the same glorious sunshiny skies above us, and the same electric air about us, whether in the atmosphere or in the people. There is the same warm-hearted appreciation for any little public service one may have been able to render, and the same truly American readiness to pardon mistakes in recognition of an honest motive. There is the same open-handed hospitality from all classes of a community that permits political differences to interfere less with its social good-will and genuine friendliness than any other on the face of the globe.

In this very club there are probably now, as there always were in the past, more Democrats than Republicans. Political critics were accustomed sometimes to point to that as a fair measure of my personal influence. It seemed to me a fairer measure of that broad-minded tolerance which characterizes men of the large world, and which lies at the very foundation of our democratic institutions, a genuine belief in the maxim of the immortal Scotchman, that whatever the difference in birth, or in fortune or in faith, "a man's a man for a' that."

BACK AGAIN WITH FRESH EYES.

There is one advantage of a long absence from home that furnishes a certain satisfaction. You come back to your own country with fresh eyes. And it is amazing what things you see, and how much better you see them. Never did I realize so fully the beauties of our incomparable Central Park as when I came to it, after a three years' absence, fresh from the Bois de Boulogne. The man is a public enemy who would deface or curtail it; and I hope this club and all men of good taste and good will in this whole community will support the spirited young president of the Park Commission, and his colleagues, in their resolute defence of it against every specious scheme of spoliation, from whatever quarter it may come.

Then there is our architecture. We are apt, in a shamefaced way, to say, "Well, New-York must look rather crude, after the splendid architecture of the great European capitals." But the fresh eye tells a different story. It does not deceive us by saying that we have here a Louvre or a Madeleine, or a Place de la Concorde, or even a Hotel de Ville. But it does startle us with the revelation of an unsuspected beauty in such a shabby old gem as the City Hall; it does make an old newspaper man feel pretty well satisfied with Printing House Square, to say nothing of Wall-st. and Broadway; and it does show a variety and a beauty of architectural effect uptown that begins to warrant us now in being as proud of the exteriors of our houses as we long have been of their interiors.

And do you know that, to a man who has been haunting the old book-shops on the Quai Voltaire and behind it, or the bric-a-brac shops beyond the Place de la Republique or the old site of the Bastile, or who has occasionally, on nights of political excitement, explored the heights of Montmartre, or the byways of the Faubourg St. Antoine, the streets of New-York do not look as badly, in many quarters at least, as he had expected. We have imitated Parisian methods in asphalt to unexpected advantage. If now we could only impart the efficiency of the Parisian broom!

This morning I read in the newspapers that we were to have the pleasure of the company here this evening of my distinguished successor near the Government of the French Republic. This afternoon he told me he had been summoned to Boston. I should have been glad to extend to him here my congratulations and best wishes. When I saw him last he was in the midst of his successful diplomatic work in the fruitful Pan-American Congress. I wish him the same success and the same enjoyment in the brilliant capital for which he is now nominated. And I take this opportunity to reassure him as to any fears concerning it which our new-paper dispatches for the last few days may have aroused. He need have no apprehensions that Paris will be blown up and scattered to the winds before he gets there. It has been a long time building, and it will not be destroyed in a hurry. Neither need he accept too literally the story that a few explosions of blasting material have stampeded the Parisians. They have seen some serious things in their day, and they are not easily stampeded. The city that went through the Reign of Terror, that knew both the glory and the downfall of the greatest soldier since Caesar, that endured the siege by the Germans, and its own Commune, has learned several things from this varied experience—among them, how to deal with lunatics and mobs. Personally, I should feel safer myself to-morrow in the company of my friend the Prefect of Police in Paris than I should on one of the boats of my other friend, John H. Starin, on the next Fourth of July picnic. Whatever happens to-morrow—and most likely it will be nothing—Mr. Coolidge will find himself, when he presents his credentials, in what will be still the gayest, the pleasantest, and the most beautiful city of the world, and he will find there a welcome as cordial as the national friendship it represents is real.

THE OLD PLACE KEPT FOR HIM.

It is a great pleasure in returning home after a long absence to find that one's place has been kept for him, that he has not been forgotten, and that, while the procession has certainly moved on without him, it can still give him room in its ranks. It is a peculiar pleasure to be received here. What reminiscences do not the place and the surroundings call up; what memories of this hall, and of the older one in Irving Place, next door to the Academy of Music, when life was young and joy was unconfined. There we greeted Canon Kingsley and Lord Houghton and Rubinstein and the King of the Sandwich Islands—but one of them left now, and he a sovereign in art. Here we greeted Froude and Matthew Arnold and Henry Irving and Count de Lesseps, and William S. Gilbert and Sir Arthur Sullivan, and what a host beside. And to name only three of our own people, can any one fail to remember with a tender reverence our last dinners here to John Brougham, Lester Wallack and John Gilbert? Ah! me,—in spite of the Lotos Club, the world is growing old!

I cannot thank you too much, Mr. President, or the club you so worthily represent, for the kindness which has marked every detail of this most gracious reception;—for the care with which you have gathered many old friends to meet me, and for the effort to bring still others. Two of your letters to-night, not to allude to many others, have touched me profoundly: the most generous words of George William Curtis and Edmund Clarence Stedman.

But I must bring this rambling talk to a close. I am not here to night to entertain, even if I could, but to be entertained. And besides, there has been just a little too much of my voice heard in the land for the three weeks or more I have been on American soil. I have no wish to wear out my welcome, and I mean to stay here some time. Plainly the hour has struck for a brilliant flash of silence from me. I thank you a thousand times for all your good-will and your good opinions—would that I deserved them better. I rejoice with you in the prosperity of the good old club, and I drink to the good health, happiness and long life of its president and of all its members.

EX-MAYOR ABRAM S. HEWITT.

When Mr. Reid resumed his seat, Mr. Lawrence introduced ex-Mayor Abram S. Hewitt, who spoke as follows:

Mr. President and Gentlemen of the Lotos Club: Your president said he was reluctant to interrupt the proceedings by the sound of any other voice than those which have already been heard. I share with him most profoundly in that regard, and I thought and think now that it is one of the privileges of old age to be allowed to rest in quiet contemplation, and in the pleasure of hearing others talk for his in-

struction. Sir, I feel the poverty of thought, and more particularly of words, which comes to those who have fought the battle of life and been retired. Still, it is easy to perform the duty which we all come here to-night so willingly to perform, in saying to Mr. Reid how lonesome we have been in his absence, and how the sense of loneliness, no amount of talk, political or otherwise, has been able to make up.

Mr. Reid and I have been friends for many years, and, although we have had our political differences, they have never invaded for one moment the sacred domain of friendship. When I have made the great mistakes of my public career, I say now that no one came to me so frankly and so freely in private and besought me to see the error of my ways and begged me to repent and go to than Mr. Reid. (Applause.) And I will say now that if I had followed his advice, on more than one occasion, it would have been better for me and perhaps for the country.

When Mr. Reid was selected to fill the distinguished office which he has just resigned, I think no one rejoiced more than I did, and no one believed more than I did that the Administration had put the right man in the right place. (Applause.)

In the early history of our country Jefferson and Adams and other of our Presidents thought that foreign Ministers were not of much use, nevertheless, they always sent men abroad to fill those offices to get rid of troublesome politicians at home. (Laughter.) There are many examples in our country, the best known of which is John Randolph—who was sent to Russia to die, and who came back home to die, to the great gratification of his friends. (Laughter.) But there was another reason. When the Diplomatic bill was attacked on the ground that the salaries were too great and that our country ought to discontinue its foreign Ministers, I had charge of the bill, and I pointed out to the House—and I never heard any objection made afterward, although I see it has occurred on an occasion quite recently—that it was quite necessary to educate our Ministers whom we sent to foreign ports, and I must say that the Republican Administration (which has succeeded the exceedingly able and patriotic Democratic Administration) has made a great discovery, namely, they have selected men who had been already trained in a greater school than any foreign community or any government under which the ordinary rules of diplomacy exist; they have selected men trained in an editorial capacity. They have picked out the men who know every trick and every motive which influences human actions. (Applause.)

I think that the very acme of human intelligence was exhibited by the President when he chose as the man to represent us under very peculiar difficulties in the Court of France a man who was born and bred in Ohio, and who had been graduated in the city of New-York in the midst of our local politics. (Laughter and applause.) I knew perfectly well that whatever he did would be well done, and that all he did as Minister to France would redound to the credit of his country. (Applause.)

Now, you are also familiar with what Mr. Reid has done and we are also grateful to him for what he has done, because he has obtained an enormous trade for this country in France, and I do not think it necessary to speak at any length upon his work there. I find that his views have been enlarged in some particulars since he left us, and that he is absolutely prepared to consider how the reciprocal trade between France and the United States might be increased; and he even suggested that the proposition made by France, of the universal exchange of products between the two nations, might be and would be for the advantage of this country rather than that of France.

Now, for the Editor of The Tribune to have arrived at the conclusion that a foreign treaty can be advantageous to anybody and that it is not a crime that ought to be suppressed, is in my mind, evidence of the enormous value that is derived from sending editors abroad as the representatives of our great nations. (Laughter and applause.)

I found in his address which he made yesterday or the day before, before the Republican State Convention, that he has arrived at some admirable conclusions, which he stated to his fellow-delegates. I think they really are of practical value, not only to the Republicans, but to the Democrats. They were the result of experience. He advised his party to get together. (Laughter.)

Now, I do not know any man of my acquaintance now living—perhaps I may know some who are dead—who have got together as many good things as Mr. Reid has. Before he went abroad he got a newspaper together, and connected with that newspaper he got a group of editors and reporters without a superior as a corps—perhaps without an equal—in any like establishment in the world. (Applause.) He got a fine building, and if I may be permitted in his presence to say it, he got a charming wife and a most admirable family and a bena ideal of a father-in-law. (Applause.)

Well. I know that I am willing to sacrifice myself on the altar of republican institutions if that is to be the result, and if I am to achieve as many delightful and pleasant things as my friend, Mr. Reid. (Laughter.)

Now, with his profound knowledge of international relations, and with the reputation which he has acquired, not only in America, but in America, there is no telling to what heights he may attain. If it should happen that the people of this country should, in a spasm of extraordinary intelligence (laughter), recognize the enormous advantage which it would be to them by securing in the highest executive office of the land the services of so trained a diplomat, so wise a statesman as Mr. Reid, there is at least one Democrat in this broad land who will not say him nay, and who will feel that virtue has had its reward. (Cheers and applause.)

CHARLES STEWART SMITH.

Mr. Hewitt's speech was well received, and at its close hearty cheers were given for the ex-Mayor of New-York, held in so high respect by all the citizens of the metropolis.

Viscount Paul d'Abzac then made a few felicitous remarks.

Then Mr. Lawrence called upon Charles Stewart Smith, president of the Chamber of Commerce, who said:

Does it not occur to you, Mr. Chairman, that considering all the dinners, receptions, fetes, etc., that have been tendered to Mr. Reid since his return, he has had about "taffy" enough to turn the head of a man less sensible than your guest? I have been an attentive reader of and listener to all that has been so well said in praise of his public and social life. I find that the whole range of his virtues has been thoroughly exposed and laid open to the admiring gaze of his friends. I have been trying almost in vain to think of something nice and complimentary that would be slightly novel and not entirely a chestnut. Fortunately I call to mind some conversation had with your guest some years ago in Paris, in which he gave me some idea of the difficulty he had in securing a passport for the American hog to the markets of France.

In discussing this matter with the Minister of Foreign Affairs, that gentleman said, "Well, what has Monsieur le Ministre Americain to offer to France in return for this great concession which you desire for this important product of your country? Can you admit free or reduce the duty upon French wines?" "I fear not," replied Mr. Reid. "We are fast becoming a large wine-growing country, and it is not probable that Congress would consent to that." After deliberation Mr. Reid said to his friend: "I think we might and should admit French pictures free," and it is very much to the credit of your guest that he threw the great influence of his journal and made strong personal exertions with the lawmakers in Washington in favor of abrogating this ridiculous embargo upon light, knowledge and refinement. (Applause.)

I think, Mr. Chairman, that the country is to be congratulated upon the appointment of T. Jefferson Coolidge as successor to Mr. Reid at Paris. I have known Mr. Coolidge for twenty-five years; he is a well-equipped gentleman of remarkable executive powers; he has the reputation of accomplishing what he undertakes. I know of no man in the country who could fill the office of Minister to France with more ability, grace and dignity than Mr. Coolidge. (Applause.)

MURAT HALSTEAD'S WIT.

The next speaker upon whom Mr. Lawrence called was Murat Halstead, who spoke as follows:

Mr. President and Gentlemen of the Lotos Club: In the interest of journalism my remarks have been reduced to typewriting. (Laughter.) The able and able-bodied editors of Brooklyn—and I may speak with some confidence for two of them—are willing to fight it out on this line with the honored guest of the evening, if it takes all summer. (Laughter.) This is the third time we have rallied, and if we are still further allured with invitations to fascinating feasts, we shall persistently respond with an appreciative acceptance and advance "while glow the heavens with the last steps of day" across the Bridge, resolved to do our duty, and return to the shadows of our churches before the hour when our goodly city is overwhelmed with the Sunday newspaper. (Laughter.)

The Ohio Society had the honor of dining the ex-Minister to France, and the physically large and intellectually intense Brooklyn editors were there representing both sides of the Mississippi Valley. (Applause.) The delights of that dinner have not faded, and we shall not, I trust, here and now resume those reminiscences and recollections that are stimulated by the blossoming of the buckeye tree, that is the chestnut of France, with intoxication in its efflorescence. (Laughter.) And yet one may speak gently of the southwestern corner of Ohio. I shall modestly refrain from giving a list of the men born there who have turned their faces to the light of the East and entered into public life on the Atlantic frontiers. It may not be inappropriate to mention that the author of "Ohio in the War" had embarrassment in the superabundance of material for his huge and handsome volumes. the rush of riches beginning with Generals Grant, Sherman and Sheridan. (Applause.) After the sword came the pen.

When I recite the fact that my pen flourished a good deal in the course of the war, I am moved rather by a sense of justice toward others, than a spirit of vanity as to myself. I ascertained early and was reminded late, that the candid historian is not constantly approved by the conquering hero; and I was not always solitary in my part of the country in that experience of information. (Laughter.)

During several years I have received from the young gentlemen who are alleged to be pursuing their studies in the numerous and various institutions of learning that adorn and to a certain extent illuminate our country communications requesting views upon Schools of Journalism. I have never returned an adequate answer, but shall now attempt doing so. Incomparably the great school of journalism was war correspondence, written on the field, and in that school the guests of the Lotos this evening, graduated with high honors. (Applause.) I did not have the advantage of the school, being graduated, as it were, in another. In these days before the War when the moon, as there is Southern authority, was constantly larger than she has been since. (Laughter.)

GENEROUS WITH THE TRUTH.

In his brilliant speech at the Ohio Society's dinner—pardon these frequent references to dining out—Mr. Reid referred to me as his "old opponent." I had several old opponents, and remember them keenly and kindly, but I have often had to confess a weakness in the wearing away of my hatefulness. It is hard to hate a man more than ten or fifteen years—or twenty or thirty years—and Mr. Reid has been the opposite of a hateful man—cne, indeed, abounding in courtesies. He has had personal prejudices, but they were generally in favor of, rather than against, people. He occasionally killed his enemies with kindness. He has had experiences of being reviled for the truth's sake; and one of the lessons to be sometimes taught in the high schools of journalism is the part of practical wisdom to tell the truth with considerate reservations.

The first time I knew Mr. Reid to be heartily and aggressively abused, I knew just as well as he that his offence was recklessness in writing that which was so. Nearly everybody knew what the matter was, but a majority of his fellow-citizens and co-laborers did not rush to his rescue. I managed to look on with composure and saw him at last rescue himself. That is what a fellow has to do when he gets into a scrape for forcing too many facts suddenly upon the people. I shall not tell what the fight was about. I was not "in it." (Laughter.)

Allow me the use of the editorial "we" for a paragraph. We of "The Cincinnati Commercial," had blown into the war from our office a good deal of talent, and were proud of our letters from the front. Mayor Bickham was there, and Mr. Plimpton was there, and our circulation was becoming almost appalling. Our competing contemporary, "The Cincinnati Gazette," did not get left by any means as often as it should. (Laughter.) Its pages contained a stream of letters that were offensively interesting and signed "Agate." We did not like that kind of pebble. It sparkled too much, and there was a suspicion that the derned thing might be a diamond. (Laughter.)

At last, weary of this competitive well-doing, we inquired who the author of these unwarranted effusions was, and the answer shall be accurately reported. "The Agate letters are written by a long-legged youth from Xenia, named Reid" (applause); and as to where he come from, he was a graduate of the Butler County Oxford, and had been editing a small but savage Republican paper at Xenia.

It seemed preposterous that there should be an eruption of journalism like that on the head waters of the Litt'e Miami. That part of the country had been remarkable for the Yellow Springs, the burning of a beautiful article of lime, the location of a powder mill that blew up quadrennially (augater), the birthplace of the Indian chief Tecumseh, from whom General Sherman was named, and for the production of an excessive allowance of original poems, in ballad form. (Laughter.) Xenia, as a fountain of poetry, was a terror of editors, and supplied the stuffing for many waste-baskets.

I must say, in parenthesis, the black powder and white lime are still burning on the old sites, and the poetry has declined in quantity, but improved in quality. I hasten to say, if Mr. Reid ever wrote po try, he was never within my knowledge caught at it. When the "Agate" correspondence became familiar, it was recollected that several notable editorials had appeared in "The Xenia News." One of them of the few first, if not the very first, that presented the name of Abraham Lincoln as a possible President of the United States. (Applause.)

Mr. Reid's return to enjoy a restful time at home, it is clear, will prove the same sort of success that he had in sailing away for a quiet time abroad. Perhaps he is not fitted for a career of repose. He seems already to have supplied a long felt want in the politics of the State. The Big Four is a Larger Five; and the improvement is auspicious. (Laughter and applause.)

ST. CLAIR McKELWAY.

Mr. Halstead's speech was of that kindly character which one successful journalist bestows upon another. And he was followed by another journalist, across the East River, who said:

Mr. President and Gentlemen: Not long ago I was at a dinner given to the guest of honor as an Ohio idea in the city of New-York. A week later I was at another dinner as a homebringing to the returning Minister of the United States to the Government of France. To-night I am glad to help out, by in part helping in, a dinner to Whitelaw Reid. (Laughter.) We do not here toast the immigrant. We do not here drink to the diplomat. We just greet and meet the man. He is here denuded of dignities. He is here stripped of accessories. Here not what he has been or done or suffered is celebrated. What he is—himself as he is—engages our regard. The Government found out of what stuff he was made by sending him abroad. (Applause.) We knew the secret beforehand, for we had taken his measure at home. The Ohio Society and the Chamber of Commerce applauded him because he had taught the French the Star Spangled Banner, by his skill with a whistle made out of the tail of an American pig. (Laughter.) Pork was the impelling principle of their approval. Though hearty in spirit, their acclaims were, so to speak, hoggish in cause. (Laughter.) The Lotos Club forgets that he was an envoy, for they know him in the higher role of an ex-president. They discount his skill as a negotiator of treaties, for they recognize his far greater skill as chairman of their

Governing Committee for so long a time. Three years in Paris as Minister are as nothing to fourteen years here as the chief of this club. The difficulties of the former position are small compared with the exactions of the latter. What are fifty years of Europe to twelve months of Lotos administration? (Laughter and applause.)

When Whitelaw Reid went to Paris he had to be received by the President of that Republic; but what was that to him who in your name here received the kings of song, the sovereigns of art, the wonder workers in the realm of literature, the monarchs of the aesthetic world? Goodlier and greater company has been greeted here by him than there greeted him. (Applause.) If to Paris good Americans go when they die, to New-York good foreigners may come in order that they may feel life is worth living. But America forbears to receive them, until the Lotos Club has set its seal of approval upon them. The Lotos Club is the clearing house for the intellect, conscience and taste of the United States. What passes here is pure gold. What fails to pass here has alloy in it. You hold a brief for the hospitality of the Nation. You are informally licensed to discriminate between the meritorious and the meretricious on behalf of the people. You establish the standard, conformity to which is par, and a falling below which is a retirement from circulation. Your club did this under Whitelaw Reid's presidency. It has adhered to his policy since his departure. It only follows its function when it recognizes that he has won his right to be received where in your name he did receive.

WELL-TRAINED FOR DIFFICULT PLACES.

I do not know what further honors await him. He learned how to be president by running this club. He learned how to be vice-president by holding that office in the Ohio Society. His duties as diplomatist were begun when he negotiated how to live, as he has elsewhere said, on less than fifteen dollars a week. His skill in arbitration must have been severely taxed to enable him here to keep the peace between the House Committee and the chef and how to reconcile the apprehensions of the treasurer with the growing figures against the names of the boys on the bulletin board of the club. (Laughter.) A newspaper man may have somewhat drawn on his fine points, but that is nothing to the skilful administration of a club of authors, artists, musicians and poets—to say nothing of publishers and bankers. (Applause.) Here he was elected to high place for fourteen years. I wish he would tell us who the inspectors were; how he stood in with them: whether he was elected before the oils closed or after the count had been polled. (Laughter.)

I am sure you are all glad that he has been a successful man. If his success has been built on the sacrifice of any one else's rights, I have yet to learn of it. (Applause.) It has certainly not come to him by the detraction of others, nor is their condemnation, or hatred, or jealousy mixed with it. It seems to me to have been an entirely legitimate success, based on pluck, industry, fair play, hold-on and a purpose to magnify the scope of general journalism, minimize the asperities of political journalism and end the idiocy of personal journalism. (Applause.)

"Sir," said a man to Benjamin Franklin, "so and so has the faculty of common-sense." "Common-sense," replied the philosopher, "is not a faculty. It is the equilibrium of all the faculties." To me it seems that this legitimately successful man has an equilibrium of all the faculties. He has sentiment, but not so much as to make him weak. He has regard to usage, but not so much as to make him a slave to routine or a serf to superstition. He has taste, but not that overplus of it which deprives his prose of teeth with which to bite. He has judgment, but not such a rigid quality of it as to deny him the pleasure of taking chances on a noble impulsiveness. He has learning, but his knowledge is organized for use, not stocked for storage amid ever-gathering dust. He has levity which is so far restrained as to save him from ever becoming the clown of occasion. He has humor without buffoonery. He has wit without malice. He has seriousness without priggishness. He is a Presbyterian without asceticism: a Republican without bigotry; a politician without jobbery; an American who is the friend, but not the bully, of his country. (Applause.)

There are other editors who hit harder, but they hurt their hands more than the heads of their antipathies. There are other editors who plunge more desperately, but the rapidity of their development lacks uniformity. There are editors who make themselves more a part of their work, but none whose work preserves its likeness so well as his does when he is away from it. I am glad he has been successful, for he has been worthily successful. I am glad he is not poor, for he has surmounted poverty without trickery and he infuses affluence with no arrogance. I wish he was worth a hundred million dollars and could not sleep until he gave me half of it. (Laughter.) He would, however, never find in any journal edited by himself a cure for insomnia. (Laughter.)

TIME TO GO TO WORK AGAIN.

Now that you have welcomed him home, he will have to go to work. The early confirmation of the nomination of his excellent successor to France will leave him without excuse much longer to refrain from journalism. He cannot forever insist that his goods are not yet through the custom house. Unless he is suspected of undervaluation, they should have been through weeks ago. (Laughter.) He cannot always maintain that his town residence is in a chaotic confusion. That remark, pretty soon, will be regarded as a proof of verbal rather than mural decoration. He cannot much longer suggest that the sea burn is not yet off his face. Pigmentary possibilities are not eternal. (Laughter.) Nor can he apologetically allude to the incomplete condition of his farm. Between you and me. I do not believe it is a farm at all. I believe it is an estate. He lived in a palace in Paris and called it a house. He is quite capable of living in a chateau in Westchester County and calling it a hut—of preempting a township up there and referring to it as a few acres. (Laughter.) All these pretexts will soon have to be dropped from texts. I do not mean scriptural texts, for of them he concedes a monopoly to another. (Laughter.) I mean political texts. He will have to show his hand in the Tribune, and that right early.

He eulogized "Protection" at Albany, but to the Ohio men he spoke of the most significant example of "Free Trade" in the world—our interstate commerce. (Applause.) We who differ from him will stand no such juggling with words. Is he for Harrison? Or is he for Blaine? We will give him until after the Minneapolis Convention to answer, but not a day more. Does he hope that the other side will nominate Cleveland or that they will nominate Hill? We pause for a reply, subject to the decision of the next Democratic National Convention. (Laughter.) All these questions must be met. He must be heard on them. Merely because he has not to France, he cannot claim a right to take French leave of living questions and burning issues. When again he puts on the armor, may the support he has had from all parties as a Minister broaden and better his advocacy of one and temper his zeal against the other. May the largeness of his country's heart, which he has felt beating against his own, convince him that patriotism is peculiar to neither party and is predicable of both. May the difficulties he finds in flooring Republican abuses make him charitable toward Democrat derelictions, and may he hold so close a rein on prejudice as at any time to be able to rally the best thought on his side with the best thought on the other side for the righteous administration which should be demanded of all public servants, whatever their politics, when once they have been clothed with the duties of representation and with the obligations of rule. (Loud and continued applause.)

JAMES W. ALEXANDER.

Everybody present pronounced Mr. McKelway's speech one of the highest order, and he was heartily applauded during its delivery and when he sat down. Then William Winter, of The Tribune staff, read a poem. Mr. Winter's poem was pronounced by those who heard it one of the best he had ever given upon an after-dinner occasion. Then Mr. Lawrence introduced J. W. Alexander, who said: There was not one word said in my invitation about making a speech. I do not complain of this, because a deaf, dumb and blind man ought to have heard

and seen enough of our distinguished friend, Mr. Reid, to be able to pronounce a eulogy upon him without preparation. But I wonder why I was discriminated against and made to speak on the spur of the moment, when Mr. Hewitt, and Mr. Smith, and Mr. Halstead and the others have evidently been getting ready for months. (Laughter.)

I see by your book that the Lotos Club was organized to promote social intercourse between journalists, artists, musicians and members of the theatrical profession. But there is not one word about the American Hog! Not that I am classifying myself under that head (laughter), although one might be happy to belong to a body for which the guest of the evening has shown such a decided partiality. (Laughter.) He has certainly lifted up that commodity from a condition of degradation and made it distinguished reversing the sentiment expressed in the lines of Hudibras:

"For truth is precious and divine,
Too rich a pearl for carnal swine."

But there are others who have enjoyed our friend's kindly influence besides the American Hog and besides the privileged classes who form the constituency of the Lotos Club. As to artists, for example, there is a great mass of the American people who haven't money enough to buy pictures, haven't skill enough to paint, haven't taste enough to judge, and haven't sense enough to keep quiet. (Laughter.) This large and influential body I suppose I represent to-night. (Laughter.) I don't know whether impressionists come under the head of artists or not. In fact, it is hard to get a definition of what an impressionist is. An artist in New-Jersey combed his mustache with a lead comb and then went out to walk in the moonlight with a young lady. When they came into the bright light of the parlor her face looked like one of Whistler's etchings, and they said he was an impressionist. (Laughter.)

But never mind the definition. The nine hundred and ninety-nine artless ones out of every thousand I represent in doing honor to our accomplished friend, and we are sure to be right, "for art may err but nature cannot miss." Then, as to musicians and theatrical people, we cannot all belong to that class, but we are all going to the fair for the benefit of the Actors' Fund, and we can all be wafted into fairyland by the magic of Padcrewski, and I represent all those who know nothing technically of music or the drama but admire them nevertheless.

PECULIARITIES OF THE JOURNALIST.

And then as to journalists. I see that they come first in eligibility in the constitution of the Lotos Club. And well they may! It is not given to all of us to be journalists, but what a profession it has grown to be! When you have done something that you want to keep out of the papers, it seems as if everybody was a journalist, and your front doorstep is invaded by them. (Laughter.) When you have a little "ad" which you want to insert gratis, it seems as if there was not a journalist in the land. (Laughter.) I represent the large class who would like to be journalists. We look with awe upon that mysterious personage who, shrouded under the impenetrable protection of the imperial "we," wields a power which may well excite the envy of a Czar! Perhaps no one of the class commands more wonder than the man who gets up the Sunday edition. (Laughter.)

The journalist occupies a niche far higher than the poet. The poet would seem to achieve greatness in proportion to his incomprehensibility (laughter); the journalist in proportion to his truth and force. (Applause.) I saw a statement in a newspaper lately that Walt Whitman wrote his poems on a tablet held in his lap. "We think our subscribers should have the advantage of this statement," said the editor, "because nobody can tell by reading one of Walt Whitman's poems what it is written on." (Laughter.) The force of the editorial "we" was observable in a paragraph in a Western paper which stated that Sam Jones said: "Next to a pretty woman I like a fast horse." "We don't," commented the editor; "when we are next to a pretty woman, we like that kind of a horse that you have to build a fire under to get him off of a snail trot.'' (Laughter.)

Not to dwell on journalists in general, let me say that, speaking for the masses who are not journalists, I am proud to be able to pay tribute to the journalist who has honored himself and his profession by showing to what noble ends that profession may lead when practised by a true, scholarly and devoted man. I congratulate you, Mr. President, that the same man who began as a journalist, showed how a pure and able paper could be made to succeed, and was called to represent his country and did it to his and his country's credit, is the one whose name comes first in the list of the organizers of the Lotos Club, was for many years its president, and is to-night its welcome guest. It could be said of him during the years when he guided The Tribune, as Bulwer said of one of his characters: "He seemed an embodied journal, including the leading articles, the law reports, foreign intelligence, the court calendar, down to births, deaths and marriages." To account for his success one has only to remember that he was a plant sprung from the soil of Ohio, watered by the wisdom of Horace Greeley and ripened under the sunshine of the Lotos Club. (Applause.)

I am reminded by the name of your club of the story of Ulysses and his companions, who, after they had sojourned among the lotos-eaters and partaken of their food, forgot their native land and never wanted to go home again. I hope that now that Mr. Reid has again tasted the food of the Lotos Club, he, too, will be overcome with that happy languor and will be contented to stay among us and never leave us again. (Applause.)

Mr. Alexander was followed by General Wager Swayne. Paul Dana also spoke.

WILLIAM H. McELROY.

Then W. H. McElroy, of The Tribune staff, said:

Mr. President and Gentlemen of the Lotos Club: As a New-Yorker whose bump of local pride is well developed, I naturally hail with enthusiasm my fellow-citizen, who is your guest of honor, since he has lent distinction to the metropolis and to our commonwealth. In a public place abroad, of great dignity and responsibility, he has been demonstrating of late years what he had previously demonstrated at home, that there is no better way of getting first-class work done in a first-class manner than by inducing a newspaper man to do it. (This assertion is made in spite of having written some pieces for the newspapers myself.) (Laughter.) "No pleasure is comparable," says Lord Bacon, "with the standing upon the vantage ground of truth." (Laughter.) Were it not for this I should hardly venture in this company, which contains so many foremost representatives of the other professions, to lay stress upon the fact that the strong and brilliant diplomatic career which just now is inspiring so many eulogies is the career of one who is primarily a journalist and only incidentally a diplomatist.

It might not be in good, in truly good, taste, further to dwell upon this fascinating thought, fascinating to a newspaper man. I shall only ask you to bear in mind, if you please, not necessarily for publication, but as a guarantee of your discriminating appreciation, that the two most successful Ministers to France from the United States have both been press men, to wit, our esteemed back number Benjamin Franklin and our esteemed contemporary, Whitelaw Reid. It would not be strange in the circumstances if an impressionable young journalist, given to magnifying his profession, should be made to exclaim, with one eye on Paris and the other on the record of our late Legislature: "Let me make the newspapers of a nation and I care not who concocts its laws." Something has been said about the grand Exposition which is to be held in Chicago next year.

It makes some of us think of an interesting little incident, not wholly unconnected with your guest of honor, of the earlier Philadelphia Exposition. One morning a young fellow from one of the Territories who was doing the Art Department, halted before an imposing figure in bronze. He took a fancy to it and was anxious to know whom it represented. Accordingly he went to one of the officials, who kindly explained: "That's Rienzi, the last of the tribunes." Instead of thanking his benefactor the young fellow laughed him to scorn, saying: "No yer don't. My pop's taken The Tribune ever since she started, and I happen to know that the last of the tribunes ain't no Ry-en-zee, but a man named Whitelaw Reid." (Laughter.)

It is understood in the newspaper rows of the country—a rose by any other name, but never mind—than Mr. Reid has determined at an early day to re-enter journalism. Assuming the report to be correct, I feel warranted in affectionately assuring him in behalf of his former associates the country over, that for a young man of capacity, industry and staying power who is good at climbing, there is always room at the bottom. (Laughter.) But I must stop lest I be accused of the intention of making a speech.

Just a word or two more. No student of values has yet determined how much glory is glory enough for one man. It was the favorite boast of one of the rulers of Rome that he found the Eternal City with brick and left it marble. Mr. Reid found the American hog persona non grata to France, but when he left the animal, France was calling it mon cher ami. (Laughter.) My very last word is this: there is no verdict so significant, so conclusive as the verdict of the jury of the vicinage. As one of the jurymen from the panel in the tall tower, I trust I may remark, without being accused of disregarding the proprieties, that those who know Whitelaw Reid best value him most highly. (Applause.)

COLONEL THOMAS W. KNOX.

Mr. McElroy was followed by Colonel Thomas W. Knox, who said:

There is a mistake in calling any one to speak for the old members of the Lotos Club, and the mistake reminds me of a little story. An old toper once heard a discussion in which some one denounced a certain brand of whiskey as bad; when he heard the remark he interrupted the conversation by saying: "Excuse me, gentlemen, there is whiskey that is better than other whiskey, but there is no bad whiskey." (Laughter.) Now I would say to our most worthy president: "Excuse me, there are members of the Lotos Club that are younger than other members, but there are no old members." (Applause.)

We are all of us young, especially when we meet as we are met to-night. The guest of the evening is a young man; it is true that he has a history and a past behind him, but he has the capacity and the promise of a future that will make the past seem very insignificant. I well remember my first meeting with him. It was only a short time ago, just after the battle of Shiloh, of which he had written one of the best battle descriptions that appeared in the newspapers during the war. His ambition then was to serve "The Cincinnati Gazette" so well that it would send him to Washington as its correspondent after the war was over. He obtained his wish and went to Washington as the "Gazette's" correspondent, and from Washington he came to New-York, as we well know. History is said to repeat itself; perhaps in about ten months from now he may get back to Washington again. (Applause.)

This dinner to-night is not only a welcome home for our former president, but it is also an anniversary of which he may not be aware. Exactly twenty years ago to-day, on the 30th of April, 1872, he was put up as a candidate for membership in the Lotos Club. A little history may not be out of place by way of information to our younger members and of reminiscence to some who are not so young. In the second year of the club dissensions arose, and the dissensions resulted in a split. Every member was arrayed on one side or the other of the fight, and some were on both sides of it; we had elected a president who refused to serve, and it was impossible to choose a president from our number as it then was.

In this emergency we decided to follow the example of distracted countries on the other side of the Atlantic when they invite a foreign prince to be their king. We determined to go outside of the club and invite some gentleman who was identified with literature, art or journalism, to become one of us and immediately take office as our president. The invitation was given to Mr. Reid, and I had the honor of bearing to him the invitation on the 29th of April, 1872. He said he would consider it and give me an answer on the following day. His answer was favorable, his name was at once bulletined, he was elected to membership on the 16th of May, and he was elected president two days later, eighty-eight votes being cast and all of them in his favor. An hour after his election he was installed into office, and from that time onward there was no more disunion in the Lotos Club. (Applause.)

Before his election the disgruntled malcontents started a rival club which had a struggling existence of a few years and then became one of the clubs that had been. The effect of the formation of the rival club was to stimulate the members of the Lotos to do all in their power for its prosperity, and there can be no doubt that the stimulus of opposition was of great benefit to us.

Those of us who have been members of the club from its beginning cannot fail to regard the growth of the Lotos with a good deal of satisfaction, and a considerable share of that satisfaction belongs to our former president, whose counsels were always prudent and at the same time showed his confidence in the club's strength and ability. More than once he solved in a few minutes questions that had puzzled the directory for days and days together, and more than once in a meeting of the club he converted into the happiest of happy families what had threatened to be a very turbulent bear-garden.

There are not many now of the membership of twenty years ago, but I contend, as I did when called to my feet, that we are not to be classed as old members. We are all young and adhere to the motto of the lotos-eaters which you will find on the first page of the club manual:

"In the afternoon they came unto a land,
In which it seemed always afternoon."

FROM THOSE WHO COULD NOT COME.

Mr. Coolidge, Mr. Reid's successor at Paris, was expected to be present, but he was obliged at the last moment to decline on account of appointments elsewhere, which rendered it necessary for him to leave the city at an early hour last evening.

Many letters of regret were received, some of which are as follows:

FROM PRESIDENT HARRISON.

Executive Mansion,
Washington, April 13, 1892.

Mr. John Elderkin, New-York City.

Dear Sir: The President directs me to acknowledge the receipt of your letter of the 12th, inviting him on behalf of the Lotos Club, to attend a dinner to be given in honor of the Hon. Whitelaw Reid on the evening of Saturday, April 30. He has already promised, if possible, to visit New-York for the occasion of the cornerstone laying of the Grant monument on the 27th, and does not feel that he could leave again so soon as the 30th. Please accept his sincere thanks for your friendly remembrance. Very truly yours,

O. L. PRUDEN, Assistant Secretary.

THE FRENCH MINISTER.

Legation de France aux Etats-Unis.
Washington. 14 Avril, 1892.

Monsieur: Je m'impresse de vous exprimer tout le regret que j'éprouve de ne pouvoir accepter la gracieuse invitation que vous avez en l'obligance de m'envoyer pour le 30 Avril. J'ai pris pour cette date des engagements qui me mettent dans l'impossibilité de me rendre a New-York. J'ai deja du d'ailleurs, decliner une autre invitation qui m'avait ete adre se pour le meme date. Agreez, je vous prie, avec tous mes remerciments pour votre aimable pensee, l'assurance de ma consideration le plus distinguee. PATENOTRE.

(Translation.)

Monsieur: I desire to express to you my regret at being unable to accept the gracious invitation which you have been so kind as to send me for the 30th of April. I have made engagements for this date which render it impossible for me to be in New-York. I have already declined another invitation which was given me for the same date. Accept, I beg you, with my thanks for your kind thought, the assurance of my most distinguished consideration. PATENOTRE.

GEORGE WILLIAM CURTIS.

West New-Brighton, Staten Island, N. Y.,
April 21, 1892.

My Dear Sir: An engagement in Baltimore for the evening of the 30th of April makes it impossible for me to accept the friendly invitation of the Lotos Club to join in its welcome to Mr. Reid on that evening. But no single voice will be missed in the general acclaim. Few American Ministers abroad have been received on their return with so general and hearty a congratulation, and it is due not only to the ability and success with which he has conducted important international negotiations, but to the American spirit in which he has represented America. Mr. Jefferson said that every American foreign Minister ought to be recalled at least after seven years of service, lest he should become too Europeanized. But if Mr. Reid tarried seventy years in the world that Jefferson thought so fascinating, we should not have feared for him such a fate nor have doubted that wherever he might go America would go with him. Yours very truly,

GEORGE WILLIAM CURTIS.

EDMUND C. STEDMAN.

New-York, 137 West Seventy-eighth-st.,
April 22, 1892.

Mr. John Elderkin, Secretary of the Lotos.

Dear Mr. Elderkin: After accepting with alacrity the Lotos invitation to the dinner in honor of Mr. Reid, I am sincerely grieved to write that it suddenly becomes out of my power to be with you at a festival so sure to be memorable. I shall be absent from the country at the date named, but certainly should put off my departure if it were possible. I should wish, indeed, to lift my voice with you all on the 30th—when all will be Jacobites for once, no longer singing "Here's a health to them that's awa' " and "He's been lang o' coming !" but "Carle, now the king's come :" and

"Sir Charlie he has come,
We'll h e a jub'lee year,"

—over and beyond the admiration which I share with you for the official success of your ex-president, whether as your chief or as the country's legate. I enter very deeply into the spirit which will set the note for your dinner-talk—the note of personal affection. For it was my good fortune to become somewhat intimate with Mr. Reid in the morning of his promise and aspirations. He honored me with his friendship thirty years ago, and at an age when one shows exactly what he is and what he is likely to be. From that time to this I have been indebted to him for loyal counsel and comradeship; and having watched the stages of his career, there is one matter of which I am well qualified to speak:

Mr. Reid has been called "lucky." Well, I think he is so. The Romans demanded that a commander should be "brave, skilful, fortunate," putting the chief attribute last, for the sake of emphasis. But what I wish to say is that Mr. Reid has ably and manfully earned, from the outset, every leaf of his laurels, every jewel in his wreath, by the most resolute and able work—the kind of work which, when superadded to notable endowments, inspired by sincere convictions, and maintained by a will-power amounting to genius, is irresistible.

Without character, conviction, patriotism, self-discipline, a true Americanism, no American—not even an editor possessed of his inborn literary style—could have the unbroken success which has come to Mr. Reid; none without a genuine loyalty to friends, and an unaffected love for letters and art and the Arcadians who pursue them, could so have endeared himself to those of us who seek the peaceful bays while he guides the war-galleys upon the rolling seas. And as for will-power!—whatever he still desires, that shall he have. We hear that his party has greater honors in store for him. If he really wishes to accept these, the party is shrewd enough to tender them. For Mr. Reid's way is that of General Crawford, who, as Wellington said when a commissary complained that the General had threatened to hang him if such a thing were not done. "undoubtedly would carry out his threat, for I have never known him to break his word !" Faithfully yours,

EDMUND C. STEDMAN.

Others who wrote were Colonel John Hay, Cornelius N. Bliss, Charles A. Dana, Horace White, Joseph H. Choate, Isaac H. Bromley, Daniel Dougherty, Frederic R. Coudert, the Rev. Dr. Henry Van Dyke and Seth Low,

THE NEW-ENGLAND DINNER.

IN NEW-YORK DECEMBER 22, 1891.

ADDRESSES BY J. PIERREPONT MORGAN, THE
REV. JOSEPH H. TWITCHELL, THE REV. DR.
HUNTINGTON, ISAAC H. BROMLEY,
CHAUNCEY M. DEPEW, GENERAL
PORTER AND CONGRESS-
MAN DALZELL.

At the New-England Dinner the attendance was
very large, 450 covers being laid at Sherry's. It
was not until 10 o'clock that the president, J.
Pierrepont Morgan, succeeded in opening the way
for the speeches of the evening, which were intensely enjoyed by the large assemblage.

When the coffee was served Mr. Morgan arose
and, calling the assemblage to order, said:

Members of the New-England Society: Again I
welcome you to our annual banquet. During the
year which has just passed, prosperity has reigned
within our borders. The treasurer reports funds in
his hands amounting to close upon $90,000.

The regular annuities to widows and children of
deceased members applying therefor have been paid
and your Charity Committee, by wise discretion, have
expended the money placed at their disposal, amounting to about $2,500, in relieving the necessities of
New-Englanders who have been found suffering and
in distress. Twenty-six of our members have been
removed by death (eleven less than last year),
and it speaks well for the character and virtu-
ous lives of the members of this society when I say
that with scarcely an exception those who have passed
away had lived for more than three score years and
ten, and have left behind them a record worthy of
their origin and of the community in which they lived.

During the year seventy-five new members have
been elected, and the total number upon our rolls at
the present time is 1,530. (Applause.)

Having thus made to you every official report I will
not longer detain you and we will proceed to the
regular toasts of the evening. I will call upon the
Rev. Joseph H. Twichell, of New-Haven, Conn., to
respond to the toast, "Forefathers' Day."

MR. TWICHELL SPEAKS.

Mr. Morgan then introduced the Rev. Mr.
Twichell, who said:

Mr. President and Gentlemen of the New-England
Society: The posture of my mind the last fortnight
relative to the duty of the present hour—which, indeed,
I was proud to be assigned to, as I ought to have been,
but which has been a black care to me ever since I
undertook it—has a not inapt illustration in the case of
the old New-England parson, who when asked why he
was going to do a certain thing that had been laid
upon him, yet the thought of which affected him with
extreme timidity, answered: "I wouldn't if I didn't
suppose it had been foreordained from all eternity—
and I'm a good mind not to as it is." (Laughter.)
However, I have the undisguised good will of my audience to begin with, and that's half the battle. The
forefathers, in whose honor we meet, were men of
good will, profoundly so: but they were, in their day,
more afraid of showing it, in some forms, than their
descendants happily are.

The first time I ever stood in the pulpit to preach
was in the meeting-house of the ancient Connecticut
town where I was brought up. That was a great day
for our folks and all my old neighbors, you may de-

pend. After benediction, when I passed out into the
vestibule, I was the recipient there of many congratu-
latory expressions. Among my friends in the crowd
was an aged deacon, a man in whom survived, to a
rather remarkable degree, the original New-England
Puritan type, who had known me from the cradle and
to whom the elevation I had reached was as gratifying
as it could possibly be to anybody. But when he saw
the smile of favor focussed on me there, and me, I
dare say, appearing to bask somewhat in it, the dear
old man took alarm. He was apprehensive of the
consequences to that youngster. And so, taking me
by the hand and wrestling down his natural feelings—
he was ready to cry for joy—he said: "Well, Joseph,
I hope you'll live to preach a great deal better than
that!" (Laughter.) It was an exceedingly appropriate remark, and a very tender one if you were at
the bottom of it.

That severe, undemonstrative New-England habit,
that emotional reserve and self-suppression, though it
lingers here and there, has mostly passed away and is
not to be regretted. As much as could be has been
made of it to our forefathers' discredit as has been
made of everything capable of being construed un-
favorably to them. They to whom to what they call
the cant of the Puritan is an offence themselves have
established and practise a distinct anti-Puritan cant
with which we are all familiar. The very people
who find it abhorrent and intolerable that they were
such censors of the private life of their contemporaries, do not scruple to bring to bear on their private
life a search-light that leaves no accessible nook of it
unexplored, and regarding any unpretty trait espied by
that unspearing inquest, the rule of judgment persistently employed—as one is obliged to perceive—tends
to be: No explanation wanted or admitted but the
worst. (Applause).

Accordingly, the infestive deportment characteristic
of the New-England colonist has been extensively in-
terpreted as the indisputable index of his sour and
morose spirit begotten of his religion. I often wonder
that in computing the cause of his rigorous manners
so inadequate account is wont to be made of his
situation, as in a principal and long-continuing aspect substantially military; which it was. The truth
is, his physiognomy was primarily the soldier stamp
on him.

HIS STRUGGLE FOR EXISTENCE.

If you had been at Gettysburg on the morning of
July 2, 1863, as I was, and had perused the
countenance of the First and Eleventh Corps exhausted
and bleeding with the previous day's losing battle,
and the countenance of the Second, Third and Twelfth
Corps getting into position to meet the next onset
which everybody knew was immediately impending,
you would have said that it was a sombre community—
that Army of the Potomac—with a good deal of grim-
ness in the face of it; with a notable lack of the play-
ful element; and no fiddling or other fine arts to
speak of.

As sure as you live, gentlemen, that is no unfair
representation of how it was with the founders of the
New-England commonwealths in their planting period.
The Puritan of the seventeenth century lived,
moved and had his being on the field of an undecided
struggle for existence—the New-England Puritan most
emphatically so. He was under arms in body much
of the time; in mind all the time. Nothing can be
truer than to say that. And yet people everlast-
ingly pick and poke at him for being stern-featured
and deficient in the softer graces of life.

It was his beauty that he was so, for it grew out of
and was befitting his circumstances. And I, for one,
love to see that austere demeanor so far as it is yet
hereditary on the old soil, and some of it is left—thinking of the origin. It is the signature of a fighting far-
more than of an ascetic ancestry—memorial of a new
Pass of Thermopylae held by the latest race of Spartans
on the shores of a new world. (Applause.)

It may be doubted if ever in the history of mankind was displayed a quality of public courage, of
pure indomitable pluck, surpassing that of the New-

England plantations in their infant day. No condition of its extremest proof was lacking. While the Bay Co ny, for example, was in the pinch of its first wrestle with nature for a living, much as ever able to furnish its table with a piece of bread, with the hunger-wolf never far away from the door; and behind that wolf the Narragansett and the Pequot at what moment to burst into savagery none could tell—in the season when mere existence was the purchase of physical toil, universal and intense, and of watching night and day, there came from the old country, from the high places of authority, the peremptory mandate: Send us back that charter! Under that clause of it granting you the rule of your own affairs, you are claiming more than was intended or can be allowed. Send it back! And what was the answer? Mind, there were less than 5,000 souls of them, all told; less than 1,000 grown men. On the one hand the power of England; on the other that scrap of a new-born State; sore-pressed with difficulties already.

What was the answer? Why, they got out some old cannon they had and mounted them, and moulded a stock of bullets, and distributed powder, and took of every male citizen above the age of sixteen an oath of allegiance to Massachusetts—and then set their teeth and waited to see what would happen. And that was their answer. It meant distinctly—Our charter, which we had of the king's majesty (and therefore came we hither), is our lawful possession, fair title to the territory we occupy and the rights we here exercise. And whoever wants it has got to come and take it. Surrender it we never will! (Applause.)

THEIR GRIT AND GALLANTRY.

Nor was that the only time. Again and again during the colony's initial stage, when it was exceeding little of stature and had enough to do to keep the breath of life in it, that demand was renewed with rising anger and with menaces; yet never could those Puritans of the Bay be scared into making a solitary move of any kind toward compliance with it. David with his sling daring Goliath in armor is an insufficient figure of that nerve, that transcendent grit, that superb gallantry. Where will you look for its parallel? I certainly do not know. (Applause.)

They used to tell during the war of a colonel who was ordered to assault a position which his regiment, when they had advanced far enough to get a good look at it, saw to be so impossible that they fell back and became immovable. Whereupon (so the story ran) the colonel, who took the same sense of the situation that his command did, yet must do his duty, called out in an ostensibly pleading and fervid voice: "Oh, don't give it up so! Forward again! Forward! Charge! Great heavens, men, do you want to live forever?" (Laughter.)

How those first New-England Puritans we are speaking of were to come off from their defiance of the crown alive could scarcely be conjectured. The only ally they had was distance. The thing they ventured on was the chance that the Royal Government, which had troubles nearer home, would have its hands too full to execute its orders 3,000 miles away across the sea by force. But they accepted all hazards whatso ever of refusing always to obey those orders. They held on to their charter like grim death, and they kept it in their time. More than once or twice it seemed as good as gone; but delay helped them; turns of events helped them; God's providence delivered them, they thought: anyhow they kept it; that intrepid handful against immensurable odds, mainly because in lay not in the power of mortal man to intimidate them. And I contend that, all things considered, no more splendid exhibition of the essential stuff of manhood stands on human record. They were no hot-heads. All that while, rash as they appeared, their pulse was calm. The justifying reasons of their course were ever plain before their eyes. They were of the kind of men who understood their objects.

The representative of an English newspaper, sent some time since to Ireland to move about and learn by personal observation the real political mind of the people there, reported on his return that he had been everywhere and talked with all sorts, and that as nearly as he could make out, the attitude of the Irish might be stated about this: "They don't know what they want—and they are bound to have it." (Laughter.)

But those unbending Forefathers well knew what

they wanted that charter for. It was their legal guarantee of the privilege of a spacious freedom, civil and religious, and all that they did and risked for its sake is witness of the price at which they held that privilege. It was not that they had any special objection to the interference in the province of their domestic administration of the king as a king: for you find them presently crying "Hands Off!" to the Puritan Parliament as strenuously as ever they said' it to the agents of Charles I. It was simply and positively the value they set on the self-governing independence that had been pledged them at the be ginning of the enterprise.

And who that has a man's heart in him but must own that their inspiration to such a degree, with such an idea and sentiment in the time, place and circumstances in which they stood, was magnificent? Was the inexorable unrelaxing determination with which they, being so few and so poor, maintained their point somewhat wrought into their faces? Very probably. Strange if it had not been. Of course it was. But if they were stern-visaged in their day, it was that we in our day, which in vision they foresaw, might of all communities beneath the sun have reason for a cheerful countenance. (Applause.)

THE RESULTS OF THOSE HEROIC YEARS.

They achieved immense great things for us, those Puritan men who were not smiling enough to suit the critics. The real foundation on which the structure of American national liberty subsequently rose was laid by them in those first heroic years.

And what a marvel it was, when you stop to think, that in conditions so hard, so utterly prosaic, calculated to clip the wings of generous thought, they maintained themselves in that elevation of sentiment, that supreme estimate of the unmaterial, the ideal factors of life that distinguished them—in such largeness of mind and of spirit altogether. While confronting at deadly close quarters their own necessities and perils, their sympathies were wide as the world. To their brethren in old England, contending with tyranny, every ship that crossed the Atlantic carried their benediction. Look at the days of thanksgiving and of fast with which they followed the shifting fortunes of the wars of Protestantism—which were wars for humanity—on the continent! Look at the vital consequence they attached to the interest of education; at the taxes that in their penury, and while for the most part they still lived in huts, they imposed on themselves to found and to sustain the institution of the school! (Applause.)

"Child," said a matron of primitive New-England to her young son, "if God make thee a good Christian and a good scholar, thou hast all that ever thy mother asked for thee." And so saying she spoke like a true daughter of the Puritans.

They were poets—hose brave, stanch, aspiring sons, whose will was adamant and who feared none but God. Only, as Charles Kingsley has said, they did not sing their poetry like birds, but acted it like men. (Applause.)

It was their high calling to stand by the divine cause of human progress at a momentous crisis of its evolution, and they were more worthy to be put on duty at that post. Evolution! I hardly dare speak the word, knowing so little about the thing. It represents a very great matter, which I am humbly conscious of being about as far from surrounding as was a simple-minded Irish priest I have been .old of, who, having heard that we were descended from monkeys, yet not quite grasping the chronology of the business, the next time he visited a menagerie, gave particular and patient attention to a large cage of our alleged poor relations on exhibition there. He stood for a long time intently scrutinizing their human-like motions, gestures and expressions. By and by he fancied that the largest of them, an individual of a singularly grave demeanor, seated a. the front of the cage, gave him a glance of intelligence. The glance was returned. A pa'pable-wink foll'wed, which also was returned, as were other like signals; and so it went on until his reverence, having cast an eye around to see that nobody was observing him, leaned forward and said in a low, confidential tone: "Av ye'll spake one w-u-r-d, I'll baptize yo, begorra!" (Laughter.)

But, deficient as one's knowledge of evolution, scientifically and in detail, may be, he may have attained to a not unintelligent perception of the all-embracing creative process called by that name as that in which, in the whole range of the advancing universal movement of life, what is ascends from what was, and fulfils it.

And what I wish to say for my last word is that, whoever of us in tracing back along the line of its potent and fruitful resources that which is his noblest heritage as an American and a member of the English race leaves out that hard-featured forefather of ours on the shore of Massachusetts Bay in the seventeenth century, and makes not large account of the tremendous fight he fought which was reflected in the face he wore, misses a chief explanation of the fortune to which we and our children are born. (Loud applause.)

DR. HUNTINGTON S WORDS

At the close of Mr. Twichell's address, Mr. Morgan introduced as the next toast "Unrealized Yankee Notions," and the Rev. Dr. W. R. Huntington responded as follows:

When, some weeks ago, a personal friend and valued parishioner called at my house to invite me to be present here to-night and to speak, I said to him, "My dear sir, I will do anything to oblige you. You have but to command me, as you know, and if you say 'accept,' accept I will. But, to tell the honest truth, of all the various kinds of public speaking, the one kind I especially loath and detest is after-dinner speaking; and the reason is, I never have caught the knack of it. I don't know how to do it."

"Yes, yes," said my friend, the representative of this society, "we know that, we know that; but then you needn't say much. Make it short." (Laughter.) Said I, "I will." I am of the opinion that my parishioner had the best of me. It is wholesome discipline, now and then, for a man to be taken at his own estimation.

By ano.her consideration I am admonished to be brief. There is a tradition, and some of you gentlemen are old enough to authenticate it, that at a New-England Society dinner, fifty years ago or thereabouts, a predecessor of mine in the rectorship of Grace Church —I don't mean Bishop Potter, but Bishop Potter's predecessor's predecessor—got himself into very hot water indeed by making a spirited reply to a previous speaker who had antagonized one of his ecclesiastical beliefs. The matter was taken up outside, and there followed a controversial war in the public print the like of which had scarcely been heard of since Cotton Mather's day. Now, how do I know that if I were to go on at any length I might not, by pure accident, and without in the least intending it, say something clever and draw upon myself speedy retribu'ion at the hands of the journalists to-morrow? (Laughter.) But, however it might have been in 1844, the ministers of churches below Fourteenth-st. have nowadays no leisure for theological contention. Their whole energy has to be devoted to shepherding their flocks for fear the sheep may run away to green pastures further up the island. (Laughter.) Nevertheless, finding myself here and on my feet, I should like, notwithstanding the thinness of the ice, to say a few things that appear to me not wholly irrelevant to the occasion.

NEW-ENGLANDERS STILL NEW.

I have had a feeling for some years past that we New-Englanders were acquiescing quite too readily in the conclusion that our last work was drawing to a close; tha. as a distinctive race, a peculiar people, if you please, we were about ready to be mustered out of service. What with the Boston elections and the dismal letters to "The Evening Post" from the hill towns of Massachuse.ts, offering us abandoned farms for a song, some of us had become prematurely and, as I think, needlessly possessed of a fear that the Yankee might be going the way of the mastodon and the dodo. (Laughter.) But it is a great mistake for any man or any family of men to settle down to the conclusion that there is nothing left in life to be accomplished, to

"rust unburnished," as Ulysses puts it, so long as it is possible to "shine in use." No, nothing will persuade me that the Yankee is functus officio quite yet. It may become necessary for him to change h's habitat, he may be driven out of New-England, but in that event he will make a newer England somewhere else. In fact, that is just what he has been doing for the last 100 years, making newer Englands all over the Northwest. (Applause.)

Not long ago I was visited by one of the great army of interviewers, with the request that I would furnish him with material for half a column. "But what is it to be all about?" I natura.ly asked. "Well," said he with an air of embarrassment such as I have seldom observed on the part of the representatives of the press, "Well, I am asking various men in official positions here in the city to write out their views of the way in which they would like to pass the evening of their days." This seemed to me a little hard upon a man of my years, so I replied: "Certainly you shall have my views, but I am afraid that they will scarcely fill out your half-column, for I can express them in three words —'in the harness.'" (Applause.)

I am bold to think, Mr. President, that in so declaring myself I spoke for my kind, spoke as the gene.ic Yankee. The thought is not to be entertai.ed that a race which has been as active as ours has been in the past should be induced, either by fatigue or by the reactionary influence of a too-great prosperity, to fold its hands and sit idle for the rest of the world's lifetime. Why, sir, the very significance of our name forbids. Do you happen, I wonder, to have heard of the latest and most approved derivation of the word "Yankee"? You remember that in old times the dictiona.y makers had a theory that "Yankee" was the Indian corruption of the French name for the English. The explanation was that the word had come down from Canada by the way of Lake Champlain, undergoing transformation at the hands of fur-traders and scouts in the passage. But the learned Dr. Skeats, of the University of Cambridge, nas changed all that, for he assures us in the supplement to his "Etymological Dictionary of the English Language" that "Yankee" comes from a Norwegian word which means quick-moving, active, spry; and then Dr. Skeats adds with a generous recognition of what has happened in recent nautical history, which in a' Englishman is worthy of all praise, "This goes to show a Yankee is much the same as yacht." (Laughter.) Now, sir, do you imagine that this "Yankee," this quick-moving, this active, this spry personage of the past, intends to be or will consent to be the great do-nothing of the future? I will not, for ' cannot believe it.

THE YANKEE IDEALIST

The truth is that the typical Yankee is, always has been and always will be an idealist. It is in his blood. Arthur Hugh Clough, the Oxford scholar-poet, who made his home for a while under the walls of Harvard a generation back, writing to his English friends his impression of Massachusetts, said: "There is something in this climate that breeds mysticism." But Clough was wrong; the mysticism, by which he meant what I just called idealism, was not in the air, as he imagined; it was in the blood. The men whom he denominated mystics because of their power of discerning things invisible, had brought their mysticism with them across the sea from the same land whence Clough himself had come. It was an affair of the heart, not of the lungs. Yes, in spite of the prevailing popular opinion to the contrary, in spite of the widespread belief that practicality is the distinguishing note of the New-Englander, I make bold to say again that the truly representative Yankee is first, last and always an idealist. The Yankee notions which best deserve the name are not those which strew the counters of the mercantile world "from China to Peru," not mousetraps, axeheads, clawhammers, Waltham watches and Waterbury clocks, but rather those notions of the mind which in the phrase of present-day philosophy we call ideas. (Applause.)

The forefathers whose day we are keeping came over here with their heads chock full of dreams; but it was a kind of dreaming that meant business. (Applause.) There was that hungry look in their eyes, which in old times gave men the name of seers. But though they saw visions, they were not visionaries. They were men of the sword and of the book, as our statutes and our pictures rightly represent them. The Bible was their dream book, the sword their implement for hewing in pieces whatever might stand in the way of their dreams coming true. (Applause.) I know that it has become the fashion of late years to poke fun at the Puritans, but I confess that although myself one of those very malignants whom they would have been glad to exterminate with that sword of theirs, I cannot make up my mouth to speak lightly of them. The profoundest view of the history of the United States is that which sees in it a continuation of the history of England. It is more, but it is that. How pathetic, when we stop to think of it, that name " New-England." They left the old England because they thought—mistakenly, as it has turned out, but they honestly thought she was past saving—they left the old England and they came to this untenanted coast that they might build an England new. They had set their hearts on solving the problem of the perfect commonwealth. In the algebra by which they tried to work it out the two known quantities from which they started were righteousness and intelligence. These were the A and B of all their calculations. But it must in honesty be confessed that in spite of their best efforts and our best efforts the X and Y of the problem have never yet been ciphered out. They are unknown quantities still.

MAKING GREAT PROGRESS.

Not that we have made no progress toward the coveted solution; we have made great progress. Witness that best of all flattery, which at this very moment the old England is paying to the new, the flattery of imitation. I would give a pine-tree shilling to witness an interview between Governor Winthrop and Lord Salisbury. How amazed the Puritan would be to learn of the concessions made by Lords and Commons, within a single generation, to the principles of Massachusetts Bay. (Applause.)

And yet the best of Yankee notions remain still unrealized both in Church and State. For how can we so much as approximate to that perfect commonwealth after which those forefathers of ours aspired, so long as our great cities are given over to misrule and our Christianity is chiefly militant against itself? We have become a Nation of great cities; therefore our municipal failure is our political failure. We have had our eyes opened to the fact that our religion is nothing unless it can show itself a social force; therefore our ecclesiastical failure is our spiritual failure.

Ah, Mr. President, let us never " go back on" the idealism which is our birthright, never pause or falter until in the State we shall have enthroned righteousness, and in the Church shall have established peace. When these things come to pass, when we have thrown to the moles and to the bats our " rings," " bosses" and " machines," and when we have brought together beneath one roof the descendants of the men whose watchwords under Charles were loyalty and reverence, and the descendants of the men whose watchwords under Oliver were righteousness and truth, then, all his best notions realized, our happy Yankee may sing his nunc dimittis—then, but not till then. (Prolonged and loud applause.)

ISAAC H. BROMLEY.

The next toast announced by the president was " Connecticut's Part in the Business," and Isaac H. Bromley responded as follows:

Notwithstanding all that has been said at this table for the last eighty-six years by persons who pay $50 to begin with and $10 annually thereafter for the privilege of treating the transaction with levity, I cling with childlike faith to the belief that there actually were Pilgrim Fathers, and that they did land. (Laughter.) I believe they were serious persons—no one can doubt it who has seen pictures of them in public places—and I hope you will agree with me when I say that the time has manifestly now arrived—Massachusetts having elected a Democratic Governor two years in succession—when we should begin to treat them seriously and inquire what on the whole they were driving at. (Laughter.) Let us consider them for a moment as historic personages; real folks with mud on their boots and a look of earnest waiting for the dinner horn; instead of painted persons on a canvas, or brass heroes on a horse block who never did a square day's work in their lives, but put in their time leaning on a gun while the women folks did the chores. (Laughter.)

The Pilgrims were just ordinary common folks; for the most part, lean, lank, hatchet-faced and slab-sided; and 270 years ago they were not cheerful persons to live with. No more are some of their descendants now. But they meant business from the word go; from the Plymouth Rock pullet to the Plymouth Rock pants. (Laughter.)

It has been remarked of them on one or two occasions that they builded better than they knew; reference being had to the fact that whereas they came over here for the purpose of establishing one religion, there are now within five miles of Boston something like 500, not including recent cleavages and new inventions. Taking a broader and more elevated view, we may safely say that they builded differently from what they knew. It is not likely that they foresaw in their wildest dreams the filling in of the Back Bay. Had they projected in their imaginations that large body of made land held down in many places by bronze specimens of mediaeval and wholly evil art (great laughter), it is doubtful if they would have come ashore; in which case one cannot help inquiring what would have become of the secretary of this society. (Applause.) Nor could they have conceived of the enormous improvement there would be in the breeding and culture of the domestic dog. In 1620 in the neighborhood of Plymouth and around Massachusetts Bay there was but one variety of dog, and that one of so furtive and elusive a character that the artist who photographed the scene of the landing, as shown on the certificates of membership of this society, was unable to secure anything but his bark; which was on the sea, and is represented at anchor in the engraving about a sixteenth of an inch from Plymouth Rock. (Laughter.) To-day more than a hundred varieties of dogs of the most useful and ornamental character may be seen on Commonwealth-ave. in Boston, attending to their several pursuits under the superintendence of ladies of the highest culture wearing spectacles. (Laughter.)

ANOTHER SURPRISE FOR THEM.

Nor could the Pilgrims have ever dreamed that 270 years from the day of their landing the members of the different trades and professions in Boston from retail junk dealers up would d'ne together every Saturday and make speeches to and about each other of the most lofty and ennobling character.

Nor that the thirst for precise and accurate information concerning the entire universe would be so absorbing as to fill Tremont Temple during the Joseph Cook season with entranced audiences, yearning in desire to follow Joseph Cook like a sinking star beyond the utmost bounds of human though.

It is not likely that they would have banished Ann Hutchinson so abruptly if they could have foreseen the organization in less than 300 years of a Question Club which can ask more questions at one session concerning the operation of the tariff than any candidate for office can answer in the two months before election. For poor old Annie's chief trouble was an inquiring mind.

They builded, indeed, more than they knew and differently from what they supposed. William Brewster was a man of stubborn will; had he been permitted to look with prophetic vision down the ages, to see in his mind's eye the vast accumulation of conflicting religions, the numberless varieties of the domestic dog, the irregular eruptions of Back Bay art, the Saturday dinners, the Cook lectures and the Question Club of to-day, he might not have wished himself back in Scrooby, but he certainly would have stood on his head in the Mayflower's cabin upset by the prospect and torn with conflicting emotions. (Laughter).

In the plaintive warble with which Dr. Chauncey Depew broke his long silence on the occasion of the dinner of the St. Nicholas Society at the opening of

the present season (great laughter), he is reported to
have expressed his regret that his ancestors who
settled on this island had no historian, except Washington Irving, who had not treated the early Dutch
with the seriousness they deserved. In this respect
he thought they were at a disadvantage as compared
with other colonists, whose stories had been told by
sober-minded writers in a stately and dignified style.
We can well understand how the accuracy of Cotton
Mather and the veracity of Samuel Peters would have
better suited the Doctor's austere taste than the jocu-
larity of Irving. (Laughter.) But Dr. Depew, who
was not without early educational advantages, must
know that it was by their own fault that the early
Dutch, instead of marching with stately tread across
the historic page, go limping over it with a wooden
leg. For it is well authenticated that the Brewsters
and Bradfords and the rest intended to settle here at
some point near the Hudson River, but the early
Dutch who were here before them bribed the pilot of
the Mayflower to tingle them up between Cape Cod
and a stern and rockbound coast. That is the way
the early Dutch lost all the good historians. (Laughter.)

SEEKING FOR PLYMOUTH ROCK.

Had not the early Dutch bribed the pilot of the Mayflower the Pilgrim Fathers would have landed on Pot
Rock instead of Plymouth Rock, and Bradford or
Winslow, or Winthrop or Cotton Mather would have
written Knickerbocker's History of New-York, but
the Dutch would not have cut so much of a figure in
it. The "stern and rockbound coast" of Mrs. Hemans
would have been different, and the inestimable being
shortly afterward conferred upon earth's stricken ones
would have been known as Hellgate Elixir instead of
New-England Rum. (Great laughter.)

The Pilgrim Fathers never lacked for historians.
They were not the Fletcher of Saltoun sort of men,
who if they could but make the ballads of a nation
cared not who made the laws; they were rather of
the type of the modern newspaper man who cares not
who throws the bomb if he only gets the "scoop."
(Laughter.) They kept diaries, and when they said
anything definite about the designs of Providence—
which they were always doing—somebody made a
memorandum of it; partly for the benefit of the
historian, but chiefly for the guidance of Providence.
(Much laughter.) It was also the habit of the Pilgrim
Father when he had said anything final and conclusive about election, predestination, foreordination or
whispering in meeting, to go immediately and sit for
his picture before he lost the expression. The result was that the historians—and the woods round
Massachusetts Bay have always been full of them—
not only had down fine what the Pilgrim Father said,
but a picture of him while he was saying it. That is
the reason why the histories of New-England are so
full; also why they are chiefly confined to what happened around Massachusetts Bay. There were other
localities in New-England, to be sure, places where
persons who had migrated from round the Bay were
saying and doing things which turned out to be worth
while; but they had no shorthand writers or portrait-
painters and kept but few diaries, so the materials for
their story are more scanty and they have not figured
so largely in spoken speeches or printed books.

Perhaps another reason why the attention of the
world has been so focussed upon Massachusetts is that
its vowel sounds lend themselves so readily to the uses
of the orator and rhetorician. There's such a long and
impressive roll to the words "The Commonwealth of
Massachusetts" that the citizen when he hears it at the
end of a Thanksgiving proclamation stretches out at
least two inches longer in his pew, and thanks God
for having been born there instead of in Connecticut
or Rhode Island. Since Mr. Webster, in a burst of
admiration for the State which he adorned by his genius
and enriched by his promissory notes (much laughter),
said, "There she stands! Look at her!" mankind has
been engaged in the contemplation of that tableau as
representing all there was of New-England. Only once
in awhile a modest voice has spoken from the sisterhood
of New-England States, saying, "We, too, are here."
(Laughter and applause.)

ABSOLUTE SUCCESS ACHIEVED.

The Plymouth and Massachusetts people started in,
as we all know, to establish religious freedom. Between
1620 and 1632 they had so far succeeded that nobody
had any voice in the direction of civil affairs except
church members, and among these, religious freedom had
found so firm a footing that any person who believed as

they did was at perfect liberty to say so. (Great laughter.) In 1632 there was an influx of new colonists
under the lead of Thomas Hooker and Samuel Stone
who settled in Dorchester, Watertown and Newtown.
These people had views of their own on several questions, and especially upon that rather important one of
the separation of Church from State, which afterward
exercised so potent an influence in the organization of
civil government in America. They were not dispu-
tatious nor quarrelsome—Cotton Mather called them
"the judicious Christians"—but they soon saw that the
differences upon this very vital and fundamental question would be fatal to the peace of the community; so
in 1634 they applied to the General Court for "liberty
to remove." It took the General Court a year to bring
itself to grant the request, so strong was the desire of
that body to strengthen and enforce upon the minds of
the new colonists the principle of religious freedom.

In the spring of 1636 the movement of "judicious
Christians" from the Bay country began, which has
been in progress in varying volume ever since, the last
authenticated case having occurred in October of the
present year. The Newtown people, to the number of
a hundred, under the lead of Hooker and Stone, were
the pioneers. They settled at Windsor, on the banks of
the Connecticut, whither they were soon followed by
the colonists of Dorchester and Watertown, so that the
original population of the three Bay towns was practically transferred to Windsor, Hartford and Wethers-
field by the spring of 1637. They found some very
early Dutch at Hartford, but, the hint being conveyed
to them that they were a trifle too early, they retired
in good order, leaving only an odor of profanity and a
name for "Dutch Point." (Laughter.)

It was the "judicious Christians" of these three
towns who erected the model of a pure Democracy,
then unknown, upon which the American Republic
was built. Not in the cabin of the Mayflower, where
the "subjects of our dread sovereign Lord, King
James," made their famous covenant and compact; not
in the Massachusetts Bay Colony, whose head and chief
had said he did not conceive that God had ever ordained
democracy as a fit government either for Church or
Commonwealth, but in Pastor Hooker's study, in 1638,
in the sermon preached to the General Court, upon the
lines of which the Connecticut Constitution of January,
1639, was formed—was government of the people, for
the people and by the people born on this continent.
(Great applause.)

Here was the beginning of the first democratic
commonwealth, the first formulated assertion of the
people's right to rule, the first effective blow at
class privilege. Here was the disseverance of Church
and State, here the establishment of town government,
the beginning of a federated system, the inauguration
of the plan and model upon which the constitutions
of all succeeding commonwealths and of the United
States, were formed. (Applause.)

ONE PHASE OF HISTORY.

The first proceeding of the General Court organized
by these "judicious Christians" was to take decisive
action in the matter of the Indian disturbances, which
the parent colony had been "puttering with" and only
aggravating, for a year or two previous. The Connecticut General Court formally declared war against
the Pequots on May 1; on May 10, Captain John Mason
was on the march with his small force, and in three
weeks' time he had settled the whole business, made
an end of the Pequot tribe and given to New-England
forty years of peace. This would seem to be an important transaction. But, except as John Mason told
the story himself, in a modest and unheroic way, some
years afterward, it is almost unrecorded. The history
of that period deals chiefly with the hero who shoved
Thomas Morton out of the country for disturbing the
Puritan peace, and killed two or three bad Indians in
a personal encounter. Miles Standish lived among
people who wrote history; John Mason among those
who made it. (Applause.)

From that time the little State organized by the
"judicious Christians" has gone on doing solid, useful
work in the world. Steadfast without bigotry, brave
without boasting, earnest without fanaticism, positive
without dogmatism, her well-descended sons trace back
their lineage with pride to the "judicious Christians"
who came out with Hooker and Stone from the three
Bay towns in 1636. The word which Napoleon could
not do without, but which Wellington never needed,
does not bedizen the fair pages on which the story of
Connecticut is told. No glories flaunt themselves along
that simple record of the natural and orderly growth
and progress of a commonwealth of common men. The

ier migration. when in obedience
.t thee out of thy country and
i from thy father's house unto a
thee," the Father of the Faithful
ie Chaldees, is not more simply
f the journey of Hooker and his
: wilderness to the river. They
.t treading any shining path, but
ashion to day's works in the
n Mason to the Pequot War; so
n to Bunker Hill; so that wise,
merchant, Jonathan Trumbull, by
n and tireless activity gathered
.news of war when the struggle
.n every crisis and at every high
ore than 250 years the steady-go-
gmen of the efirst democratic com-
continent, unknighted and un-
by aught but sense of duty, have
d done day's works in the world.

ie glow of conscious pride which
.kens I seem to take but a local,
not insensible to the debt which
.ountry owe to the Bay Colony, or
.ind owes to New-England as a
some of us who think it may not
.ccasion like this to recall the cir-
.ocmmonwealth founded by the
.;" is the mother of democracy:
.s and statesmen, of scholars and
.ul inventions, and above all of a
.ngmen. And there are some of
.ner border-line without a thrill of
.ve say, "Thank God, this is our
.tinued applause.)

PEW ON CRANKS.

of the Puritan " was the next
.y M. Depew having arrived, he
.iereto and spoke as follows:

authority in Europe on diseases
in an article in our newspapers
very one who displays unusual
.ind superiority is undoubtedly in-
true the diagnosis of this dis-
.lienist, I am now addressing an
.if selected lunatics. (Laughter.)
.nc the most prominent feature to
The newspapers are incomplete
.icles of his achievements. He
.ige over ordinary mortals in that
.interviewed. The editor of the
.n Yankee of the Yankees, is
.that the word "crank" is not to
.Anglo-Saxon or early English, but
.od things which the Puritan pos-
.1 the Dutch. (Laughter.) While
.that Shakespeare and Milton were
.ne American progress have ad-
.er. (Laughter.) As we have
.it .hreatens to empty our prisons.
.ay was to lock up people who
.roperty, or did deeds of violence on
.ry period, but .he new idea sends
.im to come out to a few
.of the professional gentlemen who
.iderful cure, and the terror of the
.the victims of these experiments.
.an who tries to assassinate an
.to dynamite a millionaire, or who
.drakes" of other people's money
.and therefore irresponsible. The
.t kind of a crank. The most im-
.faith was individual responsibility.
.iting the sinner here as a propara-
.riculation in that lurid university
.ling to his view, no superiority in
.s secured graduation. (Laughter.)
.i of crank was a person who when
. never failed to keep it before the
.sary could be very disagreeable in
. contemporaries, and who never
.the Dutchmen invented the word
.ment in Holland. (Laughter.)

.REHENSION OF WORDS.

.ributed so much to false history as
. The Stuart kings persecuted the
Puritans because they would not accept the religion
of the throne. But these royal personages had no
religion as the devout Puritan understood the word.
They were dissolute in morals and depraved in conduct. They arrayed all the powers of the State on the
side of forms, whose substance was that the king ruled
the Church; but the Puritan placed against their
authority his conscience, which held that God governed
the King. The established order of things was loyally
accepted by the classes and the masses, and for the
aristocracy and the gentry, for the men in the professions and in business, for all which with us stands for
capital and vested rights, it seemed both heresy and
treason to preach reform. The prayers of the Church
at that time were like the affidavits of candidates now
as to election expenses, the margins were larger than
the texts. (Laughter.)

The Puritan who was ready to fight and willing to
die for the privilege of worshipping God as he thought
right was the phenomenal crank of the period. He
was a perambulating can of moral dynamite, whose explosion might liberate the souls and minds of men. He
was beyond dispute the most disagreeable of human
beings to all that constituted the social and political
power of his day. In the unequal contest of these
he and his coreligionists were persecuted, imprisoned,
executed or exiled. But his fight was not for time, but
for eternity. Stuart kings are dead: their thrones have
been taken from their sons, and their power transferred
to a house alien in blood and faith; but the sons of the
Puritans govern half the world, and their principles are
the vital and energizing forces with the other half.
(Applause.) When the Mayflower sailed from Delftshaven there were thirty sovereigns governing Europe,
whose names filled all the requirements of contemporary
fame. The departure of the Mayflower and her cargo
of 120 passengers made no more impression upon the
politics or affairs of Europe than did the parting of the
waters beneath her keel upon the Atlantic Ocean. For
271 years the fight has been hot between the cranks
and the kings. The monarchs are forgotten, and their
kingdoms and principles merged or lost; but the leaders
of the Pilgrim band are for the New World the canonized
saints of civil and religious liberty. (Applause.)

THE PURITAN APPRECIATED.

The Dutchman saw the splendid quality of the raw
material which came among them for refuge. They
understood that crankiness indicates surplus energies
and determined to prepare it for power by opportunity
and education. They gave the free school to the Puritan children. They gave the free press to the Puritan
writers, free churches for the Puritan religionists, and opened the
trades for Puritan artisans. The Dutch declaration of
independence was a liberal education in liberty, and the
Dutch Republic a model for State sovereignty and National power. (Applause.)

After Pastor Robinson and Elder Brewer and their
flocks had been five years in the kindergarten of
freedom and toleration, the best of the leaders
were admitted to the University of Leyden.
The college authorities apportioned to each of
them, according to the custom of the university,
two tuns of beer every month and ten gallons of wine
every quarter, or forty gallons of wine and twenty-
four hogsheads of beer each year. Such was the hospitality of the Dutch, and such the capacity of our
Puritan forefathers. (Laughter.) The orators who
every year at this banquet indulge in pleasing fictions
of the amazement and horror of the forefathers if
they should drop in on these feasts have not studied
history. By the time the ancestor had laid his degenerate descendant under the table his own mind
could only have reached the period of severe medi-
tation. (Laughter.) In an age when trading companies were apportioning the New World and coloniz-
ing it for commerce and profit, for the Pilgrims to
select the most unhospitable section of the Atlantic
coast for settlement, solely that they might enjoy freedom of conscience in the wilderness, seems heroic
now, but was esteemed folly then. According to the
standard of the time it might be fanatical, but it was
not business. (Laughter and applause.)

The charter they framed on the Mayflower, for the
first time in the construction of government, proclaimed an organization upon the basis of just and
equal laws. For that they would have been executed
for high treason in any country in the world except
Holland. The tremendous success of their experiment is the strongest lesson to us not to fear the
truth because of its advocates or our prejudices.
(Applause.) These men were the stoned and derided
prophets of their period, and the accepted guides of

ours. Pastor John Robinson was not only the broadest-minded preacher in that bigoted period, but he had the elements of crank heresy even of our day. The words of his parting sermon to the Pilgrims the night of their departure from Delftshaven might have disturbed an ecclesiastical convention now. He said : " And if God should reveal anything to you by any other instrument of His, be as ready to receive it as you were to receive any truth in my ministry : but I am confident that the Lord hath more light and truth yet to break out of His holy Word. The Lutherans, for example, cannot be drawn to go beyond what Luther says ; and whatever part of God's will He hath further imparted to Calvin they will die rather than embrace : and so the Calvinists stick where he left them. This is a misery much to be lamented, for though they were precious shining lights in their time, God hath not revealed His whole will to them."

A PURITAN PASTOR'S LIBERALITY.

This glorious recognition of progress and declaration of open-mindedness to research and revelation, this courageous confidence that light, more light, purifies the atmosphere and illumines truth was not the expression from Faneuil Hall of yesterday, but the utterance of a Puritan pastor of nearly three centuries ago. It might have been both the text and argument of the defenders of Phillips Brooks and Dr. Briggs.

The forefathers did not comprehend then the full force of their liberal leader's teachings, but his lessons have blossomed and fruited in their descendants until New-England has found as many paths to heaven as there are Yankees on the earth. (Laughter and applause.) The trials, persecutions and isolation of the Puritans so centred their thoughts in and upon themselves that they could die for their own liberty ; but the devil was their enemy and all who disagreed with them were his followers. When at Lexington the farmers fired the shot that echoed round the world, they had exorcised the devil and could fight and die for equal liberty for every man. They burned Mrs. Rebecca Nourse at Salem for witchcraft ; but 260 years afterward they erected a monument to her memory. The Puritan could always be relied on to compensate and satisfy any one he had wronged —if you gave him time. (Laughter.)

The Puritans were not traders or men of commerce, but State builders. In their straits for money they sent Captain Miles Standish to London. He succeeded upon the pledge of all New-England as security, including, of course, Plymouth Rock, in raising 150 pounds sterling at 50 per cent interest. Now, whether money is wanted to build a railroad or to help prevent a financial cataclysm in England, the sons of the Pilgrims are the lenders of the cash. They return good for evil by reducing the rate of interest. (Laughter and applause.) The acknowledged head of Yankee bankers is the president of your society. He has established a higher rule of honor, based upon Puritan principles, that if millions of railroad bonds agreed to be taken at a price cannot be marketed when the company is ready to deliver them, though the engagement is only a verbal promise, not enforcible at law, the word of a Yankee banker is a contract under seal. (Applause.)

SOMETHING ABOUT FANATICS.

" These quarters are very pleasant," said an inmate of Bloomingdale Asylum, " but I do not like Dr. Brown, because he called me a fool."

" Oh," I replied, " Dr. Brown is a perfect gentleman, and you must be mistaken."

" Well," argued the lunatic, " I overheard the doctor say that I had a congenital and abnormal development of the cerebellum, and if that is n't calling a man a damned fool, I don't know what it is." (Laughter.) The Puritan has enjoyed the just repute as a fanatic of the highest distinction as a crank, but whether it was the King or the Church which encountered him they never after the battle thought him a fool. He never threatens the life of the individual or takes private property ; but if commerce or business or vested interests are entrenched in moss-covered rings, he takes the ring, no matter who or what it hits or hurts. He shakes the business world by throwing over tea in Boston Harbor ; but by that he vindicates an immoral principle and creates a nation. He throws conservative pulpits into convulsions or terror when he proclaims that bleeding Kansas needs not Bibles but rifles. (Laughter.) He knows that when the question is whether a great victory shall be dedicated to freedom or slavery, the border ruffian

requires discipline with Winchesters before he is prepared for the Bible lesson. Our polite conditions have not removed his crankiness, and I hope never will. He can become popular with party leaders and office-seekers by laboring for Civil Service reform, and can still arouse their dormant consciousness and forces by boldly charging that an attempt to defeat the popular will, as expressed in the votes of the people, by quibble or trick, and in order to carry a Legislature, is an assault upon the suffrage and a subversion of the ballot. All hail the Puritan cranks, the Miltons, the Cromwells, the Hampdens of the Old World, the Otises, the Adamses, the Lloyd Garrisons, the John Browns, the Abraham Lincolns of the New. They are for humanity and the elevation of light and liberty. (Loud cheering and long-continued applause.)

GENERAL PORTER'S REPLY.

Mr. Morgan then called upon General Horace Porter to speak to " Sires and Sons." General Porter said :

I have acquired some useful experience in attending New-England Society dinners in various cities. I dine with New-Englanders in Boston ; the rejoicing is marked, but not aggressive. I dine with them in New-York ; the hilarity and cheer in mind are increased in a large degree. I dine with them in Philadelphia ; the joy is unconfined and measured neither by metes nor bounds. Indeed it has become patent to every observer that the further the New-Englander finds himself from New-England the more hilarious is his rejoicing. (Cheers and laughter.) Whenever we find a son of New-England who has passed beyond the borders of his own section, who has stepped out into the damp cold fog of a benighted outside world and has brought up in another State, he seems to take more pride than ever in his descent—doubtless because he feels that it has been so great. (Laughter.)

The New-England sire was a stern man on duty and determined to administer discipline totally regardless of previous acquaintance. He detested all revolutions in which he had taken no part. He was always ambitious to acquire a reputation that would extend into the next world. If he possessed too much piety it was tempered by religion ; while always seeking out new virtues he never lost his grip on his vices. (Laughter.)

When he landed at Plymouth he boldly set about the appalling task of cultivating the alleged soil. (Laughter.) His labors were largely lightened by the fact that there were no agricultural newspapers to direct his efforts. (Laughter.) By a fiction of speech which could not have been conceived by a less ingenious mind, he founded a government based upon a common poverty and called it a commonwealth. (Laughter.) He was prompt and eminently practical in his worldly methods. In the rigors of a New-England winter when he found a witch suffering he brought her into the fire ; when he found an Indian suffering he went out and covered him with a shotgun. (Laughter.)

The discipline of the race, however, is chiefly due to the New-England mother. She could be seen going to church of a Sabbath with the Bible under one arm and a small boy under the other. When her offspring were found suffering from spring fever and the laziness which accompanied it, she braced them up with a heroic dose of brimstone and molasses. The brimstone given here was a reminder of the discipline hereafter ; the molasses has doubtless been chiefly responsible for the tendency of the race to stick to everything, especially their opinions. (Laughter.)

The New-Englanders always take the initiative in great National movements. At Lexington and Concord they marched out alone without waiting for the rest of the Colonies, to have their fling at the redcoats, and a number of the colonists on that occasion succeeded in interfering with British bullets. (Laughter.) It was soon after observed that their afternoon excursion had attracted the attention of England. They acted in the spirit of the fly who bit the elephant on the tail. When the fly was asked whether he expected to kill him he said : " No, but I notice I made him look round." (Laughter.)

THEIR RESPECT FOR IMPOSSIBILITIES.

Such are the inventive faculty and self-reliance of New-Englanders that they always entertain a profound respect for impossibilities. It has been largely owing to their influence that we took the negro, who is a natural agriculturist, and made a soldier of him; took the Indian, who is a natural warrior, and made an agriculturist of him; took the American, who is a natural destructionist, and made a protectionist of him. They are always revolutionizing affairs. Recently a Boston company equipped with electricity the horse-cars, or rather the mule-cars, in the streets of Atlanta. When the first electric-motor cars were put into service an aged "contraband" looked at them from the street corner and said: "Dem Yankees is a powerful sma't people, first they come down h'yar and freed de niggers, now they have done freed de mules." (Laughter.)

The New-Englander is so constantly engaged in creating changes that in his hand even variety becomes monotonous. When a German subject finds himself oppressed by his Government he emigrates; when a French citizen is oppressed he makes the Government emigrate; when Americans find a portion of their Government trying to emigrate they arm themselves and spend four years in going after it and bringing it back. (Laughter and applause).

You will find the sons of New-England everywhere throughout the world, and they are always at the fore. I happened to be at a French banquet in Paris where several of us Americans spoke, employing that form of the French language which is so often used by Americans in France, and which is usually so successful in concealing one's ideas from the natives. There was a young Bostonian there who believed he had successfully mastered all of the most difficult modern languages except that which is spoken by the brakemen on the elevated railroad. (Laughter.) When he spoke French the only departure from the accent of the Parisian was that "nuance" of difference arising from the mere accidental circumstance of one having learned his French in Paris and the other in Boston. The French give much praise to Molière for having changed the pronunciation of a great many French words: but his most successful efforts in that direction were far surpassed by the Boston young man. When he had finished his remarks a French gentleman sitting beside me inquired. "Where is he from," I replied. "From New-England." Said he, "I don't see anything English about him except his French." (Laughter.)

A TRIBUTE TO GENERAL SHERMAN.

In speaking of the sons of New-England sires. I know that one name is uppermost in all minds here to-night—the name of one who added new lustre to the fame of his distinguished ancestors. The members of your society, like the Nation at large, found themselves within the shadow of a profound grief and oppressed by a sense of sadness akin to the sorrow of a personal bereavement as they stood with uncovered heads beside the bier of William T. Sherman: when the echo of his guns gave place to the tolling of cathedral bells: when the flag of his country which had never been lowered in his presence dropped to half mast as if conscious that his strong arm was no longer there to hold it to the peak: when he passed from the living here to join the other living commonly called the dead. We shall never meet the great soldier again until he stands forth to answer to his name at roll-call on the morning of the last great reveille. At this board he was always welcome. The same blood coursed in his veins which flows in yours. All hearts warmed to him with the glow of an abiding affection. He was a many-sided man. He possessed all the characteristics of the successful soldier; bold in conception: vigorous in execution, and unshrinking under grave responsibilities. He was singularly self-reliant, demonstrating by all his acts that "much danger makes great hearts most resolute." He combined in his temperament the restlessness of a Hotspur with the patience of a Fabius. Under the magnetism of his presence his troops rushed to victory with all the dash of Caesar's Tenth Legion. Opposing ranks went down before the fierceness of his onsets, never to rise again. He paused not till he saw the folds of his banners wave above the strongholds he had wrested from the foe.

While mankind will always appreciate the practical workings of the mind of the great strategist, they will also see in his marvellous career much which savors of romance as well as reality, appeals to the imagination and excites the fancy. They will picture him as a legendary knight moving at the head of conquering columns, whose marches were measured not by single miles, but by thousands: as a general who could make a Christmas present to his President of a great seaport city; as a chieftain whose field of military operations

covered nearly half a continent; who had penetrated everglades and bayous; the inspiration of whose commands forged weaklings into giants; whose orders all spoke with the true bluntness of the soldier; who fought from valley's depth to mountain height and marched from inland rivers to the sea. No one can rob him of his laurels, no man can lessen the measure of his fame. His friends will never cease to sing paeans in his honor, and even the wrath of his enemies may be counted in his praise. (Prolonged applause.)

CONGRESSMAN DALZELL.

The next and final toast was "New-England in Congress in Early Days," and Congressman John Dalzell, of Pittsburg, Penn., spoke in response. He said:

There is comfort to me in the thought that this is not an occasion where one can be expected to say anything new, if, indeed, there be anything new under the sun. What new thing can be said of New-England history, New-England heroes or traditions?

Have they not been embalmed by her own sons in classic prose and stirring verse? If we must say trite things, it is our privilege to say them in connection with the story that never grows old, the story of Liberty. If we may not enrich the world with new thoughts, we can, at least, enrich ourselves by dwelling again on the heroism, the fortitude and devotion which dedicated a new continent forever to the cause of civil and religious freedom. As lovers of liberty and of the heroic of our kind, we may light anew our torches at the altar whose fires, kindled on the bleak New-England coast, now make splendid with their light a world's horizon. Precious are the human virtues of courage and conscience that bud and blossom even in the lost cause; but how inestimably admirable are these same virtues when their fruitage continues to ripen to the advancement of human progress and of all that makes life worth living. (Applause.)

There are two or three thoughts connected with the relation of early New-England to our system of government of which I would speak in very brief terms and merely by way of outline.

Because it is so that the thirteen original States of the Union became the United States under the system of government with which we are familiar, it by no means follows that their union on that basis was the thing originally most natural and obvious. Many circumstances existed to keep them apart as separate independencies. Diversities of race, religion, habits of life and thought, of material interests, claims of superiority, one over another, mutual jealousies, all these were considerations against merger into a single nation. True, there were influences existing in an opposite direction, such as common dangers, and finally a common tyranny of the mother country. But it is unto New-England really that history carries us in our search for the most potent sources of the Union, which was cemented on the basis of man's equality. (Applause.) Hers were the people most imbued with the spirit of independence, rendered most hardy by the struggle for liberty, educated most thoroughly in the practice of self-government. The co-operation between the colonies that became habitual had its inception in New-England precedents. The first Confederacy on this side of the Atlantic was a New-England Confederacy. It was Massachusetts that originated the scheme of committees of intercolonial correspondence that resulted finally in intercolonial action and the Continental Congress. It is not robbing others of the credit due to them—which was great—to assign to New-England id as the place of leadership in the movement which culminated in a more perfect Union; and, besides, the day is long since past for sectional jealousies between those who follow now the same flag. The American issue of Puritan and Cavalier is heir to the glory of both Houses. Were I speaking from a narrow view, I should tell you of the sterling virtues, the pioneer spirit and the religious love of liberty that carried the Scotch-Irish across the Alleghenies, to plant church and schoolhouse southward and westward in the onward march of civilization. Too recent is our experience to draw distinctions founded upon race and place, since on many a battlefield of our Civil War, memorable for courage, men of all races, fighting for the right as they saw it, have proved by the testimony of blood that there is no name like the name American. (Applause.)

WRITTEN CONSTITUTIONS.

To New-England we must go for the origin of written constitutions. Magna Charta, the Bill of Rights, the habeas corpus, mark the milestones in the march of Saxon liberty: but the conception is a Yankee one of an instrument in writing which, covering the whole field of government, should secure liberty by defining the limits of power. Charters for corporate purposes of greater or less importance reach far back into history, but these emanated always from the king. Written constitutions from the true and only source of power, the sovereign people, as practical measures, were born of New-England experience and jealousy of power. The inventive genius which has become the characteristic badge of Americanism has not found its only opportunities in the field of mechanics. (Applause.) It is not alone of that material kind which would coin brains into dollars. It is practical in its higher reach and loftier purpose, looking into the security of political rights, and the preservation of the ends which wrote early New-England and the New-England of to-day—which means a continent—on the world's map of civilization. Two years before the Long Parliament opened the fight between the divine royalty of the people and the assumed royalty of the kings, the "free planters" of Connecticut gave to history its first written Constitution. That was a "farmers' alliance" worthy of place and of power, and its Constitution was one that called for the intervention of no Supreme Court in its construction, since it prescribed that, as to all matters not provided for therein, they should be governed by the laws of God.

For my part, I much prefer the original idea of a written constitution as a chart of government, to the modern monstrosity of our day, which, under the name Constitution, gives to us a code of laws.

That our forefathers in convention assembled proceeded, as of course, to set up a Government within the framework of a written Constitution is due to New-England ideas and precedent. (Applause.)

While it is true that our Constitution embodies principles proved by long experience to be conservative of rights, it is also true that it had to deal with conditions altogether new in human experience. No other people have had interests to be cared for like the interests of the American colonists. The problem presented was to make a Nation, and at the same time preserve, so far as might be, the autonomy of the States. Home rule was too sacred a possession in colonial eyes to be put in peril. (Applause.) The equality of the contracting parties was not to be destroyed to the detriment of any.

RESULT OF CONTESTS.

Hence the contest between the small States and the large ones. Hence the threatened danger of no union at all. To constitute a Legislature with two Chambers offered no solution to the difficulty; since representation upon the basis of either wealth or population preserved the disparity instead of avoiding it. And here light broke upon the darkness from the Connecticut Constitution of more than a century before. Provision was therein made for representation in one House from townships and in the other from the people of the whole State. And this New-England idea, known to history as "the Connecticut compromise," by adoption and adaptation, resulted in the scheme which makes one house of our National Legislature the representative to-day of the people of the districts and the other the representative of the states. (Applause.) I would that our Constitution makers had followed their model even more closely. I would that they had made Senators the representatives of States, but chosen by the people of the States, without interposing between the elector and his Senator the uncertain and oftentimes the servile and corrupt votes of a State Legislature. And so far as that is concerned, I can see no reason why a machine-ridden and boss-ridden people, if any such there be, should not even now go back, or go forward rather, to the Connecticut plan.

New-England's strongest mark on the Federal Constitution is the clause giving National control to the regulation of commerce. Strongest, I say, because of the far-reaching importance of that power as now exercised. No man not familiar with its tremendous reach can appreciate the extent to which it makes us a Nation as contra distinguished from an aggregation of States. By means of it we have free trade between forty-four States and our Territories. Free trade in a commerce by the side of which the commerce of any other Nation dwindles to a comparative insignificance; since our internal commerce, it is stated, is in value twenty-five times our foreign commerce; a commerce, therefore, that is double the entire foreign commerce of all the other Nations on the globe, and ten times more than that of Great Britain. (Applause.) Free trade upon our railroads and rivers, upon ocean and gulf, and upon the great lakes. This power to regulate commerce, reaches not only to traffic foreign and domestic; it has relation to the currency, to the telegraph and the mail, to immigration, to harbors and channels, to our rivers, and the bridges over them, to the men and the vessels that navigate them, to the creation of corporations in connection with interstate commerce, and to the exercise of the eminent domain, even without authority from the States, and within their lines. (Applause.) This great and all-pervading power went into the Constitution at the instance of commercial New-England, which agreed with the South in return therefor that a twenty-year lease of life should be given to the slave trade. And now the slave trade and slavery belong to the buried past, while the Nation marches to new conquests in the world's great battle for commercial supremacy. (Applause.)

LOYALTY TO INDIVIDUAL RIGHTS.

The glory of our early New-England lay in its loyalty to individual right and in its unvarying obedience to the laws that secured it. I appreciate the fact that this is a place where the discussion of partisan politics is wholly inappropriate. But it is the most appropriate place in the world to take counsel as to our country's weal. (Applause.) And so, my countrymen, standing for a moment on a platform higher than that of party, advocating no particular scheme of legislation, laying blame at no man's door, eager only to provoke thought and advance justice, let us ask ourselves the question—how true are we to the men who, in the Mayflower's cabin, not only signed a compact to enact wise laws, but embodied therein the promise of "all due submission and obedience" thereto? Claiming to be worthy sons of worthy sires, shall we shut our eye to the fact that a fundamental provision in our organic law is to-day a dead letter, seemingly impossible of execution?

Must it be forever that a Nation, boasting itself the consummate flower of the hardy New-England tree of liberty, shall belie in practice its declaration of freedom, and while its claims for the whole people the divine right of sovereignty, confine that sovereignty in fact to some of the people only? Surely, surely, here is a problem demanding honest recognition, that it may meet successful solution, to the sacrifice of all time-serving considerations, at the hands of patriotic Americans. For, as faith without works is vain, so are empty professions without performance, but sounding brass and a tinkling cymbal. An habitually broken law is the prelude to utter lawlessness, and a standing notice of coming retribution.

Right forever on the scaffold
Wrong forever on the throne,
Yet behind that scaffold
Standeth God, within the shadow
Keeping watch above His own.

The purpose of every such occasion as this is education and inspiration. Education from a conning anew of the lessons of human experience and inspiration from the courage and the conscience of those of that elder day, to the end that we work out, with the courage and the conscience of Americans worthy of their past, the problems that face us in the present and for the future. (Loud and prolonged applause.)

MR. MORGAN'S FAREWELL.

On the conclusion of Mr. Dalzell's speech, Mr. Morgan, on surrendering the gavel as president of the society, appropriately addressed his successor, Daniel Rollins, as follows:

My Dear Friends: The hour has come which comes to every one who has had the honor of filling the chair, when I must turn over to my successor his badge of office and resign, in his favor, the emoluments and honors of office.

It is my happy privilege to do this in favor of one whom you have unanimously elected to fill the chair; one well known to you all; whose name is a household word among you all and to whom, I am sure, you will gladly extend the honor and courtesies bestowed upon his predecessors.

To you, my dear friend, I extend the hand of welcome. For many years we have worked together in our respective offices on behalf of the society, and our official intercourse has been such that its memories will always be pleasant, while life beats; but beyond this, I feel that a personal friendship has grown up, which nothing can ever sever, and for which I am glad at heart. I must also thank you for the kindness you have personally extended to me by assuming, on my behalf, the social duties of the presidency during my term of office, which, owing to a deep domestic affliction, it was impossible for me to perform myself.

On behalf of the society, I extend to you its welcome to the chair, and hand you the badge of office, and I myself take my place with our venerable ex-presidents who surround us. Members of the New-England Society, I propose the health of the Hon. Daniel G. Rollins, president of the New-England Society, and call for three cheers and a bumper.

NEW-YORK AND THE FAIR.

REPRESENTATIVE GATHERING AT DELMONICO'S.

SPEECHES BY CHAUNCEY M. DEPEW, GEORGE R. DAVIS, W. T. BAKER, JOHN BOYD THACHER, GORTON W. ALLEN, CHARLES S. SMITH AND OTHERS.

On December 22 New-York's World's Fair Commissioners gave a dinner to 100 guests at Delmonico's for the purpose of arousing interest in the great exhibition and of securing the moral support of influential merchants, bankers, railway presidents and manufacturers for a proper representation of the Empire State at Chicago. Mr. Depew began the speechmaking at 9 o'clock, as follows:

The New-York Commissioners are very glad to welcome you here to-night. The National Commission for the creation and promotion of the World's Fair, or Columbian Exhibition, consists of three members from each State. The New-York members, Mr. Thacher, Mr. Allen and myself, have invited you to meet us, not on account of the general interests of the exhibition, for its success as a whole is assured, but we wish to consult with you as to the proper provision which should be made for such a representation of our State at the exhibition as would be worthy of its position among our sister commonwealths. (Applause.)

Unfortunately with us the question has been obscured by political claims and considerations which have not entered into the councils of other States, and which have no place, legitimately or illegitimately, in the consideration of the duties which devolve upon us. (Applause.)

This exhibition is destined to be not only the most phenomenal presentation of the industries, the arts, the sciences, the education and the civilization of this and other countries, but its character is in all respects purely national. The success of the Columbian Exhibition must not be impaired or retarded by local ambitions or jealousies anywhere. (Applause.) So far as New-York is concerned she has none. (Applause.) She has not acted in this matter before, because the time had not yet arrived. She is now prepared to do her part in her own imperial way. (Loud applause.)

Whenever a new State is organized there is always fierce competition among rival cities for the position of capital of the commonwealth. When the selection is made controversy is forgotten, and the fortunate place becomes thereafter the centre of the official and legislative life of the State. New-York was the first capital of the United States and continued so for many years. The South and the West fiercely contended for a change, and of course as the result of the controversy New-York lost. Nevertheless she still remains the first city of the continent and the centre of its enterprise and financial strength. Her size and grandeur always have and always will unite all places to dispose of her as the most dangerous competitor before indulging in their own rivalries. But since Washington became the Capital New-York has been proud to be represented there by her ablest statesmen, and to do her part to promote the glory and grandeur of the Republic. (Applause.)

The great West beyond the Alleghanies, which has made such marvellous growth in the last half century in population and agricultural and industrial wealth, demanded and received the World's Fair for the city of Chicago, which city is in itself the most phenomenal exhibit of American energy, enterprise and civilization. (Applause.) Whether the Exhibition had been at New-York, Chicago, St. Louis or San Francisco, it would have been, as it is now, the plain duty of each State to do its best to promote an enterprise which means so much for the industrial, agricultural and educational interests of our country. (Applause.)

The Centennial Exhibition of 1876 was a worthy celebration of the completion of the first 100 years of our independence. The country was still staggering under the bankruptcy of the fearful panic of 1873, but the exhibition placed our business upon its feet and infused life and health into our credit. It distributed to the remotest corners of our country that instruction which materialized into new sources of employment and development, and brought into circulation millions of dollars which otherwise would have lain dormant or idle.

WHAT AN EXHIBITION DOES.

The exhibition two years ago at Paris saved the French Republic from political destruction by turning the commercial distress which was prevalent throughout France into happy and prosperous times. Three hundred millions of dollars or more were in that instance released from savings banks and stockings or brought in from other nations to swell the tide of French profit and progress.

Our Columbian Exhibition comes at a most opportune time. The unprecedented crops which our fields have produced this year and the equally unprecedented demand for our food products abroad will give us for twelve months an exhilarating period of prosperity. Farm mortgages will be paid off, new enterprises will be started, old railroads will be extended and new ones will be constructed. Values will rise in market price, everybody will be richer, and in accord with the temper and spirit of our people credit will be strained to the utmost to realize the largest returns from these phenomenal commercial opportunities. In the ordinary course of financial experience over-trading and over-confidence, with probably different relations another year between the farm and the markets of the world, would be followed by a corresponding collapse. But this great industrial exhibition at Chicago will take up the frayed threads of opportunity, too lavishly employed, and weave them into new cables to draw the car of American progress. The vast movement of peoples over railways, the stimulus given to business at cities and railway centres, the hundreds of millions of dollars brought into active use which would otherwise be unemployed, will save us as a Nation from the dangers which threaten, and crystalize into permanency thousands of enterprises which otherwise would fail from lack of confidence or capital.

The citizens of Chicago are to be complimented and congratulated upon the courage and forethought which have characterized their local preparations for this grand event. They have already expended ten millions of dollars of their own money, and their patriotism and resources are not yet exhausted. But the expense of this national enterprise should not be wholly borne by the locality where Congress has placed it. The nation should do its part to second the efforts of the citizens of Chicago to make this World's Fair Exhibition surpass in every respect any ever yet held in any country. (Great applause.)

The grounds devoted to the Fair are more than three times greater in area than the acres which the Exhibition had at Paris in 1889. The buildings are more numerous and very much larger than the ones which astonished the visitors at the French Capital. The floor space in these magnificent structures will be five times greater than at the Centennial Exhibition at Philadelphia, and double that of the French Exhibition at Paris. The cost of the preparations for the Centennial was about five millions of dollars, of the French Exhibition about ten millions, but for the Exhibition at Chicago it will be seventeen millions. The buildings themselves will be an industrial exhibition of the highest character. They are designed by the most distinguished of American architects. In proportion and grandeur they excel the famed structures o. other lands. By modern invention and the plastic art the architect is enabled to impress upon the eye all the effects produced by the genius of Phidias and Praxiteles. (Applause.)

WHAT THIS COUNTRY WILL HAVE.

Our exhibition will be unique and distinct from its predecessors at London, Paris, Vienna, Berlin in its superb recognition of woman and her work. (Applause.) A structure equal in size and appointments to any except the Machinery Hall at Paris, and designed by an American girl, will demonstrate by its architectural beauty the advance of women in this field, and the departments housed in this superb structure, where woman's work will be displayed, will fitly show what the United States has done to ennoble and dignify womanhood, and give her opportunity to make her way in the arts and industries. (Applause.)

At the Centennial Exhibition at Philadelphia, Morse's telegraph comprised almost the sum of our knowledge of electricity, but a building at Chicago twice as large as Cooper Institute, devoted entirely to electrical appliances and inventions, will demonstrate by the advance in one department the enormous progress of the country in every department since then.

At the time of the Centennial Exhibition we had 45,000,000 people; now our numbers reach the grand total of 64,000 000. Then we had thirty-seven States, but we have since added seven stars to our flag. Then the product of our farms in cereals was about $2,200 000,000; now it is over $4,00,-000,000. Then the output of our factories was about $5,000,000.000; now it is over $7,0,0,000,000. Such progress, such development, such advance, such accumulation of wealth and the opportunities for wealth—wealth in the broad sense, which opens new avenues for employment and fresh chances for independence and for homes—have characterized no other similar period of recorded time. (Applause.)

It is an insult to the intelligence of our State to ask what should be the place of New-York in this grand exhibition. First in population, in manufactures and almost in agriculture, first in all the elements which constitute a great and growing commonwealth, her place in the emulous and friendly rivalry of sister States in this grand exhibition should be that which nature and the enterprise of her people have given her. (Great applause.)

Our markets are West, our competitors are West. We must remove any prejudice that may exist against our trade, and then command the markets by the superiority and cheapness of our product. The opportunity is before us to suffer great loss or gain incalculable advantage. But aside from ma erial considerations, New-York has never failed when patriotic effort was demanded to respond with volume and enthusiasm which sustained her imperial position. (Applause.) In the presence of this representative body, speaking for them and through them for the people of the Commonwealth, I can say to the country East and West, and North and South, "New-York will be at the Columbian Exposition, and she will be there in the full grandeur of her strength and development." (Prolonged applause.)

IT WILL BE INTERNATIONAL.

The Columbian World's Exposition will be international because it will hospitably welcome and entertain the people and the products of every nation in the

world. It will give to them the fullest opportunity to teach us, and learn from us, and to open new avenues of trade with our markets, and discover materials which will be valuable in theirs. But its creation, its magnitude, its location, its architecture and its striking and enduring features will be American. The city in which it is held, taking rank among the first cities in the world after an existence of only fifty years, is American. The great inland fresh-water sea, whose waves will dash against the shores of Jackson Park, is American. The prairie, extending westward with its thousands of square miles of land, a half-century ago a wilderness, but to-day gridironed with railroads, spanned with webs of electric wire, rich in prosperous farms, growing villages, ambitious cities, and an energetic, educated and progressive people, is purely American.

The Centennial Exhibition of 1876 celebrated the first hundred years of independence of the Republic of the United States. The Columbian Exhibition celebrates the discovery of a continent which has become the home of peoples of every race, the refuge for those persecuted on account of their devotion to civil and religious liberty, and the revolutionary factor in the affairs of this earth, a discovery which has accomplished more for humanity in its material, its intellectual and its spiritual aspec s, than all other events since the advent of Christ. (Loud cheering and prolonged applause.)

The next speech was delivered by ex-Senator T. W. Palmer, president of the World's Columbian Commission. Other addresses were made by J. Seaver Page, George R Davis, director-general of the Fair; W. T. Baker, president of the Chicago local commission; John Boyd Thacher and Gorton W. Allen, New-York Commissioners, and Charles S. Smith, president of the New-York Chamber of Commerce.

ADDRESS OF THE DIRECTOR-GENERAL.

Here is what George R. Davis said:

Mr. Chairman and Gentlemen : Being called upon in my official capacity as Director-General of the World's Columbian Exposition, through your courtesy, I wish to express my appreciation of your consideration in extending to me an invitation to be present at this banquet in the great metropolis of the Nation, and to assure you of my pleasure at the opportunity to meet face to face and to clasp the friendly hand of so many gentlemen of New-York, and of other States, men distinguished in National and international affairs who with me are equally desirous that the World's Fair of 1893 shall be in every way a success; shall in every way express to the world the productiveness of American soil, the wealth of American genius, the breadth of American intellect, the warmth of the American heart, the generosity of American people and the superior qualities and characteristics of our great democratic form of government over all other forms of government in the world. (Applause.)

Standing in such a distinguished presence and with such a subject calling us together, I feel sure that all thought of local interest and of all personal ambitious ends will have no place among us, and, that we shall be inspired by the single ambition that we are brothers of one family, seeking to build up and improve the father's domain, and by so doing build up and improve ourselves. (Applause.)

As the key to our thought we may ask the general question, what is the intent of the World's Fair? What lesson is it to inculcate? What influence is it to exert upon the world and upon our Nation? As a general answer, it may be said that the World's Columbian Exposition is intended to express our gratitude to all Nations of the earth that have in any way promoted our prosperity and made our National life possible. Under the gracious Providence which Mr. Lincoln, in his farewell address to his neighbors in Springfield, appealed to ; that Washington at all times relied upon, without which he could not have succeeded—under this Providence we are indebted to all of the Nations of the earth for our place and station in the world. Our country has gathered profit alike out of the successes and misfortunes of other Nations and governments of the world.

OTHER NATIONS NOT JEALOUS.

As a general statement, it may be said that the Nations of the earth which have contributed to our National success are not jealous of us, but they are rather proud of the part they have had in our up-building, and the greater the success of the World's Columbian Exposition, the greater will be the glory reflected upon these Nations. An inferior Exposition would naturally lower us in our own estimation and would subtract from the renown of the nations that had helped us.

The Exposition is to be American sunshine and soil, American skill and genius, American scholarship and thought against all the world, and the world will be the prouder and all the better if we gain the victory.

Any consideration of our indebtedness to the nations of the world must of necessity lead us to reflect upon the leading character who stood out as the representative of the best thought of these nations, and who pushed their people out to our assistance. Fourteen hundred and ninety-two, eighteen hundred and ninety-two and three! These dates, spanning 400 years, bring Spain and Columbia together, and lead us to acknowledge our indebtedness to Spain.

The education of Columbus in the great schools of his time and his experience in navigation gained by his several voyages upon the Mediterranean; the valuable charts, journals and memoranda of a distinguished navigator, which came into his possession through his fortunate marriage; his great struggle for a livelihood when residing at Lisbon, the very centre of geographical speculation and adventure, all conspired to incite the adventurous spirit of Columbus, and it was here that he first felt the inspiration and declared that "there was land to the westward," and that a faithful voyaging in that direction would land the navigator on the eastern shores of Asia.

The story of Columbus is familiar. His repulses and discouragements were great, and it was some ten years later that we find him weary, leading by the hand his little motherless son Diego, when, overcome with fatigue and hunger he asked for bread and water for his famishing child at the convent of Larrabeda. Here he was welcomed by the brother superior and bountifully supplied. The brothers of the convent became interested in his schemes, so much so that the brother superior then and there promised that he would exert on behalf of Columbus such influence as might be necessary to secure to Columbus a hearing before Ferdinand and Isabella, which promise this brother superior faithfully fulfilled.

This incident in the life of Columbus has always impressed me with the sense of gratitude that the world scientific, the world commercial and the world religious, and more especially the debt of gratitude the people of this country of ours owe to the brothers of this convent, and especially to the brother superior, for on this incident and the faithfulness of this superior to his promise swings the door through which Columbus passed to the discovery of this continent. (Applause.)

True, many years passed during which Columbus struggled when his appeal to the Spanish court was not listened to, aye, when turned adrift with the admonition, "trouble the Nation no more," aye, when all others had apparently shut the door of hope in his face, Isabella called him to her presence and assured him that she would assume the undertaking for her own crown of Castile and would defray the expenses of the perilous voyage from her own means. Who can estimate the debt of gratitude that this country owes to the Spanish people, and to the great and generous-hearted Queen, who when all others failed gave herself to the great undertaking that opened this continent to the people of the world?

SPAIN'S INTEREST IN THE FAIR.

It gives me pleasure to state that the Government of Spain is deeply interested in the success of the Exposition, and she will make an exhibit which will reflect honor upon the Queen and the country which assisted Columbus to cross the unfurrowed seas and open America to the world.

Nor is it possible for us to speak of our indebtedness to Spain without remembering Italy, whose dominion once swayed from the source of the Euphrates to the Pillars of Hercules at Gibraltar, under whose bright blue skies the eyes of Columbus first saw the light of day. Therefore to Italy as well as to Spain must America made acknowledgment. Italy will be here with an exhibit of the rich treasures of her classic land.

Then there is Germany, that land of music and mathematics and of subtle thought; that land which has given name and character to some of our leading States; that land whose thrifty sons and daughters are scattered by the million over our vast domain. What does this country owe to the German? Perhaps if we let the light fall upon Sigel and his heroic followers, we will pause before we seek in common figures to compute the uncounted debt. Germany is to be with us in '93 with a magnificent display of the resources of that great Empire. Austria will be with us. The tens of thousands of former subjects from both upper and lower Austria who are of us will gladly welcome the representatives of their home country and the display promised from Austria-Hungary will be superb in every respect.

Then there is France; the land of genius, scholarship, art and politeness. What does this country owe to France? There came to this country in 1777 a young son of France, who became a very close and intimate friend of Washington, and in 1780 he was intrusted by the Congress of the United States, with the defence of the State of Virginia, and when in 1784 he visited this country, his tour was one unbroken triumph, and the name of Lafayette was upon the lips of every one. (Applause.) Then it is in her generous and tasteful statue in the very doorway of this great city casting a light far out upon the stormy deep, telling of the love that the young Republic of France bears for the Republic that Lafayette helped to establish. (Applause.) The most generous appropriations are being made by the French Republic to enable that Nation to make an exhibit that will be worthy of her great history. (Applause.) There is not a class of people among us (and there are many) more earnest or more anxious for the success of the Exhibition, nor more tasteful and helpful in their suggestions than are the sons of France.

Already the Turkish Government—or rather the Ottoman Empire—has made choice of its position on the Exposition grounds, as indeed have many others. One of her leading sons said the other day that the Columbian Exposition of '93 will enable Turkey to prove to the world that she is not the "sick man" of the nations, but a strong and growing nation, loving liberty, progressive and powerful. Russia, that land of teeming millions of diversified people and multiplied tongues; Russia, from where her brow is bathed in the cold waters of the Arctic Ocean to where her feet rest in the waters of the Black and Caspian seas, will be here. Russia is interested in us; we are interested in Russia. Russia has ever been our friend, and in the hours of our darkest trial it was no little comfort to every true American heart to know that the great navy of Russia was sleeping quietly in American waters. The great Russian Government will be with us in '93 and through the Exposition the nations of the earth will come to know more of Russia and her peoples, and will love her more because of her exhibits.

Then there are Sweden and Norway and Denmark. We have no more industrious, peaceful, thrifty population among us than the great and growing Scandinavian population. These countries will be here with fine exhibits; their representatives have already visited us.

Then there are Holland and Belgium and Switzerland and the other Continental Nations of Europe, they will be here.

THE BRITISH EMPIRE WILL BE REPRESENTED.

Great Britain will be with us; the Nation that has given us more of her subjects, and more of whose sons and daughters are among us than any other Nation of the world; the Nation that is one with us in blood, in spirit, in language and in love of constitutional government; one with us in literature, in science and in art; that Nation which is related to us by ties that neither time nor war nor revolution can sever. (Applause.) Her Shakespeare is our Shakespeare; her Byron is our Byron; her Milton is our Milton; her Tennyson is our Tennyson; her Gladstone is our Gladstone; her Edwin Arnold is our

Edwin Arnold; and "The Light of Asia " and "The Light of the World" are a literary food for all of our sons and daughters. Great Britain will be with us; her treasures of mine and sea will be here; her treasures of literature, art, science, will be here; her treasures from India, Australia, British North America, the Cape, from all her Colonies, and from all her islands in the sea, will be here. Treasures from England and Ireland, Scotland, Wales will be here. (Applause.) The representative wealth and genius and skill of her 500,000,000 of subjects will be here, and she will be our greatest competitor in the race for first place among the millions of the world, and such competition demands the perfect unity, broadest liberality on the part of every State in the Union and on the part of the Congress of the United States that the Exposition may be in every respect what every foreign nation will be delighted to have it and what every true American desires it to be.

I have not spoken of China nor of Japan, not that I am forgetful of the relations they as nations sustain to us and we to them. Japan stands in the foreground in wonderful example of the swift progress of modern developments and education. These Governments will be here. The Exposition means to Japan and China everything. It means all of those moral blessings which invariably accompany the era of invention. Nor have I spoken of the vast nations that lie south of us, nor is it perhaps necessary that I should. Their hearts are all with us in being one with Columbus. The Central and South American Republics hanging to the great Andes like basket panniers, filled to overflowing with precious stones, the cereals, gems and metals; to these countries the display of resources at Chicago will strengthen and encourage reciprocal relations and attract more strongly the attention of eager capital. (Applause.)

WHAT THIS COUNTRY OWES TO ITSELF.

We owe much to ourselves to the upbuilding of the great Republic, and to the States and Territories of our own country; to the people of North America, to the institutions, to the commerce, to the quick civilization, the benefits of the Exposition must be sweeping in their extent and universal in their application. The new States of the far West, side by side with Territories knocking at the door of Statehood, will bring their best offerings of gold and silver and wheat and grain to this latter industry to be christened by the people of the world and receive the benediction of their assembled sisters. The States of the boundless prairie and of the lofty mountain region will prove by the excellence and the abundance of their products that the secrets of our National prosperity and explain why "westward the course of empire takes its way." Raw material will meet its natural complement, machinery; and the result will stimulate the production and advance both. The new South, the marvel of our day, according to your distinguished orator and statesman, Mr. Depew. " the land of promise for the young men," will be given ample opportunity on the grounds of this Exposition to present an illustration of her last thirty years' progress. Once again cotton will meet corn, and to their mutual advantage, and the exhibits from that country will greatly surprise even those acquainted with the resources of the South, and eventually divert broad and rich streams of money to their proper lodging place. To these great States contiguous to Chicago and of which Chicago is a great influential and commercial centre, the Fair cannot fail to be of incalculable benefit. Proximity will permit these States to present large exhibits at comparatively small cost, and £20,000,-000 of their people through the perfection of railroad facilities can be conveyed to the gates of the Exposition at small expense. The Eastern States; none will receive greater benefits from the great Exposition than the States of the Atlantic coast. And in this participation your own State, the Empire State in a far higher than a political sense, has gained the title of the pivotal commonwealth. She leads among the Atlantic States in population, in commerce and in wealth. Her harbor is universally regarded as the gateway of this Nation. Through it will pass the majority of exhibitors and sightseers from abroad, all of whom will enjoy her hospitality. She [will reap largely of the benefits of the Exposition without any of the attendant disadvantages. She will maintain before the world her high rank as a producer, and arm in arm with the great sister State of the prairie will present to the Columbian Exposition the representative wealth and greatness of this Nation. (Applause.)

Indeed, it is my thought that the Exposition is not only going to draw the sister nations that are near us closer together, but I believe it will draw all nations of the earth nearer together, and that it will cement the States of the Union together so closely that thereafter there will be no North, no South, no East, no West, no black, no white, no German and no Irish, but one cemented American Nation under one flag, and that bearing across its stars and stripes in letters of livid light that the nations of the world can readily read, " Peace on earth, good will to men." To such a consummation let us unitedly work. (Applause.)

WHAT W. T. BAKER SAID.

W. T. Baker made the following address:

I presume there is no urgent demand on this occasion for an extended reference to the birth of the World's Columbian Exposition. The circumstances attending the legislative creation of the project are perhaps better known in this neighborhood than all that has been accomplished since. The Exposition appears to have been neglected, if not forgotten, for awhile by some who were equally anxious with ourselves in the first place for its promotion. It even appeared at one time that there was some trace of bitterness because the Exposition was located further west or north than those not imbued with the Chicago spirit of prophecy and confidence would have had it, but if such there has been it has disappeared, and with

"No fears to beat away—no strifes to heal,
The past unsighed for and the future sure,"

we are going steadily forward with the co-operation in all needed ways of all the people of the Nation. (Applause.) The form of organization under which we are operating has appeared to many at a distance to be somewhat complex, and it may be well for me to explain at the outset what otherwise may be confusing.

The act of Congress, approved April 25, 1890, providing for the Exposition, states in the preamble that "such an exhibition should be of a national and international character, so that not only the people of our Union and this continent, but those of all Nations as well can participate." And to carry out this intention the Congress provided two agents to do its will. The first is a commission consisting of two Commissioners from each State and Territory of the United States, appointed by the President on the nomination of the Governors of the States and Territories respectively, and eight Commissioners-at-Large, appointed by the President.

DUTIES OF THE COMMISSION.

The board so constituted was designated the World's Columbian Commission. The duties of the Commission relate to exhibits and exhibitors, or, as stated in the act, " to prepare a classification of exhibits, determine the plan and scope of the Exposition, appoint all judges and examiners for the Exposition, award all premiums, if any, and generally have charge of all intercourse with the exhibitors and representatives of foreign Nations."

The other agent recognized by the act of Congress is the World's Columbian Exposition, a corporation organized under the laws of the State of Illinois. This corporation has to do mainly with ways and means, the erection of buildings, the maintenance, protection and policing of the same, the granting of concessions, the collection and disbursement of all its revenues, and fixing the rules governing the Exposition. It is composed of upward of 28,000 stockholders, and is controlled by a board of forty-five directors. These directors have been chosen from among the active business-men of Chicago, and are every one of them men who have made an honorable success of the pursuits which they have followed in finance, commerce and manufactures, and are giving their time and their best energies to the success of the Exposition. Their names are many of them known wherever American commerce has been permitted to extend, and I think it proper to add that they have been selected quite regardless of political affiliations, and that politics never has been and never will be considered in the management of the business of this corporation. (Applause.) The

Board of Directors is divided into thirteen standing committees having jurisdiction over the several departments of the commission and the directory, and all expenditures are directed and scrutinized by them as closely as is done in the private affairs of the best managed mercantile establishments. They know that they are charged with a great public trust, and having accepted its responsibilities will welcome investigation of their conduct of that trust to the last detail.

The jurisdiction of these two bodies, as to the details of the work, somewhat embarrassing at the outset, was settled by a compact between them and they are working together harmoniously and effectively. Under this compact fifteen grand departments were determined upon, the heads of which are appointed by the Director General, who is the executive officer of the commission, and all expenses, except the salary of the Director General, are paid by the World's Columbian Exposition Company.

WHAT WAS REQUIRED OF CHICAGO.

In order that the City of Chicago might enjoy the honor conferred upon her by having the Exposition located in her midst, she was required to furnish an adequate site acceptable to the National Commission and ten millions of dollars in money, which was, in the language of the act, considered necessary "for the complete preparation for said Exposition." This obligation the citizens of Chicago promptly met. (Applause.) The adequate site and $10,000,000 were provided, and on evidence thereof the President of the United States issued his proclamation inviting the nations of the earth to participate in the Exposition. The $10,000,000 is provided for, first, by subscriptions to the capital stock of the corporation in excess of $5,000,000, and a municipal appropriation by the City of Chicago of $5,000,000. Of the capital stock subscribed for 60 per cent. has been called, resulting in the payment into our treasury of $3,347,000. The city appropriation is available when required, and our first draft upon it for $1,000,000 will be paid February 1 next. The remaining 40 per cent. of stock subscriptions will be called whenever our increasing requirements make it necessary.

As the work has developed it has grown upon the comprehension of all engaged in it. The classification provided and the plan and scope as determined by the commission were so comprehensive that the $10,000,000 which Congress thought sufficient, and which Chicago has provided, has been found entirely inadequate to produce such an Exposition as was contemplated when the nations of the earth were invited to join us in celebrating the 400th anniversary of the discovery of America. The act of Congress specifically stipulates that "the buildings proposed to be erected shall be deemed by said commission adequate to the purposes of said Exposition." It is necessary, therefore, either to amend the classification and limit the scope determined upon by the commission, or largely exceed the amount deemed necessary by Congress when the Exposition was ordered. We believe the commissioners have acted wisely and with a due sense of their responsibility, and we have felt that the pride and patriotism of the people would justify them and protect us in producing such an Exposition as would do honor to the great event which we shall commemorate.

VAST SIZE OF THE EXPOSITION.

Every department of the Exposition will be produced on a scale greater than has ever been accomplished even where each was made the subject of a special exhibition. This is notably the case in the Departments of Agriculture, Transportation, Electricity, Mines and Mining, Horticulture, and the Department for Woman's Work. A large space has been accepted by the Government for its exhibit, and the buildings to be constructed will be such as will do credit to their surroundings. The Navy Department is building a model cruiser, which will appear to be afloat alongside the pier constructed for it off the shore of Lake Michigan. It has been said that the son in order to be as good as his father must be better, and we are justified in saying that an Exposition to be equal to those which have preceded it must excel them all. What has been done heretofore in other Expositions would not do for us. There were really no beaten paths to follow, no precedents to guide us, only a lofty purpose to make the Exposition worthy of the occasion and equal to the expectations of the Government that gave it being.

The Exposition grounds cover an area of 633 acres;

the buildings erected by the Exposition will cover 103 acres, and there will be approximately twelve acres covered by buildings not erected by the Exposition. The Exposition grounds have a frontage on Lake Michigan of 1 3-4 miles, and there is within the grounds, exclusive of lake frontage, five miles of docks and two and one-half miles of navigable watercourse, which during the Exposition will be perambulated by boats of every description for the pleasure and convenience of visitors. There are eleven main buildings, all of which have reached an advanced stage of construction, so that no doubt exists as to our ability to complete them in time for their dedication in October next as required by law. The largest building is about a mile around it, and its central aisle has a clear span of 368 feet and 206 feet high. The Machinery Hall of the Paris Exposition if placed within this aisle would have a space 6 feet wide on each side and 11 feet on each end, with 50 feet clear for ventilation above its roof. There will be used in the construction of this building 6,000 tons of iron and steel. These figures may mean much or little to you, but for the purpose of comparison I may state that the Eiffel Tower required but 7,000 tons, and only 3,000 tons were used in the Brooklyn Bridge, and 5,600 in the great railroad bridge at St. Louis. The heroic dimensions of all the buildings have only lately been realized as they have begun to loom up in their perfected outlines. The Exhibition buildings already planned, including annexes, require a consumption of 18,000 tons of iron and steel, and have a total floor-space of upward of 6,320,000 square feet, or 135 acres.

The buildings primarily projected, including landscape improvements, have all been contracted for at a saving of about $2,500,000 from the architects' estimates, but the growing necessities of the enterprise have required the erection of others not at first contemplated at a cost of about $1,900,000. For the protection of these buildings and their contents, and to supply fountains and all the daily requirements within the grounds, we have provided for a possible supply of 64,000,000 gallons of water daily, which will be carried through 20 miles of mains from six inches to three feet in diameter. Ten miles of these pipes are already laid, and power in place for pumping 3,000,000 gallons of water daily under pressure of 100 pounds per square foot. For supplying power for machinery, etc., we have provided for boilers having a water evaporating capacity equal to 25,000 horse-power, and engines for generating electricity, 18,000 horse-power; for driving line shafting and isolated exhibits, 2,000 horse-power; for compressed air, 3,000 horse-power; and for pumps, 2,000 horse-power. Electrical force will be supplied as power to the amount of 3,000 horse-power. The system of sewage projected will be extensive and complete. We are preparing for the treatment of 6,000,000 gallons of sewage every twenty-four hours, the precipitated matter of which will be burned and only clear water allowed to escape. The lighting of the grounds and buildings is estimated to require the use of 7,000 arc lights and 120,000 incandescent lamps.

THE BEST ARCHITECTURAL TALENT SECURED.

In planning the grounds and buildings we have employed the highest architectural genius in America, including three of the foremost artists of your own city. The Board of Architects, ten in number, first met in conference with Mr. Frederick L. Olmsted, our landscape architect, and agreed upon a general plan, each accepting an assignment of one grand building. The economy of the new material used by us for exterior covering has enabled us to give the the architects an open field for the exercise of their genius. When each had completed his individual plan further conferences were had, and all were made to harmonize without cost to the artistic beauty or individual worth of each. The result has been an ensemble of land and water, of nature and art, that in its completed state will, I believe, be more beautiful than anything yet created by the hand of man. (Applause.) We shall have no Eiffel Tower or other meretricious attractions to allure the multitude, but there will be no lack of entertaining features of a high order, and our grounds and buildings will be an exhibition in themselves. This exhibition of the genius of American architects will be a revelation to the world, and for years to come its beautiful forms will inspire students and its details will be copied wherever public buildings are erected. In the grand court in particular the glories of the Taj-Mahal will be eclipsed at every step, and your children's children will tell the traditions of its splendor. (Applause.)

The estimated cost of the completed structures, including landscape, statuary, fountains, terminal facilitics, police and fire stations, and all that may be necessary for the comfort and convenience of visitors, will be $15,117,500, exclusive of the cost of administration, which is estimated at $2,770,000, up to the opening of the Exposition, May 1, 1893.

The money contributed by Chicago to this great national enterprise is being expended with a view solely to the interests of the Exposition. Every contract has been let to the lowest bidder, regardless of where he hailed from. Competition has not been restricted to any section, and owing to our unsurpassed facilities for transportation from every direction contractors in all parts of the country from the Atlantic to the Pacific have had an equal opportunity with our own, and have availed themselves of it to such an extent that 31 per cent in numbers and 36 per cent in amount of all our contracts have been awarded outside of Chicago. Contracts have been let already in Philadelphia, New-York and Boston, in San Francisco, Seattle, and Omaha, in Minneapolis and Duluth, in Kansas City and St. Louis, in Leavenworth and Louisville, in Birmingham, Ala.; in Milwaukee, Detroit, Cleveland, and Pittsburg; in Wilmington, Del.; Plainfield, N. J.; Jackson, Mich., and in Stamford, Conn.; in Rome and Florence in Italy, in Paris, Constantinople, London, Edinburgh and Berlin. In keeping the workshops busy and labor satisfied in eighteen States are we not demonstrating that this is not a Chicago Fair, but is, as Congress intended it to be, a national and international enterprise? (Applause.) In exceeding the expenditure at first considered adequate for the purpose we feel that we have done our duty. We know that our completed work will satisfy the highest expectations of the people, and we believe that we are justified in asking of the Congress of the United States such assistance and recognition as the circumstances of the case demand. About $3,000,000 has been appropriated by the several States for their proper representation, and nearly $4,000,000 already by foreign governments.

THE RESPONSE FROM FOREIGN LANDS.

A year and a half ago we began our work in foreign fields, and knowing our ability to comply with all requirements made by Congress we anticipated the official invitation of the President of the United States by sending commissioners to the Far East, to Japan, the Orient and the Latin-American countries, and have the most gratifying reports from all. The official invitation of the President has been accepted by nearly every nation on the earth, and even in the few countries where there has been no official acceptance the individual interest and enterprise of the people are at work, so we apprehend that none will remain unrepresented. Mr. James Dredge, of the Royal Commission of Great Britain, accompanied by Sir Henry Wood, its secretary, and Herr Wermuth, of the Imperial Commission of Germany, have made personal visits to Chicago and returned home full of enthusiasm for the work. Nearly every nation in Europe has informed itself by the personal observations of official representatives who have approved of the preparations made by us, and will aid their people to make complete and artistic exhibits. The Latin-American Department, which was organized at an early date, has aroused enthusiastic interest in Mexico and all the South American Republics. The archaeological treasures of Old Mexico and Yucatan have been resurrected and the tombs of the Incas ransacked for the benefit of the great Exposition, and if we had nothing to show beyond the exhibits in this department we should still have a marvelous exhibition. (Applause.)

As to the exhibits from our own country we have no misgivings whatever; in fact, applications for space already received indicate that the large plant that we have provided may be inadequate for all who may desire to exhibit. This may result in such a pruning as will admit only the cream in all departments, and, at any rate, it justifies the extensive preparations which we have already made. It is our ambition, it is our purpose to make the Exposition in the highest and best sense educational. While the present stage of development of science and the arts will necessarily be represented on the largest scale, yet we shall not forget the beginnings of things. We expect the Exposition to be not simply a bazaar but an illustrated history of the progress of 400 years. And visitors to the Exposition will not be limited to the consideration of material things. The World's Congress Auxiliary, organized by our directory, has for its motto "Not Things but Men." Its object is to provide for the proper representation of the intellectual and moral progress of the world by the consideration of living questions by the leaders in all the chief departments of human achievement. The series of congresses will continue through the Exposition, and will, we be-

lieve, invite the thinking men and women of every land to its councils. These discussions will be largely engaged in by women, and in the gatherings of the brightest intellects of the world they will have a grand opportunity of demonstrating their leadership in the moral and social reforms and the educational advancement of the race.

TO SHOW WHAT WOMEN HAVE DONE.

The Woman's Department as organized by the Board of Lady Managers is something quite unique in Expositions, and will be presented on a scale that would be impossible of attainment in any country but our own. More than a generation ago the Sage of Concord said that it was a chief felicity of our country that it excelled in women. (Applause.) What was true then is a thousand times true now. There is nothing more significant in the progress of our civilization than the great increase of the opportunities in every field of endeavor that is open to women. The Woman's Building in the great Exposition, now nearly completed, was planned by a woman architect, is embellished with sculpture and art designed by women and will contain an exhibit of woman's work that will be a marvel to all visitors. It will be a brilliant object lesson to all the world in what is being accomplished by women in the world's work, and a revelation of the extent to which she has become more than a helpmate to man. (Applause.)

The buildings of the Exposition must, according to the act of Congress, be dedicated October 12 next, on the four hundredth anniversary of Columbus's discovery. We shall be ready, and the programme of ceremonies for the occasion, to continue through four days, is already nearly complete. But the gates of the Exposition will not open till the first of May following and the ceremonies precedent to that occasion will take place in New-York. Congress has provided for a grand naval review in April, 1893, in your beautiful harbor, to which the President has invited the navies of the world. That grand pageant is not permitted to us, but we know that it could not be in better hands and will be worthy of your great city and State. (Applause.)

A TRIBUTE TO NEW-YORK.

New-York has been accused of apathy in this great work and of a lack of civic pride and enterprise which I do not believe is warrantable. I have never met the individual New-Yorker whose aims were not as high, whose public spirit was not as great as that of a citizen of any other city, and what is true of the individual must be representative of the community. It only requires the focalizing effort of a company like this to demonstrate the fact that New-York is not lacking in that civic energy that made Athens famous; that made Venice mistress of the seas and arbiter of the destinies of empires for centuries; that made Rome ruler of the world, and that is building up, a thousand miles from here on an inland sea, the commercial metropolis of this continent. (Applause.)

I believe my enthusiasm does not outrun my judgment when I say your citizens will have no grander opportunity than the present to demonstrate their patriotic public spirit in helping on a great National enterprise. It would be worth many times $5,000,000 to this dear land of ours if every generation of Americans could rally around some sentiment, some grand idea, not of war, that would unite the East and the West, the North and the South in enthusiastic accord. The dangers of sectionalism could then never threaten the stability of our institutions, and the man of New-York or of San Francisco, of New-Orleans or Chicago would lose nothing of loyalty to his city or section by being first of all an American. The people of France were united in their enthusiasm for the last great Exposition, and the value of its success to the City of Paris cannot be compared with the gain to France. Such an opportunity is presented to our people in the World's Columbian Exposition. There will be presented in friendly emulation the best results in four centuries of human progress, in which this people if unified will have the lion's share. If we are actuated by the proper spirit of national enthusiasm there is no question but what the Exposition will demonstrate our commanding position as leaders in the arts of peace before all the world.

JOHN BOYD THACHER'S SPEECH.

Here is what Commissioner John Boyd Thacher said:

Our nation is charged with the celebration of the Columbian discovery because we have best enjoyed its heritage. That discovery was meant for mankind. Two events first catch our eye in the four hundred years of authentic history made in the New World. The one is the planting of the cross on Watling's Island in 1492. The other is the planting of the standard of American liberty in Philadelphia in 1776. (Applause.) The two events were remote from each other in time and distant in scene. The actors were of different blood. The first not only made the second possible, but determined its action.

It is with the chief actor in the first event that we have to do just now. What manner of man is this our Columbus? We have of him four and forty distinct portraits. Each is a type. No two of these resemble each other. He is in mail and in silken hose; he is mild and he is fierce: he is freckled like a country lad and he is bearded like the pard; he has the bewildered look of one who never had a compass, and he has the eye through which alone destiny looks. You and I can draw him as we like. If your Columbus is only a searcher after shining gold, he is a splendid wretch. If your Columbus is only a capturer of harmless heathen to drag them after the car of religion, he is a pious trifler. A man is no better than he makes his heroes. The God who makes men and who uses men never intrusted a great purpose to a mean soul. (Applause.) The bearer may not fully know the weighty business on which he goes, but something of its meaning shines upon him and from his tempered visage enforces homage. The lonely Genoese pacing the deck of his caravel, watching for a land, and no land from day to day, must have had a glimpse of the new hemisphere and visions of its destiny. And so your Christopher Columbus and mine is, as his name implies, the anointed bearer of a blessing for mankind, a preparer and and an opener of a new world in which man should be free from his brother, true to himself and obedient to his Maker. (Applause.) It is such a man about whose statue we are to walk at this exposition. It is the tree of his planting which we are to consider as we eat of its fruits. No section, no State, no Chicago can hug this blessing to its single bosom. It is for us all. Let all the people participate in its enjoyment. (Applause.)

We do not deny our disappointment when the World's Fair winged a westward flight. We know that if the unities had been consulted neither New-York nor Chicago would have been selected, but the celebration of the great discovery would have been beneath Southern skies and where the ocean sea washes the true Guanhani. We claimed the celebration in New-York because we were the supreme city of the western hemisphere. We have lost the Fair, but our city has relinquished nothing of her supremacy. It will be mock humility now if we offer to tear down our huts to build Chicago's palace. Rather let us rejoice that we are great and strong, and that out of our fulness we may aid our sister city of the West. (Applause.) Chicago deserves our support. She has won our admiration. (Applause.) To raise ten millions of money for a sentimental purpose is a task which any metropolis might approach with hesitation. Chicago has accomplished this in a few short weeks. Our blood runs faster as we recognize this magnificent courage. and we would share in her labor that we may justly share in her glory. Nothing pertaining to humanity is foreign to the true man. We are one people. one family. When prosperity spreads her sheltering wings in the East, the West is safe and happy. When in the West the fields of grain stretch far and wide, we in the East eat bread without scarceness. (Applause.)

Chicago does not come to us with an offertory basket in her hand. She comes bringing us a flag with the colors of the World's Columbian Exposition upon its bright folds. She asks us to wave it in token of friendship and a common interest. Let the noble contention between us be from this hour which shall bear this flag furthest in its march of triumph and which voice shall loudest proclaim its glory. (Applause.)

GORTON W. ALLEN'S ADDRESS.

Commissioner Gorton W. Allen made the following remarks:

That the World's Columbian Exposition is to be an unparalleled success may as well be regarded as assured. Not because the commissioners with the local directory are of themselves able to achieve so desirable a result by their combined wisdom and enterprise, stimulated by a degree of enthusiasm that repels all thought of apprehension of failure, but because the World's Fair Exposition is the formulated expression of the universal wish of the American people. (Applause.) It goes without saying that that universal wish is, when formulated, a specific against any tendency in the direction of failure. True, we admit the word failure in our dictionaries, but it is most commonly employed as one of the extremes in human endeavor from which we measure upward actually to discover the distance between achievement and failure. The enterprise is not seeking friends for the obvious reason that it has no enemies at home or in foreign lands. (Applause.)

If there has been in the past any suspicion or doubt as to the loyal and liberal spirit of the Empire State and its chief city, in any and every way or manner, to the end that the Exposition shall be crowned with success, there is none now. Much as our people would have been delighted had the generous offer of the metropolis been accepted, the failure to secure the location has never for an instant provoked or suggested the slightest feeling of retaliation, jealousy or envy. (Applause.) On the contrary our people would be more likely to contribute more generously lest their failure to fulfil the largest expectation of Chicago should be attributed to disappointment. Do you ask me what New-York contemplates doing in aid of the Exposition? I reply that she will occupy a conspicuous place upon the site chosen, and will undoubtedly construct a building quite commensurate to the necessities of its citizens who propose to patronize the Exposition as exhibitors and visitors. Its capacity will be ample; its architectural finish will be in harmony with and not inferior to the buildings of any other State. I assure you whatever is necessary for New-York to do to accommodate her people will, I have no doubt, be done, and done as promptly as the Governor and the Legislature can be duly advised by competent authority of what is needed.

A SUGGESTION FOR GOVERNOR FLOWER.

And now, addressing myself more especially to the citizens of New-York, it occurs to me that His Excellency Governor Flower should be requested, by enactment of our Legislature, to appoint a commission, consisting of such number as should be deemed adequate, to visit the city of Chicago, and, in connection with the World's Fair Commissioners from this State, ascertain the needs of New-York State exhibitors and visitors, and, with all needful information, report to the Governor with recommendation as to the amount of appropriation deemed necessary to provide for the needs of the people, and suitably to represent the character and greatness of this great Commonwealth. In that way the Governor and Legislature can be promptly and adequately advised, and be able intelligently to provide appropriate legislation. Legislative provision for New-York's exhibitors and visitors without such information would in all probability result in grievous disappointment. So much for New-York State.

More important than any other purely financial question is that which relates to aid from the general Government to promote the Columbian Exposition. My views upon this subject are very decided, after much reflection. That the Exposition is in need of and must have financial aid, and that with reasonable promptness, is quite beyond the realm of controversy or question. I venture to assume that the general Government will give heed to the necessity of the case, and grant the required aid in some form. But in what form? That an adequate loan of any required amount can be secured from the Government by the pledge of the revenue of the Exposition, derived from the admission of the visitors, for the payment of the debt, at such time and manner and under such regulations as may be determined upon, is feasible, and without doubt it can be accomplished. It can be easily demonstrated that such security would be ample to indemnify the Government against loss or hazard, and if so it may be safely assumed that such aid would be easily within reach.

OPPOSED TO A GIFT FROM THE GOVERNMENT.

It has been suggested by some and by others urged that the Government should be requested to make an appropriation of the public money in aid of the Exposition—a gift as distinguished from a loan. This proposition, I am assured, will meet with decided opposition, and justly so, in my judgment. Many reasons will be urged against this method of relief, but of them all I refer to but one, and that will be held sufficient.

It has not passed out of the memory of the general public that when the question of locating the place for the World's Columbian Exposition was before Congress New-York State was a vigorous bidder for the contested honor and prize, and she came with an indemnity backed by her millionaires, unquestioned and unquestionable, undertaking to assume all financial burdens and responsibilities, and to preserve the general Government harmless in any emergency. Who doubts for a moment that that undertaking would have been faithfully kept? Who doubts that the city and State of New-York would have, with prodigal hand, made ample provision for all exhibitors, foreign and domestic, out of their own purse?

It has not passed out of the mind of the general public that Chicago came valiantly (and, as I believe, sincerely) to the front and promised to do at least all that the citizens of New-York promised to do, and exhibited the evidences of their ability so to do. (Applause.) No one then doubted that Chicago meant what she proposed. No one doubted that the promoters of the Chicago interest were able and intended at all hazards to keep the faith then pledged. (Applause.) Who believes now that Chicago would have been successful in that memorable yet friendly struggle, if there had been a doubt of her ability to perform what she undertook?

Were I a resident of Chicago I would repel any propositions for aid from the general Government, except in the form of a loan, secured as I have before outlined. Her fair name should not be compromised, neither her wealth nor greatness belittled by the failure to keep her promise, which won for her the prestige and honor of being the city chosen by authority of the general Government as the fittest and best-equipped for entertaining the Nation's guests while attending the greatest exposition of the achievements in the world's industries of the nineteenth century. Whatever else may be done to secure financial aid and relief, let not this be done. (Applause.)

REMARKS OF CHARLES S. SMITH.

Here is the speech of Charles S. Smith:

Mr. Chairman: I was one of the World's Fair Committee of 100 named by Mayor Grant, and also a member of the Finance Committee which did some preliminary work in securing the five-million subscription preparatory to our unsuccessful attempt to secure the Columbian Fair for New-York. We made a good fight for this city at Washington and were fairly and squarely beaten. When I heard that Chicago had won the prize, I heaved a sigh of relief and said I was glad of it, and ever since then I have been in the condition of the German in "the lager beer case." Some thirty or forty years before the qualities of that healthful and invigorating beverage were generally known to other than our German fellow-citizens, who were just introducing it in this country, a license case came before our courts, in which the question was raised if lager beer was intoxicating, and expert witnesses were called. The judge asked a portly German if a man could get drunk on lager. "Oh, nein, nein," was the reply, "I take five, ten, fifteen or twenty glasses in an evening and feel gooder and gooder all the viles." (Laughter.) Now, Mr. Chairman, I think there are a good many citizens of New-York who agree with me in feeling under great obligations to our Chicago friends for having relieved us of our immense task.

I want to contribute a few words to the truth of history regarding New-York's loss of the Fair. I admit readily that there are in both political parties some narrow-minded men who want to secure a party advantage on all questions, public and private, but I am glad after all the newspaper discussion as to the political aspect of the decision regarding the location of the Fair to say that, in my judgment, there was very little politics in it. (Applause.) Mayor Grant nominated a committee that was universally satisfactory, and it was one of the rules laid down for the finance committee that not a dollar should be appropriated or paid without their consent, and if any man thinks that Samuel D. Babcock, the late August Belmont, J. Pierpont Morgan and their associates on that committee could be influenced by political considerations in the administration of a great trust fund, I am sorry for his judgment. The truth is, it was a case of local option. The majority of the voting power in the National House of Representatives reside west of the lakes, and

they decided to use all their influence to secure the Fair for a Western city, and they got the votes.

ACTION OF THE MERCHANTS.

We had a meeting a few days ago at the Merchants' Club, composed mainly of downtown dry-goods men. As I was formerly a member of that fraternity, and as I took part in that meeting, it would not perhaps be modest in me to suggest that you could hardly do better than to indorse the wise action of the Merchants' Club regarding the co-operation of our city and State, for the dry-goods men both in New-York and Chicago are considered a wise body of men, and they generally accomplish what they undertake. (Applause.) We drafted a bill asking our State Legislature to appropriate $500,000 for the Chicago Fair, and we expect to have that bill passed and signed by the Governor. (Applause.)

Now, Mr. Chairman, we argued at the meeting I have referred to that the Columbian Fair was entitled to the hearty support of the citizens of the State of New-York on two distinct grounds: First, of patriotic sentiment; and second, of self-interest. I stated at our meeting that I had attended all the World's Fairs excepting the one in Vienna, and that the United States exhibit at all these fairs, excepting only the one at Philadelphia, was absolutely humiliating, if not a positive disgrace to our country. At the last and the greatest of all the international expositions, the late one at Paris, Edison alone half-redeemed our fame, and gave us the only exhibition which was at all worthy of the Nation. We are the largest producers of silk fabrics in the western world, excepting France, and yet we did not show a sample of silk, and in plain silk we produce an article equal to the best made in Lyons. (Applause.) We are the largest producers of carpets in the world, and in design and quality of the grade we make we are excelled by none, and yet we did not show a sample of carpet; in pile fabrics in general we were not as well represented as we often are at any ordinary state fair. Even in machinery, where we had no adequate representation, the masses in Europe had reason to conclude that we in the United States are principally producers of raw materials, with little skill in all the higher grades of manufacturing. We have some reputation abroad for sewing and reaping machines and for locomotives, but we have never challenged the attention of the world by any proper show of our ability and progress in any of our diversified industries. We must change all this by making the Chicago World's Fair creditable and representative of the high position of the United States. Then New-York City and state have almost if not quite as large a pecuniary interest in the success of the Columbian Exhibition as have Chicago and the State of Illinois.

NEW-YORK'S INTEREST IN THE FAIR.

No city, town or hamlet in this broad land can prosper without a considerable portion of that prosperity being reflected in this city and State. All foreign visitors and exhibits come through the port of New-York and our hotels and shops and railways will have all they can do during the Chicago Fair. We shall have our full share of the gains without the trouble of the Fair. Besides, as a matter of business, Chicago has with our city the largest and most intimate commercial relations of any city in our country. She is our best customer, and the great heart of New-York is too noble, too generous, to entertain any miserable jealousy of the Western progress and success. (Applause.) All commercial and financial roads in the United States lead to New-York. There is no great business establishment or corporation in any of the states of this country that is not obliged to have an office in this city, and so, Mr. Chairman, let us insist that New-York State shall do her whole duty toward Chicago in this matter. In 1775 Burke, in a great speech in the House of Commons, referring to a boy then only eight or ten years old, and assuming that he might have a long life, said: "Young man, there is America, which at this day only serves to amuse you with stories of savage men and uncouth manners; it shall, before you taste death, show itself equal to the whole of that commerce which now attracts the envy of the world. Whatever England has been growing to by a succession of civilizing conquests and civilizing settlements in a series of 1,700 years, you shall see as much accomplished by America in the course of a single life." (Applause.)

Mr. Chairman, to prove that Burke was a prophet of far-reaching vision, I have only to mention that the foreign commerce of the United States for the year ending June 30, 1891, was exclusive of gold, $1,729,-296,000. (Long-continued applause.)

JEFFERSON ON THE DRAMA.

THE VETERAN COMEDIAN TALKS CHARM-INGLY CONCERNING HIS ART.

AN ADDRESS DELIVERED AT YALE COLLEGE— AN ANSWER TO THE DONNELLY BACON-IAN THEORY.

New-Haven, April 27 (Special).—Joseph Jefferson, the veteran comedian, spoke at Yale College this evening on the subject of Dramatic Art. His address, which was full of personal reminiscences and treated the subject in an extremely agreeable and interesting manner, was listened to with close attention and evident enjoyment by a large audience.

Mr. Jefferson spoke as follows:

In my present condition I feel that I strangely resemble the village boy of New-Hampshire. It was proposed that in this same village a schoolhouse should be erected. One of the Solons who had been perhaps the oldest inhabitant, strongly opposed this barbarous introduction, and in his own simple words said: "We don't want no book larnin' in this place. I'm agin it, my wife's agin it and we'll both vote agin it, for 'tain't no account and takes a boy from his nat'ral work and chores e'en a-most as much as goin' a-fishin'. Why, there was a boy in this village years ago, as likely a young fellow as anybody ever stuck a knife into. What was his name, now? Oh, Webster. Yes, Daniel Webster. He was a peart, snappy boy, but he got it into his head that he must have book larnin'. Well, he went up to Boston, got his book larnin' and nobody ever heard on him agin."

Now, though I resemble Daniel Webster about as little in personal appearance as I do intellectually, I still fancy that I may bear a likeness to him in this one particular instance, that after I have finished my discourse in the presence of so much "book larnin'," nobody will ever hear of me again.

Charles Lamb has said that the world is divided into two classes; those who are born to borrow and those who are born to lend. If you should happen to belong to the latter class, then do it cheerfully. So do I think that the world is divided into two other parts; those who are born to entertain by their oratory and those who are not. But if you belong to the latter class, as I fear I may, do it cheerfully. Making a speech cheerfully, however, and making a cheerful speech are two very different matters.

I think it quite likely that many who are here naturally associate me with the characters I have acted upon the stage. You will possibly, therefore, recognize my voice and manner as connected with those imaginary persons, the valorous Mr. Acres or fighting Bob; Rip Van Winkle, that disreputable vagabond of the Catskills, or that grand old impostor, Dr. Pangloss, LL. P. and A. S. S. If you have derived in times gone by any entertainment from these familiar characters, you must bear in mind that in acting them I was assisted by costume, scenery and the presence of excellent performers, who surrounded me and shared for a time your attention; and besides these important auxiliaries, I had the advantage of speaking the superb and witty lines of Sheridan, Colman, Boucicault and Washington Irving. Mark the difference! I am now thrown upon my own resources, and in this impoverished condition stand before you, not as an interesting imaginary character, created by the brilliant genius of these immortals of the past, but as a mere piece of uncertain humanity, who is doubtful, in his present novel position, whether he will sink or swim.

THE ACTOR PLEADS HIS OWN CAUSE.

You will then, I am sure, admit that in presenting myself before you as an orator, I have risked whatever reputation I may have gained as an actor. And as I am now on trial for this misdemeanor, it is but fair that I should plead my own cause. I propose, therefore, to turn "State's evidence," and unmask my accomplice. During my last visit to New-Haven, a deep-laid scheme was planned by which this august body was to be assaulted in open daylight, and I was chosen for the deadly work—being considered as a fit instrument of torture. You will be surprised to know that my confederate and the principal conspirator in this plot is now in the midst of this assembly, and, I fear, exulting over the widespread desolation he has wrought. If, therefore, you judge me guilty of this assassination of your time and patience, I beg you will visit your condemnation on my partner in crime, Professor John F. Weir, for in this dire scheme he is the anarchist, whilst I am only the dynamite.

Having now made a full and complete confession and placed my accomplice in the hands of justice, I feel free to proceed with my nefarious work.

I have just alluded to an actor wandering from the especial walks of his art and posing as an orator. Many actors have wondered why they have failed as readers, and quite a number who have succeeded upon the rostrum are surprised that they have failed upon the stage. Fanny Kemble and James E. Murdoch are the only actors I can call to mind who have succeeded as readers. These exceptions are sufficiently limited to prove the rule, and for the reason that peculiar qualities that are required in an actor are at variance with those which are desirable for an orator. Of course, there are some attributes that belong to each: voice, gesture, a fine articulation, presence, dignity, repose—all of these are necessary to both, but here is the great distinction: an orator impresses his audience by what he says to them. An actor is often most effective when he shows how he is impressed by what is said to him. No one talks back to the orator! He has it all to himself. He is only heard. He never listens. An actor who does not know how to listen has half of h's art to learn. When Cassio is rebuked by Othello, he must show how he is crushed by the justice of that rebuke. When Romeo breathes his love for Juliet, she betrays her ecstacy while listening to his passionate speech. You will see that this is no part of oratory. The orator is dictatorial. He is not made to listen, therefore, he is not created to act. For instance, I would consider Mr. Levy, the cornet player, an orator in music. In his solo he would be grand and impressive, but in an orchestra he would be a nuisance—for every man is a nuisance who is continually blowing his own horn.

ORATORY NOT DISPARAGED.

I beg you will not for a moment think that I disparage oratory. On the contrary, it is a glorious gift. I only mean to draw the distinction between the rostrum and the stage. Acting has been called, erroneously, I think, one of the mimic arts. I do not consider that good of any kind is displayed by mimicry. It is generally conceded that imitators are seldom fine actors, though they are usually great favorites with the public. I confess that I enjoy the exhibitions of this kind of talent exceedingly. There is something very attractive and even strange to see one man display the voice, manner and expression of another—particularly if that other be not yourself. We may enjoy the imitation of our dearest friends, but our smiles vanish and our faces elongate if the mimic attempts to give "a counterfeit presentment" of the party of the first part. I have heroically tried on several occasions to enjoy imitations of myself, but have never succeeded.

These ingenious transcripts contain a slight touch of ridicule that always offends the original.

An anecdote of Mr. Buckstone, the English comedian, will serve to illustrate what I have said. At the close of a dinner party he had been given to understand that there was a person present who gave an excellent imitation of himself. Buckstone at once desired the gentleman to let the company have a test of his quality. The gentleman politely declined, saying that he might give offence; but the comedian would not let him off, insisted on the exhibition, and rubbing his hands together in great glee settled himself down for unlimited enjoyment. The imitator, seeing that there was no escape, arose and amid breathless silence begun. His hit was immense, and as he sat down the guests broke forth in loud laughter and applause; the whole table was in a roar of merriment; every one was in ecstasy except Buckstone, who looked the picture of misery.

"Well, Mr. Buckstone," exclaimed a wag, who was quietly enjoying the comedian's discomfiture, "don't you think the imitation very fine?"

"It may be," he replied, "but I think I could do it better myself."

Acting is more a gift than an art. I have seen a child impress an audience by its natural grace and magnetism. The little creature was too young to know what art meant, but it had the gift of acting. The great value of art, when applied to the stage, is that it enables the performer to reproduce the gift, and so move his audience night after night, even though he has acted the same character a thousand times. In fact, we cannot act a character too often, if we do not lose interest in it. But when its constant repetition palls on the actor, it will as surely weary his audience. When you lose interest—stop acting.

A STORY OF MACREADY.

This loss of interest on the part of an actor may not be visible in the action or pantomime; but unless care and judgment are observed it will assuredly betray itself in the delivery of the language, and more particularly in the long speeches and soliloquies. In dialogue the spirit of the other actors serves to stimulate and keep him up; but when alone, and unaided by the eye and presence of a companion, the old story fails to kindle the fire. An anecdote of Macready that I heard many years ago throws a flood of light upon this subject, and as I think it too important a one to remain in obscurity, I will relate it as I got it from Mr. Couldock, and then refer to its influence upon myself and the means I used to profit by it. The incident occurred in Birmingham, England, some forty years ago. The narrator was present and naturally listened with interest to a conversation upon art between two such able exponents of it as Mr. Macready and Mrs. Warner. What they said referred to an important scene in the tragedy of "Werner," which had been acted the evening before. Mr. Macready, it seems, had much respect for Mrs. Warner's judgment in matters relating to the stage, and desired to consult with her on the merits and demerits of the preceding evening's performance. As nearly as can be remembered, his question and her reply were as follows:

"My dear madam," said Macready, "you have acted with me in the tragedy of 'Werner' for many years, and naturally must be very familiar with it and with my manner of acting that character. I have noticed lately, and more particularly last evening, that some of the passages in the play do not produce the effect they formerly did. There is a certain speech especially that seems to have lost its power. I refer to the one wherein Werner excuses himself to his son for the 'petty plunder' of Strulenheim's gold. In our earlier performances, if you remember, this apology was received with marked favor, and, as you must have observed last evening, it produced no apparent effect. Can you form any idea why this should be? Is it that the audience has grown too familiar with the story? I must beg you to be candid with me. I shall not be offended by any adverse criticism you may make, should you say that the fault is with me."

"Well, Mr. Macready, since you desire that I should speak plainly," said Mrs. Warner, "I do not think it is because your audience is too familiar with the story, but because you are too familiar with it yourself."

"I thank you, madam," said Macready, "but how does this mar the effect of the speech?"

"Thus," said Mrs. Warner. "When you spoke that speech ten years ago there was a surprise in your face as though you then only realized what you had done. You looked shocked and bewildered, and in a forlorn way seemed to cast about for words that would excuse the crime; and all this with a depth of feeling and sincerity that would naturally come from an honest man who had been for the first time in his life accused of theft."

"That is as it should be given," said Macready. "And now, madam?"

"You speak it," said his frank critic, "like one who has committed a great many thefts in his life, and whose glib excuses are so pat and frequent that he is neither shocked, surprised nor abashed at the accusation."

"I thank you, madam," said the old actor. "The distinction may appear at first as a nice one, but there is much in it."

MR. JEFFERSON EXAMINES HIMSELF.

When I heard that story from Mr. Couldock it struck me with much force. I knew then that I had been unconsciously falling into the same error, and I felt that the fault would increase rather than diminish with time if I could not hit upon some method to check it. I began by listening to each important question as though it had been given me for the first time, turning the query over in my mind and then answering it, even at times hesitating as if for want of words to frame the reply. I will admit that this is dangerous ground and apt to render one slow and prosy; in fact, I was accused, and I dare say quite justly, of pausing too long. This, of course, was the other extreme and had to be looked to, so that it became necessary that the pauses should, by the manner and pantomime, be made sufficiently interesting not to weary an audience; so I summed it up somewhat after the advice of Mr. Lewes—to take time without appearing to take time.

Pantomimic action, unless it is in perfect harmony with the scene, is fatal to the effect of a delicate point. If the situation be a violent one, such as the preparation for battle in "Richard," or where Hamlet's uncle rises from his seat in the play scene, dismissing the audience, the situation being pronounced and the action strong, indifferent pantomime on the part of the actor might not be noticed in the bustle and excitement. But, to exemplify my meaning, let us take a point where the audience is called upon, not for enthusiastic applause, but for rapt attention; where the situation is so subtle that the head bowed slowly down, or a movement of the eye, will reveal the meaning. Now, at this critical point, if one of the actors should even remove his hat, or unmeaningly shift his position, he will destroy the effect. The finer the acting the more easily the effect is destroyed, just as a scratch will disfigure a polished surface that would not show on the face of a cobblestone. The audience cannot look in two places at once; the eye is such a tyrant that it distracts from the subject "then necessary to be considered," directing the attention to a useless and intrusive movement. The value of repose is so great that it is difficult to estimate it.

THE ART OF DOING NOTHING ON THE STAGE.

At rehearsal the amateur, having finished his speech, invariably asks the stage manager what he shall do next. As soon as he ceases to be the interesting figure, he should observe the action of the other characters; this is the most natural by-play and the least likely to do harm. It acts like the distance in a picture, which, by being subdued, gives strength to the foreground. But the tyro is generally fearful that he will fail to attract attention, whereas obscurity instead of prominence may at that time be most desirable. To do nothing upon the stage seems quite simple, but some people never acquire this negative capacity. It is David's speech (in "The Rivals") that terrifies Acres. How could an audience get the full value of what David says if they were looking at the face of Acres? The two characters would conflict with each other, and so rob the picture of clearness. But if Acres here will subdue his personality and sink, as it were, into the background, the audience will get the full force of what David says and become as perfectly saturated with its meaning as Acres himself. Now see how fully they are prepared to receive the expression of fear from the latter. After David's scene is over, Acres has the audience at full command—the slightest suggestion from him is taken up at once. They know his character and realize his position as vividly as he does himself; it is because they have had the full and uninterrupted benefit of the previous scene. If, during David's speech, I, as Acres, show my face to the audience or pull out my handkerchief and weep, I might gain a temporary advantage, but I should weaken David, and in the end mar the effect of my own character; and, believe me, an audience is always grateful to an actor who directs its attention in the right way. The traveller thanks the truthful finger-post, but never forgives the rascal who has misdirected him.

Nothing in art is more distressing than to see an actor attract the attention of the audience from an interesting point in the performance by the introduction of some unimportant by-play. At times this is done from ignorance, but, I regret to say, often through jealousy. This unfair spirit reflects back upon the guilty party, for the public resents it quietly while the offender least suspects it; their enjoyment has been marred, and the obnoxious cause of it has only consoled them by a display of unmeaning activity; they refuse this rubbish and inwardly mark the individual who has the impertinence to offer it. But, as two pigs under a gate make more noise than one, it is still worse to see a pair of ranters or a couple of buffoons trying to outdo each other. There is but one recompense; they are both self-slaughtered in the conflict.

As two spent swimmers that do cling together,
And choke their art.

THE PRESENT CONDITION OF THE STAGE.

I was present some time ago when there was quite an interesting conversation in relation to the stage. Many subjects were discussed and I was interrogated on a point which is of some importance. If I remember rightly the question put to me was this:

"Do you consider the stage in a better condition now than it was formerly? say from one to two hundred years ago?"

I replied that I thought the question was leading me a long way back, and that though I might with justice lay claim to a lengthened dramatic experience, the date mentioned was rather before my time. But if I am to reason from my knowledge and engraft it on the history of the past, I would unhesitatingly declare that the stage is in a much better condition now than it ever was before. The social and moral status of the whole world has undoubtedly improved, and gone hand in hand with scientific and material progress, and permit me to assure you that the stage in this respect has not been idle, but that, to my knowledge, it has in the march of improvement kept pace foot by foot with every social advance.

Even the coarse dramas of the olden time were in keeping with the conditions of the social and literary society that surrounded it. Those plays that appealed to the lowest tastes were not only welcome but demanded by the court of Charles. Old Pepys, who lived during this time, says in his diary: "I went last night to see 'A Midsummer Night's Dream'; it was a great waste of time, and I hope I shall never again be condemned to see such a poor play. Ah, give me a comedy of Ethelridge, and let us have no more of this dull, vague Shakespeare." It was not, therefore, that there were no good plays, but that the vicious public wanted bad ones, and while rakes and unprincipled gallants and vile women were the heroes and heroines of the stage, the plays of Shakespeare had been written for a hundred years. Such lovely creatures as Rosalind, Desdemona, Beatrice, Ophelia, Imogene, Portia and Juliet, together with their noble mates, Orlando, Benedict, Hamlet, Romeo, and a host of pure and marvellous creations were moulding on the shelves, because the managers had suffered bankruptcy for daring to produce them. Shakespeare says that the actors are "the abstract and brief chronicles of the times." And so the people insisted that the actors should give them an exhibition of the licentious times rather than the splendid lessons of Shakespeare. As the social world improved in its tastes the drama followed it—nay, in some instances has led it.

SHAKESPEARE OR BACON AGAIN.

There is a matter vitally connected with the stage to which I may call your attention. We are told that in every decade the shoremen that live on Long Island are stirred up with a desire to hunt for the secreted treasures of the late lamented Captain Kid, and it seems that the world has periodical attacks of a solemn question, "Did Shakespeare or Bacon write the plays that for many centuries have enlightened the English-speaking world?"

It has been said that a female descendant of Bacon at one time went so far as to try to break into the tomb of Shakespeare with a crowbar, in the hopes of finding some manuscript that would reveal the fact that her respected ancestor was the rightful heir to the fame of which Shakespeare was supposed to have robbed him. Lately a new theorist has appeared in the person of the Hon. Ignatius Donnelly. This gentleman has written a work entitled the "Great Cryptogram," in which he emphatically denies that Shakespeare wrote those plays, and insists that Bacon was their author. I am not a fair critic of the work, as I have only had extracts from it. Argument is something extremely potent. It was once proved by an ingenious writer that Napoleon never existed, but the gentleman forgot to prove that Napoleon didn't die. Surely, if he died, he must have lived.

Now, the work of Mr. Ignatius Donnelly certainly proves that Bacon wrote the plays, but it doesn't prove that Shakespeare didn't. In the first volume, the question is asked in conspicuous head-lines: "Where are the copies of the plays?" and I must admit that it is most remarkable that no scrap of paper has ever been found in his handwriting that would prove his authorship. But if the loss or destruction of the manuscript has any weight against Shakespeare's having written the plays, does it not also stand with the same force against Bacon? According to this logic, no one wrote the plays. If we accept such theories, in what a maze we are left. Under this belief, we not only lose our Shakespeare, but we do not even save our Bacon. While I respect the author's research (for all desire to unmask imposture and lay bare the truth is most commendable), I beg to reply to him:

MR. JEFFERSON'S ANSWER TO MR. DONNELLY.

Respected member of the Bar and State;
In Law and Literature profoundly great;
As you have thrust at an immortal name,
I claim the right of parrying the same.
For though I'm neither skilled in Law or Science,
The gauntlet you've thrown down in bold defiance,
(Espousing Bacon's cause armed cap-a-pie,)
I here take up to have a tilt with thee.
You pose before me as the great "I am,"
And flourish forth that deadly cryptogram;
That curious volume, mystic and misleading,
Co-jointly with your case of special pleading.
But I defy them both, for good or ill,
And stand the champion of "immortal Will."
So shall my sword upon thine own impinge,
"The croaking Raven bellows forth 'Revenge.'"
The Actor doth the Lawyer here oppose,
The sock and buskin for the woolsack goes.
Lay on, Macduff,
With all your legal stuff
And damned be he
Who first cries, "Hold! enough."
Stay: Ere we come to blows, with main and might,
I beg to scan the ground on which we fight.
The question's this, if I am not mistaken,

"Did Shakespeare or did Francis Bacon,
Inspired by genius and by learning too,
Compose the wondrous works we have in view?"
The scholar Bacon was a man of knowledge,
But inspiration isn't taught at college.
With all the varied gifts in Will's possession
The wondering world asks, "What was his profession?"
Ho must have been a lawyer, says the lawyer;
He surely was a sawyer, says the sawyer;
The druggist says of course he was a chemist;
The skilled mechanic dubs him a machinist;
The thoughtful sage declares him but a thinker,
And every tinman swears he was a tinker.
If Shakespeare was so poor a piece of stuff,
How is it Bacon trusted him enough
To throw these valued treasures at his feet
And not so much as ask for a receipt?
Such confidence is almost a monstrosity
And speaks of unexampled generosity.
Oh, liberal Francis, tell us why we find
Pope calling thee the "meanest of mankind"?
But now to Shakespeare let us turn, I pray,
And hear what h's companions have to say.
First then. Ben Jonson, jealous of Will's wit,
Paid tribute when his epitaph he writ.
If other proofs are wanting than Rare Ben's
We will consult forthwith a group of friends.
Awake! Beaumont and Fletcher, Spenser, Rowe,
Arise! and tell us, for you surely know:
Was, or was not, my client the great poet?
And if he wasn't don't you think you'd know it?
These his companions. brother playwrights mind,
Could they be hoodwinked? Were they deaf or blind?

I find it stated to our bard's discredit—
And 'tis the author of the Cryptogram who said it—
That Shakespeare's tastes were vulgar and besotted,
And all his fam'ly have been allotted
To herd and consort with the low and squalid;
But whence the proof to make this statement valid?
They even say his daughter cou'd not read;
Of such a statement I can take no heed
Except to marvel at the logic of the slight:
So, if she couldn't read—he couldn't write?
Your proofs are too confusing, and as such
You've only proved that you have proved too much.
The details of three hundred years ago
We can't accept, because we do not know.
The genea' facts we are p'epared to swallow,
While unimportant trifles beat us hollow.
    We know full well
        That Nero was a sinner,
        But we can't tell
    What Nero had for dinner.
Just take my hand and come with me
To where once stood the famous mulberry tree.
Then on to Stratford Church, here take a peep
At where the "fathers of the hamlet sleep."
They hold the place of honor for the dead.
The family of Shakespeare at the head,
Before the altar of this sacred place
They have been given burial and grace.
Your vague tradit'ons are but a surmise:
The proof I offer is before your eyes.

And oh, my comrades, brothers all in Art,
Permit me just one moment to depart
From this my subject, urging you some day
To seek this sacred spot and humbly pray
That Shakespeare's rage toward us will kindly soften,
Because, you know, we've murdered him so often.
I ask this for myself, a poor comedian;
What should I do had I been a tragedian?

I could pile up a lot of other stuff
But I have taxed your patience quite enough;
In turning o'er the matter in my mind
This is the plain solution that I find:

It surely is—"whoe'er the cap may fit"—
Conceded that these wondrous plays were writ.
So if my Shakespeare's not the very same,
It must have been another of that name.

FUTURE OF REPUBLICANISM.

MR. SUTHERLAND'S WISE AND INSPIRING SPEECH AT ALBANY.

HE DISCUSSES THE SENATE STEAL. TELLS THE COLD TRUTH ABOUT MAYNARD. SHOWS THAT REPUBLICANS ARE BEATEN ONLY BY THEIR OWN FAULT AND GIVES SOME MIGHTY GOOD ADVICE.

At the recent dinner of the Unconditional Republican Club of Albany, on the occasion of the last anniversary of Lincoln's Birthday, William A. Sutherland, the Republican nominee for Attorney-General last fall, delivered a speech in response to the toast "The Future of the Republican Party," which deserves as wide a circulation as it can possibly be given. The Tribune gave extracts from the speech the morning after it was delivered which showed its character and force, but it is such a well-knit argument in favor of that organization which is the Republican party's greatest need in this State that its appearance in full to-day will certainly be of great value. The lessons drawn from the elections that have occurred during the last twenty-five years are most impressive. Mr. Sutherland spoke as follows:

Ho who seeks to look into the future must study diligently the past. Whoever strives to forecast coming events must have intelligent appreciation of the happenings of to-day. And a student of the philosophy of politics, especially one seeking for the course by which he thinks his party shou'd steer, needs to go below the surface and learn the undercurrents moving men to, or restraining them from, political action.

We have been taught by the wise men of the party that much of Republican failure in the State of New-York has been due to other causes than those I shall discuss to-night. Some particular man, or set of men, have been selected as the scapegoats upon whose heads should rest the maledictions of earnest Republicans whenever the party has failed to achieve success at the polls. It has been said, even within my recollection, that if certain so-called leaders of the party could be deposed from their self-assumed position, the party, rising like a giant refreshed, having shaken off its burdensome load, would overcome all opp sition and rush triumphant to the position of power. But in my judgment, this argument has carried us t o far. Whatever of justice or right there may or may not have been in the attempts of one set of men within the party to depose from leadership some other set of men, and whatever of force there may or may not have been in the claim that this or that or the other man and his friends shou'd retire from a position of prominence, the balance of the argument, namely, that the mere retiring of any man or set of men would insure triumph to the party, has proved a delusion and a snare.

NOT THE FAULT OF LEADERS.

The Republican party of the State of New-York has made a record in the casting of votes that is very instructive. That record has but one exception, the year 1866. Leaving out that exception, the record is this: That the vote of the party is only polled once in four years. No matter what the issue has been, no matter how excellent the ticket, no matter whether the "leaders" were new or old, the vote of the party has not been gotten to the polls in "off" years. Many able and astute men have been giving reasons why Mr. Fassett was not elected Governor at the election of 1891, but none of them, so far as I have observed, have qualified their reasoning by any reference to, much less any admission of, this stubborn and very unwelcome fact, namely: That the Republican candidates on the State ticket of 1891 received just as loyal support from the party, and just as large a percentage of the party vote, as any other State ticket voted for in any but a Presidential year since 1860, with only one single, solitary, lonesome exception.

Mr. Fassett received in 1891 nearly 45,000 more votes than were cast for Mr. Davenport in 1865; 116,000 votes more than were cast for Governor Cornell in 1879, and nearly 50,000 votes more than our State ticket received in 1889.

In 1860 the Republican vote of the State of New-York was 362,646, as against 312,510 Democratic.

Abraham Lincoln, in memory of whom we gather here to-night with uncovered heads, and whose life and character came as a blessing to all mankind, was then elected President. I well remember, though but a boy at the time, how earnest were the Republicans of the State of New-York in 1862 to support the hands and strengthen the administration of Abraham Lincoln. They nominated for Governor General James S. Wadsworth, a widely known and highly respected resident of Western New-York; a gentleman whose noble impulses had moved him to send a shipload of provisions to the Emerald Isle, in the days of the great famine in Ireland, and whose patriotic soul had led him to don the uniform of the defenders of our flag and render heroic services in the cause of the Union. He had been Military Governor of the District of Columbia, and was close to the administration of Abraham Lincoln. He was beloved by the people; was respected by the State, and was famous throughout the Nation. No stain was upon his character; he was freely and voluntarily nominated for the office of Governor by the Republicans of the State, and Abraham Lincoln was stretching his emancipating hands toward the imperial member of the sisterhood of loyal States, asking the people of this, the greatest, the grandest and most powerful of the States, to show her loyalty, not only to the Administration but to the Nation itself, by electing James S. Wadsworth as her Governor. The Democratic vote that year for Horatio Seymour was 306,649, being not quite 6,000 less than the Democratic vote of 1860. In 1860 the Republicans had carried the State by 50,000, in 1862, however, while the Democratic vote fell off less than 6,000, the Republican vote was reduced by over 67,000, and the loyal, the brave the generous, the every-way acceptable General Wadsworth received only 295,897 votes.

REPUBLICANS VOTE ONLY ONCE IN FOUR YEARS.

There was in this falling off no rebuke intended by outraged Republicans against any bosses, nor against the Administration of Abraham Lincoln, nor against the character of the Republican candidate, nor the platform upon which he stood. There was simply and only that which has occurred in every off year but one since that date, such deplorable, and I might almost say such criminal, inattention to their political duties by many members of the Republican party, that the right was defeated and the wrong prevailed. In 1864 the Republican vote for President was 368,735, and the Democratic vote was 361,986. The year 1866 furnishes the only exception to the regular and persistent staying at home by the Republicans, no matter if even a Governor is to be elected, unless there is also a President to be voted for. The Republican vote in 1866 for Governor was only 2,420 less than the votes cast for Lincoln in 1864, being 366,315, and the Democratic vote was 352,526. In 1868 the Republican vote for President was 419,883, and the Democratic vote 429,857. For Governor in 1870, the Democratic vote fell about 20,000 from its Presidential vote in 1868, but

the Republican vote was reduced by 53,447; the Republican ticket receiving 366,436, and the Democratic ticket 399,552. In 1872 many Democrats refused to support their candidate, Greeley, and their vote was the lightest, but one, of any Presidential vote in the thirty years under review, being 387,282. The Republican vote was 440,738. But in 1874, only two years afterward, the Democratic vote went up from 387,000 to 416,391, while the Republican vote, which was cast for that gallant soldier, that sturdy patriot, John A. Dix, fell from 440,000 in 1872 to 366,074. John A. Dix was just as good a man in 1874 as he was in 1872. He was elected in 1872, but in 1874 there were 84,664 Republicans who neglected to cast their votes for his re-election.

SOME HIGHLY SIGNIFICANT FIGURES.

In 1876 the Republican electoral ticket received 489,207 votes, and 521,949 were cast for Tilden. For Secretary of State, in 1877, the Republican vote was only 371,798, being a reduction from the previous year of 117,509 votes. Of course the Republicans did not elect their State ticket. In 1879 there were 77,000 votes cast for John Kelly for the office of Governor, for which reason Lucius Robinson received only 375,790, and Governor Cornell, the only Republican Governor the State of New-York has had since 1874, received 418,567 votes. But Cornell's vote was 70,000 less than that cast for Hayes in 1876. In 1880 the Republican electoral vote was 555,554, and the Democratic vote was 534,811. In 1882 Grover Cleveland received for Governor 192,000 majority, but his vote was only 807 greater than Hancock's vote in 1880; for Cleveland received in 1882 just 535,318 votes. The Republican vote in 1882 was 342,464. Unquestionably very much of the Republican falling off in 1882 was intentional on the part of the stay-at-home voters, and yet Folger's vote in 1882 was within 76,103 as great as that cast for Cornell in 1879, a discrepancy by no means equal to many I have noted. Although Cleveland carried the State in 1882 by 192,000, and very nearly, if not quite, lost it in 1884, his vote was increased in 1884 over that which he received in 1882 by 27,730, and the official records show that he received in 1884 563,048 votes, while the official record of the vote for Blaine was 562,001. In 1885 the Democratic vote for Governor was less by nearly 63,000 than his Presidential vote in 1884. Cleveland is said to have carried the State in 1884 by the slender plurality of 1,047. Surely when 62,586 Democrats failed to go to the polls in 1885, the Republicans ought to have carried the State. They would have done so if only 12,000 out of the 71,670 stay-at-home voters who voted for Blaine in 1884, had been willing to put themselves to the very small inconvenience of travelling from their places of business, or their places of residence, to the polling places and there casting their votes. The vote for Hill was 501,462, and for Davenport 490,331. In 1888 the Republican vote for President was 650,338, and the Democratic vote was 635,965. In 1889, for Secretary of State, the Democratic vote fell to 505,694. It would seem that with 130,000 stay-at-home Democrats, the Republican State ticket in 1889 should have been elected; but the Republican vote fell from 650,000 to 485,367, and 165,000 Republicans who voted for Harrison in 1888 did not care enough about the State ticket in 1889 to go to the polls and vote. It is significant as bearing upon the meaning of that particular Republican stay-at-home vote that while leadership in the party has very often changed between 1860 and 1890, there was the same leadership, the same chairman of the State Committee and the same general situation of the Republican party in 1889 as in 1888. But see the disaster which those 165,000 stay-at-home Republicans have brought upon the party and upon the State! If they, indeed, if only 21,000 of them, had dropped their several occupations long enough to vote, a Republican Board of State Canvassers would have been elected, whom Governor Hill could not have persuaded to violate the statutes and disobey the commands of the courts. The present State Senate, which the courts said was Republican, could not have been stolen by the Democrats if our excellent State ticket in 1889 had received 75 per cent of the Republican vote of the previous year.

SOME SUGGESTIONS FOR FUTURE WORK.

In 1891 the Republican party was united. I think it is my duty as one of those who went down with the ticket to repel at all times and in all places the insinuation of the Democratic press that any faction or element or considerable number of members of the Republican party had any but the most loyal desire for the success of the ticket in 1891. I believe the party was never more united in support of a ticket than it was last fall. I challenge any man to point out in any part of the State any Republicans, sufficiently numerous to be worth mentioning, who expressed dissatisfaction with the ticket; or who manifested any desire for its defeat; or who did anything, except give the ticket their loyal and even enthusiastic support; save and only the great army of regular and ever recurring stay-at-home voters.

Fassett received in 1891 534,956 votes, being 49,589 more than were cast for Gilbert, Secretary of State, in 1889, but being over 100,000 less than were cast for Harrison in 1888; while Flower received 582,893, being 53,072 votes less than were cast for Cleveland in 1888, but about 57,000 more than were cast for Rice in 1889.

A gratifying future for the Republican party in the State and in the Nation depends upon whether an affirmative answer can be given to this question: Can we, and will we, adopt such means as will insure the polling of the full Republican vote at every election? The party in the Nation depends more than it has been willing to admit upon the Republicans of the State of New-York. During the years we have reviewed, with the exceptions of 1868 and 1876, the electoral vote of New-York has been in the majority columns of the electoral vote of the Nation; and since 1876 the electoral vote of New-York has determined the national contest. But the mere statement of the case is sufficient to prove that the continued success of Democracy in off years materially contributes to their vote in this State at Presidential elections, and materially retards the efforts of the Republicans in bringing out the Republican vote at Presidential elections. The success or failure of the Republican party in off years, in the State of New-York, bears materially upon the success of the party in the Nation at a Presidential election.

Anxious eyes will be directed toward the Empire State during the coming summer and fall, and we shall be bidden to Herculean labors by our brethren of every State, in the hope that by those labors we may again place New-York in the Republican column. Our labors this year will not be lightened, nor will our task be any less difficult, because the whole election machinery of the State is in the hands of our opponents. Hence the duty of even those Republicans who are only interested in the party from a national standpoint to come to the polls at every election, every fall and every spring, in order that when the National contest is on, the machinery of elections may not be in active and possibly corrupt operation against us.

CAMPAIGNING ALL THE YEAR ROUND.

How then can we secure the polling of the full Republican vote in an off-year?

Republicans are notoriously active at just about the close of the campaign. Democrats are active and vigilant from January 1 to the 31st of December. We suffer the Democrats to take control of the boards of Supervisors of Republican counties, and fold our hands to a little more sleep and a little more slumber, blissfully dreaming that it matters not who represents a town in the county legislature. But a few days after an important election we find Democratic Supervisors running away from the commands of the Supreme Court of the State, with election returns in their pockets, under letters of safe conduct from the Democratic Governor, and promise of swift pardon from punishment prompted by the righteous indignation of an outraged court. At the same time we see Democrats in another Board of Supervisors manufacturing, without even daring to disclose the process of manufacture, a false and fraudulent majority for a Democratic candidate for the State Senate; and a Republican County Clerk required under pain of decapitation to certify to the State Canvassers this false and fraudulent result. We see State Canvassers, elected to their high positions because Republicans were busy with some other concern on election day, eagerly reaching out their hands to receive, by personal delivery, these false and fraudulent returns but afterward refusing to receive by personal delivery (because the statutes say delivery shall be through the mails) certified copies of returns from the same county corrected after judicial examination by Democratic judges. We see some of these same canvassers actively participating in the suppression of those same corrected returns when they were afterward received through the mail at the offices of the Governor, the Controller and the Secretary of State; and we see those State Canvassers, by unanimous vote, defy the mandates of all the courts of the State and of every judge who had had those returns under examination, by canvassing the false and fraudulent returns against the mandamus of the Supreme Court unanimously affirmed by the Court of Appeals. And all these things are done simply and only to secure a partisan majority in one branch of the Legislature. In view of these recent doings, I believe the entire Republican party will welcome with eagerness the adoption of any honorable means by which hereafter the entire Republican vote can be pulled out of its apathy and brought to the polls on every election day. I believe this magnificent Unconditional Republican Club of Albany is ready to do its share in that work. Can I not ask of this club, whose name calls up the image of that great conqueror of the Rebellion, and whose membership is now assembled to do honor to the memory of the immortal Lincoln, to do what perhaps no one man can do successfully, to spring to the relief of the Republican party, and propose and carry into execution such means as will insure a live, active and fruitful campaign before every election day?

THE STATE COMMITTEE SHOULD ORGANIZE IN JANUARY.

Suppose you propose to the party that hereafter our campaigns begin on the first day of January and conclude not until somebody in every election district of the State has been called to account and given either praise or condemnation for the result of that election in his particular election district. Suppose you propose that we do not wait until after a State Convention in the fall for the appointment of a State Committee and its organization for the purposes of that campaign. We all know how this has operated in the past. After our State Conventions, with scarce an exception since 1860, I think only excepting 1870 and 1882, Republicans have gone to their homes congratulating themselves upon the nomination of an excellent ticket and their excellent prospects of success. Some time afterward the State Committee appointed at that State Convention has organized. State Committees have always promised us success down to the very eve of election, but State Committees organized at such late day have never been able to become carefully informed as to the situation in the interior of the State. In Presidential years the State Committee has usually been appointed at the spring convention, and the members thereof then knew who would have charge of the campaign. The campaign had been begun early and the vote of the party has been drawn out. The State Committee should be able in every year, at every election, to send its impulse into the uttermost parts of the State, as the heart sends the life-blood through the minutest arteries and to the smallest point in every part of the body. Too often the State Committee has been pounding away in New-York City very much like the heart-beats of a man whose extremities are encased in ice. Ought not the State Committee to be in active operation long before the holding of the State Convention? A great measure of the success of the Republican party in the County of Monroe, in which county I may say that better results were obtained last fall than in any other of the interior counties of the State, is due to the fact that for upward of ten years past the County Committee, appointed at the fall convention, has not taken office until the first day of the following January, and so has organized in January for the campaign in November. A State Committee organized in January could and should be charged with the responsibility of seeing to it that every Republican county elects a Republican Board of Supervisors in the spring. To this end, they could and should require Republican County Committees in every county, as in Monroe, to take office and to organize in January for the entire year. With County Committees in active operation for the spring campaigns, and the State Committee organized in January, we would have ample means of information as to the situation and of the needs of the party in every county and every town in the State. By beginning at once the collection of information, and the collection of funds, the State Committee could, before the first day of March in every year, place Republican newspapers in the hands of enough doubtful voters or apathetic Republicans to produce very substantial results on election day. The State Committee, organized thus early and properly supported by the party, could have, before a State Convention is even called, an actual canvass of the greater part if not all the State, showing just where the greatest efforts would have to be put forth in the fall. And a State Committee thus organized, and thus carrying on a campaign, could and should call to account at the close of its campaign all through whom it had acted and administer due condemnation to all who had failed in their duty, and hold up to the very proper and deserved commendation of the entire party every man who had discharged the full measure of his duty. A State Committee thus early organized, and knowing that from January 1 it was to have charge of the party and its campaign for that year, could and would seek the co-operation and the active interest of earnest Republicans in every part of the State. Doubtless so early an organization of the State Committee would necessitate the employment of a permanent secretary and the establishment of a permanent headquarters. But the contribution by our moneyed men of $10,000 for this purpose, in the month of January, would be of more value to the party than the contribution of $50,000 on the first day of November. The proper and legitimate expenditure of money through the spring and summer months in finding out where and who the doubtful and hesitating voters are, and in furnishing them with proper literature, and in sending missionaries personally to labor with them, is worth tenfold the expenditure of vastly greater amounts the last week of October in the hiring of brass bands or the shooting off of fireworks.

"HONEST" DEMOCRATS AND THE SENATE STEAL.

What is there that promises the hearty acquiescence of the great mass of the party in any honorable improvement in our party management?

First, there is the great and general disappointment of Republicans over the failure of last fall. And second, and far more potential, there is the uncovering which we have seen of the present management of the Democratic party in all its hideous nakedness.

To-day the Republican party has been awakened from its dreams. It has been rudely and grossly shaken into its wakefulness, and it sees with staring and astonished eyes the entire Democratic party of the State standing as the enemy of decency, of honesty, of uprightness and integrity.

When Governor Hill, a few hours after election, notwithstanding the returns at the County Clerks' offices showed eighteen Republicans and fourteen Democrats elected to the State Senate, made public

proclamation that the Senate was Democratic, men said "this man is mad," and that even Democrats would not sanction so patent a theft as the transfer of a majority of four in the Senate into a minority. But the men who said these things were all Republicans. There was no Democrat from Buffalo to, Albany nor from the St. Lawrence River to Montauk Point who lifted his voice or raised his finger or wrote a line in protest against the Governor's proclamation.

When the Deputy Attorney-General of the State of New-York hovered over the Democratic Board of Supervisors of Dutchess County, and plying his way back and forth between Albany and Poughkeepsie, steadily turned the wheel that ground out a false and fraudulent result on State Senator in that county, where was the Democratic newspaper, with the single exception of one brave little sheet in Poughkeepsie, that dared say aught against this proceeding? And who was the Democratic leader anywhere within the borders of the Empire State who lifted his voice against the iniquity?

As the conspiracy progressed step by step, and in county after county; as that conspiracy approached its completion; and when Republicans bestirred themselves to make such application to the courts as might result in undoing these wrongs; what Democratic newspaper, what Democratic leader, what single and isolated individual member of that party came forward with any word of encouragement for the opponents of the wrong, or with a syllable of condemnation for any of the wrong-doers?

FALLING DOWN BEFORE A GANG OF SHAMELESS THIEVES.

Just now, it is true, there is some little indication of activity against the chief wrong-doer, but that activity is directed only against the holding of a convention in the month of February. Very excellent gentlemen are now lifting their voices against the outrage which has been perpetrated by the naming of February instead of April as the time when the Democrats of the State of New-York should, in convention assembled, prostrate themselves before their god and their proprietor, David B. Hill. But what one of these excellent and well-intentioned gentlemen has been heard to protest against the violation by the State Canvassers of the solemn and unanimously affirmed mandates of the Supreme Court of the State? These gentlemen make loud outcries against the sort of weather in which their State Convention is to be held; but when a Supervisor, with election returns in his pocket, was dodging into darkness lest the courts should correct the wrong-doings of Mr. Hill's minions; when Mr. Hill's personal appointees and official friends were, under his evident and official direction, engineering flagrant and violent pieces of political burglary; when Mr. Hill was swinging a headsman's axe at a Republican County Clerk who refused to certify a false statement to be correct; when he was transmitting a pardon with lightning speed to one whom the Court had adjudged in contempt; and even later still, when by the slow process of the regular turn of the judicial wheel one fact after another has been brought to light, showing that Governor Hill, Deputy Attorney-General Maynard and Secretary of State Rice, if not the entire Board of State Canvassers, were deliberately strangling at the birth official returns brought forth with much labor by the midwifery of Democratic judges; even now, and in presence of this mass of colossal iniquity, the entire Democratic party stands dumb. They acquiesce in and receive the fruits of practices which Tweed never dreamed of, and which have raised the author and successful perpetrator thereof to be the only true and genuine object of the idolatrous worship of the Democratic party. Before this hideous monster of iniquity, this engineer and perpetrator of outrages almost indescribable, it seems to the Republican observer as if the entire Democratic party were prostrate in adoration.

THE RIGHT KIND OF TALK ABOUT MAYNARD.

There are, it is true, some good men in the Democracy of New-York. But their voices made no discord in the songs of praise that swelled and rose to greet every advance of the Hill conspiracy.

Not even a solitary Democrat has been heard to give

the faintest sound of protest at the indignity put upon the members of our highest court, when the command of Senator Hill moved the hand of Governor Flower to push along the judges of that court, and to seat by their side, upon a hitherto stainless bench, a creature upon whose handiwork they had but a few hours before pronounced unanimous judicial condemnation.

What Democratic member of the bar, what Democratic newspaper, what man who voted for Flower has shown that he even thought of disapproving that outrage by Governor Flower upon the Goddess of Justice, when he took the man who had stolen from the Controller's office judicially accredited election returns and dumped that man upon the bench of the court of last resort!

Thank God that the going out of this year will see him thrown off from that bench, "unwept, unhonored and unsung."

But what of the Democrats? Do they not seem to rather like these doings?

If there is a solitary Democrat in the State of New-York who even in his heart has rebelled against those astounding villanies, is he not like a trembling schoolboy in presence of his master, scarce daring to think his own thoughts, much less whisper them to his neighbor?

What a commentary it is upon the domination of Hillism in the Democratic party that with all the goings on of the past weeks the only note out of harmony with the Democratic chorus was the feeble wail at Cooper Union last night over the fact that Washington's birthday is this year to be "a cold day" for Grover Cleveland!

What a spectacle is presented by the gleeful acquiescence or else the frightened silence of his entire party when the Governor of the State, whose lips had touched the sacred volume in making oath that he would enforce the laws, nevertheless encourages, instigates and actively assists his like solemnly sworn subordinates in flagrant violations of the laws!

AN HONEST BALLOT THE GREATEST OF ISSUES.

There is yet, therefore, a mission for the Republican party to fulfil. If it shall be that virtue do not depart from our land; that integrity become not a forgotten word; and that common honesty among the common people be not swallowed up in the quagmire of official corruption; it will be because the Republican party of this State is so infused with virility as well as inspired with enthusiasm as to bring about not only the overthrow of the perpetrators of recent villany, but the continued supremacy of honest men. Even the material prosperity of the land, which depends so largely upon the success of the Republican party; even the magnificent prospects opening before us through the fruitful operation of "Blaine's reciprocity humbug"; even the golden harvests of foreign coins which we are just beginning to reap through the far-seeing statesmanship of Harrison's Administration, dwindle into insignificance compared with the moral questions facing the voters of this State this fall, and every fall, until the present masters of the Democratic party shall be completely under foot.

We have seen with surprise that party survive the leadership of Calhoun and Davis; we have wondered how it could endure the commanding presence of Buchanan and Fernando Wood; we see now that it stands as a party in chains to obey with meekness, mute and uncomplaining, the masterful will of its William M. Tweed returned to life in the person of its David B. Hill.

If we shall teach our young men to obey the laws of the land, to respect the commands of the courts, to give some heed to their official oaths, and to abstain from grand larcenies; if the coming generation of this great land shall be taught to respect virtue and avoid vice, to love the true and abstain from the false, to cherish the right and despise the wrong; this land must be governed by the party of the immortal Abraham Lincoln, the party of Unconditional Surrender Grant, the party of that king among the princes of the Nation, Roscoe Conkling; the party of the martyred Garfield, the party that numbers in its ranks "the matchless man from Maine," and the party that has given us the peerless Administration of Benjamin Harrison.

CITY OFFICIALS SCORED.

DR. CHARLES H. PARKHURST'S SCATHING WORDS.

HE DENOUNCES THEM AS "A DAMNABLE PACK OF ADMINISTRATIVE BLOODHOUNDS"—HERE EVERY CRIME HAS ITS PRICE.

New-York City's governing body, as at present constituted, received what was perhaps the most scathing denunciation of it ever hurled from a platform on the first Sunday in February at the hands of the Rev. Dr. Charles H. Parkhurst, pastor of the Madison Square Presbyterian Church. He sounded a trumpet call for Christian sentiment and endeavor to back the crusade of the press against the varied forms of vice prevalent in New-York. The responsibility for the grossness and open defiance of law that characterize the city's immorality he charged directly upon the municipal officers now in power, using the most direct of ungarnished Anglo-Saxon, and allowing no euphemism to cloak the names and character of the city officials and their relations to the criminal classes.

Dr. Parkhurst's text was: "Ye are the salt of the earth." He said:

That states illustratively the entire situation. It characterizes the world we live in; it defines the functions of the Christianity that has entered into the world, and it indicates by implication the stint which it devolves upon each Christian man and woman of us to help to perform. These words of our text occur in what we have learned to know as "The Sermon on the Mount," or what we might properly designate as Christ's statement of fundamentals. In this sermon He is putting in His preliminary work: He is laying a basis broad and deep enough to carry everything that will be laid upon it later. And it is one of the impressive features of the matter that the founder of Christianity so distinctly foresaw that practical and concrete relation with the world into which the new faith was to come, and that so early in His ministry as this He announced that relation in terms so simple and unmistakable.

Ye are the salt of the earth. This, then, is a corrupt world, and Christianity is the antiseptic that is to be rubbed into it in order to arrest the processes of its decay. An illustration taken from common things, but which states at a stroke the entire story. The reason for selecting the above Scripture, and the burden that is upon my mind this morning, is this: that current Christianity seems not in any notable or conspicuous way to be fulfilling the destiny which the Lord here appoints for it. It lacks distinct purpose, and it lacks virility. We are living in a wicked world, and we are fallen upon bad times. And the question that has been pressing upon my heart these days and weeks past has been—What can I do? We are not thinking just now so much of the world at large as we are of the particular part of the world that it is our painful privilege to live in. We are not saying that the times are any worse than they have been. But the evil that is in them is giving most uncommonly distinct tokens of its presence and vitality, and it is making a good many earnest people serious. They are asking, What is to be done? What is there that I can do? In its municipal life our city is thoroughly rotten. Here is an immense city reaching out arms of evangelization to every quarter of the globe; and yet every step that we take looking to the moral betterment of this city has to be taken directly in the teeth of the damnable pack of administrative bloodhounds that are fattening themselves on the ethical flesh and blood of our citizenship. We have a right to demand that the Mayor and those associated with him in administering the affairs of this municipality should not put obstructions in the path of our ameliorating endeavors; and they do. There is not a form under which the devil disguises himself that so perplexes us in our efforts, or so bewilders us in the devising of our schemes as the polluted harpies that, under the pretence of governing this city, are feeding day and night on its quivering vitals. They are a lying, perjured, rum-soaked and libidinous lot. If we try to close up a house of prostitution or of assignation, we, in the guilelessness of our innocent imaginations, might have supposed that the arm of the city government that takes official cognizance of such matters, would like nothing so well as to watch daytimes and sit up nights for the purpose of bringing these dirty malefactors to their deserts. On the contrary, the arm of the city government that takes official cognizance of such matters evinces but a languid interest, shows no genius in ferreting out crime, prosecutes only when it has to, and has a mind so keenly judicial that almost no amount of evidence that can be heaped up is accepted as sufficient to warrant indictment.

IN LEAGUE WITH THE INFAMOUS PLACES.

We do not say that the proposition to raid any noted house of assignation touches our city government at a sensitive spot. We do not say that they frequent them; nor do we say that it is money in their pockets to have them maintained. We only say (we think a good deal more, but we only say) that so far as relates to the blotting out of such houses the strength of the municipal administration is practically leagued with them rather than arrayed against them.

The same holds true of other institutions of an allied character. Gambling houses flourish on all these streets almost as thick as roses in Sharon. They are open to the initiated at any hour of day or night. They are eating into the character of some of what we are accustomed to think of as our best and most promising young men. They are a sly and constant menace to all that is choicest and most vigorous in a moral way in the generation that is now moving on to the field of action. If we try to close up a gambling-house, we, in the guilelessness of our innocent imaginations, might have supposed that the arm of the city government that takes cognizance of such matters would find no service so congenial as that of combining with well-intentioned citizens in turning up the light on these nefarious dens and giving to the public certified lists of the names of their frequenters. But if you convict a man of keeping a gambling hell in this town you have got to do it in spite of the authorities and not by the aid of the authorities. It was only this past week that a search warrant was issued by one of the courts in town, and before the officer with his posse reached No. 522 Sixth-ave., the action of the court reached there, and the house that is spoken of in Scripture as empty, swept and garnished, was not, in point of unadorned vacuity, a circumstance to the innocent barrenness of the gambling rooms in question. I do not say that the judge of Jefferson Market Police Court was responsible for the slip. I do not believe that he was, at least in any direct way. All that is intended by the reference is that the police court leaked. With hardly the shadow of a doubt that court, in some one of its subordinates at any rate, stands in with the gamblers, and to that degree the court becomes the criminal's protector and guardian angel. This is mentioned only as illustration of the fact that some people understand, and that all people ought to understand, that crime in this city is intrenched in our municipal administration, and that what ought to be a bulwark against crime is a stronghold in its defence. We strike the same difficulty again when we come to matters of excise. No one can have followed the crusade that has been in progress these last weeks against unlicensed saloons or against saloons that have been open in unlicensed hours, and have a solitary shred of doubt that every conviction of a saloon-keeper is obtainable only by a square fight with the constituted authorities. The police do not take the initiative. What has been done during the last six weeks has been done because the outraged sentiment of decent people voicing itself through the press has rendered it impossible for what we amuse ourselves by calling the guardians of the public peace and virtue, vulgarly known as the police, to do otherwise than bring some criminals to justice, or at least to threaten to do so. Unless all signs are misleading, your average policeman or your average police captain is not going to disturb a criminal, if the criminal has means, if he can help it.

EVERY CRIME HAS ITS PRICE.

We are saying nothing as to the connection there is between the criminal's means and the policeman's indulgence. We only state in explanation that it is the universal opinion of those who have studied longest and most deeply into the municipal criminality of this city that every crime here has its price. I am not saying that that is so, but that the more intently any man of brains scrutinizes these matters the more he discovers along this line that is of an intensely interesting nature. I should not be surprised to know that every building in this town in which gambling or prostitution or the illicit sale of liquor is carried on has immunity secured to it by a scale of police taxation that is as carefully graded and as thoroughly systematized as any that obtains in the assessment of personal property or real estate that is made for the purpose of meeting municipal, State or Federal expenses current. The facts do not always get to the surface, but when they do they let in a great lot of light into the subterranean mysteries of this rum-be-otted and Tammany-debauched town.

Near the beginning of the year the Grand Jury considered the matter of indicting the keeper of a notorious resort on Fourteenth-st. (I am giving the case as it was presented in one of our most trustworthy journals, and has, I believe, not been contradicted.) There was no legal evidence at hand that would be sufficient to convict, and the District-Attorney was asked to secure some. An innocent imagination would have supposed that he would jump at the opportunity. The request was repeated by the Grand Jury, apparently without effect. His hesitancy may have been due to either one of two causes. He may have known so much about the establishment that he did not like to touch it, or he may have known so little about it that he was sceptical as to the truth of the derogatory reports that were in circulation in regard to it. Indeed, the District-Attorney said to me in his own house four weeks ago that until after McGlory's establishment was raided he had no idea that institutions of so vile a character existed in this city. All we can say is that we must give the young man the benefit of the doubt. Such a case is truly affecting. Innocence like that in so wicked a town ought not to be allowed to go abroad after dark without an escort. But to return to our narrative.

THE GRAND JURORS AS DETECTIVES.

Our guileless District-Attorney, with the down of unsuspecting innocence upon his blushing cheek, failed to respond to the demands for evidence made upon him by the Grand Jury. The jurors themselves, therefore, assumed experimentally the character of detectives, and the proprietor of the place was soon caught, of course, in the act of illegal selling. An indictment was then found. It remained to secure witnesses that would be willing to go on the stand and testify; for while the jurors were willing to visit the place and satisfy their own minds of the illegality of what was going on there, they experienced a natural delicacy in having their names publicly associated with such a resort in the published reports of criminal procedure. Accordingly instructions were given to the captain of the precinct to procure the necessary evidence. This was followed by another touching exhibition of modesty and blushing hesitancy. The fact of it is they all stand in with each other. It is simply one solid gang of rascals, half of the gang in office and the other half out, and the two halves steadily catering to each other across the official line. The captain declared reiteratedly that evidence against McGlory was something that he could not obtain, till finally the Grand Jury threatened to indict the captain himself, whereupon the evidence was at once produced and McGlory convicted upon it. All of which is only another way of saying that the most effective allies which McGlory had in the prosecution of his vile trade on Fourteenth-st. were the District-Attorney and the captain of the precinct.

THE POWER OF MONEY AND FEAR.

Now it may be said that this method of stating the case is injudicious; that it is unwise too sharply to antagonize the powers that be; that convictions will not be obtainable if we make enemies of the men who exercise police and judicial functions. On the contrary, there are only two kinds of argument that exercise the slightest logical urgency on the minds of that stripe of bandit,—one is money and the other is fear. We shall gain nothing by disguising the facts. To call things by their right names is always a direct contribution to wholesome effects.

A steamer can only make half-time in a fog. The first necessity of battle is to have the combatants clearly and easily distinguishable by the diversity of their uniform. We want to know what is what.

Every solid statement of fact is argument. Every time you deal with things as they are, and name them in honest, ringing Saxon, you have done something. It has always been trump-card in the devil's game to keep things mixed. He mixed them in Paradise and he has been trying to keep them mixed ever since. If the powers that are managing this town are supremely and concertedly bent on encouraging iniquity in order to the strengthening of their own position, and the enlargement of their own capital, what in Heaven's name is the use of disguising the fact and wrapping it up in ambiguous euphemisms? Something like a year ago, in company with a number of gentlemen, I conferred in his office with the highest municipal dignitary of this city in regard to the slovenly and the wicked way in which he was pretending to clean our streets. In what I had to say to him at that time I addressed him as though he were a man, and as though he had the supreme interests of this city at heart; and I have been ashamed of myself from the crown of my head to the sole of my foot ever since. Saying nothing about the outrage a man commits upon himself by the conscious falsification of facts, it does not pay. Neither the devil nor any of his minions can be caught in a trap. You can hammer him, but you cannot snare him. Cajolery only lubricates the machinery of his iniquity. Petting him oils the bearings; minimizes the squeak and maximizes the velocity. Now this is not spoken in malice. It is not spoken without a recognition of the fact that there are men occupying official place in this city whose chief ambition it is to discharge their duties incorruptibly. Of course such exceptions are due to circumstances that it was beyond the power of dominant influence to control. We have referred to such exceptions only for the purpose of anticipating the charge that our indictment has been harsh and indiscriminate.

STRONG LANGUAGE ABOUT THE MAYOR.

But after all that has been said the great fact remains untouched and uninvalidated, that every effort that is made to improve character in this city, every effort to make men respectable, honest, temperate and sexually clean is a direct blow between the eyes of the Mayor and his whole gang of drunken and lecherous subordinates, in this sense—that while we fight iniquity they shield and patronize it; while we try to convert criminals they manufacture them; and they have a hundred dollars invested in manufacturing machinery to our one invested in converting machinery. And there is no scheme in this direction too colossal for their ambition to plan and to push. At this very time, in reliance upon the energies of evil that dominate this city, there is being urged at Albany the passage of a bill that will have it for its effect to leave the number of liquor licenses unrestricted, to forbid all attempts to obtain proof of illicit sales, to legalize the sale of liquor after 1 o'clock on Sunday afternoon, and indeed to keep open bar 160 out of 168 hours of every week. Sin never gets tired; never is low-spirited; has the courage of its convictions; never fritters away its power and its genius pettifogging over side issues. What voluminous lessons the saints might learn from the sinners! We speak of these things because it is our business as the pastor of a Christian church to speak of them. You know that we are not slow to insist upon keenness of spiritual discernment, or upon the reticent vigor of a life hid with Christ in God. Piety is the genius of the entire matter; but piety, when it fronts sin, has got to become grit. Salt is a concrete commodity, and requires to be rubbed into the very pores of decay. I scarcely ever move into the midst of the busier parts of this town without feeling in a pained way how little of actual touch there is between the life of the church and the life of the times. As we saw last Sabbath morning, we must have a consciousness of God, but the truth complementary to that is that we must have just as lively a consciousness of the world we are living in. Men ought to have that, and women ought to have it too. Nobody that can read is excusable for not knowing what is transpiring. And Christians of either sex ought to know it and ought to want to know it; ought to feel that it is part of their own legitimate concern to know it.

HERE IS THE PLACE FOR MISSIONARY WORK.

We have no criticism to pass on the effort to improve the quality of the civilization in central Africa, but it would count more in the moral life of the world to have this city, where the heart of the country beats, dominated in its life and government by the ethical principles insisted on by the Gospel, than to have a belt of evangelical light a hundred miles broad thrown clear across the Dark Continent. And the men and women that live here are the ones to do it. It is achievable. What Christianity has done Christianity can do. And when it is done it is going to be done by the men and women who stand up and make a business of the thing, and quit playing with it; quit imagining that somehow we are going by some indescribable means to drift into a better state of things. Say all you please about the might of the Holy Ghost, every step in the history of an ameliorated civilization has cost just so much personal push. You and I have something to do about it. If we have a brain, or a heart, or a purse, and sit still and let things take their course, making no sign, uttering no protest, flinging ourselves into no endeavor, the times will eventually sit in judgment upon us, and they will damn us. Christianity is here for an object. The salt is here for a purpose. If your Christianity is not vigorous enough to help save this country and this city, it is not vigorous enough to do anything toward saving you. Reality is not worn out. The truth is not knock-kneed. The incisive edge of bare-bladed righteousness will still cut. Only it has got to be righteousness that is not afraid to stand up, move into the midst of iniquity and shake itself. The humanly incarcerated principles of this Gospel were able in three centuries to change the moral complexion of the whole Roman Empire; and there is nothing the matter with the Christianity here except that the incarnations of it are lazy and cowardly, and think more of their personal comfort than they do of municipal decency, and more of their dollars than they do of a city that is governed by men who are not tricky and beastly.

THE VALUE OF VIGOROUS PROTEST.

But you ask me perhaps what is the use of all this asseveration and vituperation? What is the good of protesting? What is the good of protesting? Do you know what the word Protestant means? Do you know that a Protestant is nothing but a protestant? A man who protests? And did not the men who protested in the sixteenth century do a good deal? Didn't they start a volcano beneath the crust of the whole of European civilization? Wherever you have a Luther, a grand stick of human timber all afire with holy indignation, a man of God, who is not too lymphatic to get off his knees, or too cowardly to come out of his closet, confront iniquity, look it in the eye, plaster it with its baptismal name—such a man can start a reformation and a revolution every day in the year if there are enough of them to go around. Why, it makes no difference how thick the darkness is, a ray of light will cut it if it is healthy and spry. Do you know that the newspapers had not been solidly at work for more than about four weeks before the dives began to close up? Why, the truth will frighten even a policeman, if you will lodge it where David did when he fired at Goliath. Truth, with explosive enough behind it, would scare even the captain of a precinct, and chase the blushes from the callow face of the District-Attorney. We have had an example of that recently on a larger scale in the matter of the Louisiana lottery. The whole country was kindled into a flame of indignation, and the lottery men bowed before the storm. And, so far as the North was concerned, it was principally the doing of one man, too, a man who had a head, heart and convictions, and a pen and lungs to back them.

You see that these things do not go by arithmetic, nor by a show of hands. A man who is held in the grip of the everlasting truth and is not afraid is a young army in himself. That is exactly what the Bible means when it says that one man shall chase a thousand. That is the way history has always gone. That is what the Bible story of Sodom means and the assurance that ten men would have sufficed to save it. Not ten that were scared, but ten men that so had the courage of their convictions and that so appreciated the priestliness of the office to which they had been called that the multitudnousness of the dirty crowd they stood up among neither dashed their confidence nor quenched their testimony.

THE BUSINESS OF THE CHURCH.

This is not bringing politics into the pulpit, politics as such. The particular political stripe of a municipal administration is no matter of our interest, and none of our business; but to strike at iniquity is a part of the business of the Church; indeed it is the business of the Church. It is primarily what the Church is for, no matter in what connections that sin may find itself associated and intermixed. If it fall properly within the jurisdiction of this church to try to convert Third-ave. drunkards from their alcoholism, then certainly it is germane to the functions of this church to strike the sturdiest blows it is capable of at a municipal administration whose supreme mission it is to protect, foster and propagate alcoholism. If it is proper for us to go around cleaning up after the devil, it is proper for us to fight the devil. If it is right to cure, it is right to prevent, and a thousand times more economical and sagacious. If we are not as a church transcending our jurisdiction by attempting to convert Third-ave. prostitutes from their harlotry, then surely we are within the pale of our authority as a church when we antagonize and bear prophetic testimony against an administration the one necessary outcome of whose policy it is to breed prostitutes. Republicans and Democrats we have nothing to do with, but sin it is our particular province to ferret out, to publish, and in unadorned Saxon to stigmatize; and the more influential the position in which that sin is intrenched the more painstaking and pronounced requires to be our analysis, and the more exempt from hesitancy and euphemism our characterization.

OBLIGATIONS OF CHRISTIANS.

The only object of my appeal this morning has been to sound a distinct note, and to quicken our Christian sense of the obligatory relation in which we stand toward the official and administrative criminality that is filthifying our entire municipal life, making New-York a very hot-bed of knavery, debauchery and bestiality, in the atmosphere of which, and at the corrosive touch of which, there is not a young man so noble, nor a young girl so pure, as not to be in a degree infected by the fetid contamination. There is no malice in this, any more than there would be if we were talking about cannibalism in the South Sea Islands; only that having to live in the midst of it, and having to pay taxes to help support it, and having nine-tenths of our Christian effort neutralized and paralyzed by the damnable pressure of it, naturally our thoughts are strained to a little snugger tension.

A man always aims differently when he is firing at a target that is close by than he does when he is shooting at something the other side of the moon. Now this gives the Church good, solid, concrete, objective business for it to throw itself into. It would be a very boom for Presbyterianism in this city if it were understood that Presbyterianism represented conspicuously and pronouncedly integrity in high places and purity and temperance in administrative circles. It might retain in the Presbyterian fold some of the young people that are drifting off into other denominations on the ground that Presbyterianism seems to them not to be in touch with the life of to-day, and not to be showing itself equal to the demands that the times make upon it.

It might put a new spirit into the hearts of some of our clergymen, who, if they were combining their concerted energies to the task of converting dirty New-York into a new Paradise of the Western World, would surely find less fascination in shelling for men the old cobs grown in mediaeval cornfields.

I have meant to be unprejudiced in my position and conservative in my demands, but, Christian friends, we have got to have a better world, and we have got to have a better city than this is, and men who feel iniquity keenly and who are not afraid to stand up and hammer it unflinchingly and remorselessly, and never get tired hammering it, are the instruments God has always used to the defeat of Satan and to the bringing in of a better day. The good Lord takes the fog out of our eyes, the paralysis out of our nerves, and the limp out of our muscles, and the meanness out of our praise, shows to us our duty, and reveals to us our superb opportunity, making of every man and woman among us a prophet, instinct with a loving, so intense that we shall not be afraid, loving righteousness with a loyalty so impassioned that we shall feel the might of it and trust it, and our lives become this day enlisted in the maintenance of the right, and thus show that Almighty God is mightier than all the ranks of Satan that challenge His claims and dispute His blessed prayers.

TRADE WITH THE SOUTH.

SPEECHES BEFORE THE PROVIDENCE COMMERCIAL CLUB.

I. N. FORD DISCUSSES "RECIPROCITY"—SENATORS ALLISON AND ALDRICH DEFEND THE AMERICAN TRADE POLICY.

Providence, Feb. 27.—The monthly dinner of the Commercial Club to-night was attended by about eighty-five persons. The special guests of the evening were Senator William B. Allison, of Iowa; Senator Nelson W. Aldrich, to whose Senatorial campaign the meeting was calculated to give an added impetus, and I. N. Ford, of The New-York Tribune. Other leading men in attendance were Governor Ladd, Lieutenant-Governor Stearns, Secretary of State George H. Utter, Speaker Adin B. Capron, D. Russell Brown, General Olney Arnold, Colonel Samuel P. Colt and Colonel John C. Wyman. The first speaker of the evening was Mr. Ford, who spoke on "Reciprocity." Mr. Ford said in part:

Your chairman has asked me to discuss the Reciprocity policy in its practical application to manufactures. Perhaps I cannot do better than to single out some of the special industries of Rhode Island. The question will take some such form as this: How can a larger market be secured in Tropical America for engines, machinery, cotton-prints and jewelry? In a broad way the answer will be: By the exercise of American energy and business intelligence and by the reproduction of European mercantile methods now successfully employed in Southern countries.

American agricultural industries will gain the largest advantages from the Reciprocity conventions. This is natural and right, for the treaty concessions made to the export trade are grounded upon the free market opened for the agricultural products of Tropical America. There is no serious competition from Europe in this class of products, and the gain from Reciprocity will be measured practically by increased consumption caused by the cheapening of food. When an import duty of $5 75 was levied in Cuba upon a barrel of American flour, wheat bread was a luxury. When the duty is reduced to 90 cents, wheat bread will be eaten by all classes. In Venezuela flour is now taxed about 110 per cent. If the duties can be materially reduced through Reciprocity the consumption will be largely increased. In neither country will there be any difficulty in selling flour. American millers already understand the requirements of a hot, moist climate, and their brands are known in Southern markets. Increased trade is secured as soon as the high revenue duties are reduced. The same remark applies to meats, potatoes, lard and provisions of all kinds.

For general manufactures the difficulty of opening a new market is greatly increased by European competition. A barrel of flour will sell itself; a steam engine or a case of cotton prints will not. Manufactures must be adapted to the requirements of the climate, the necessities and tastes of the people, and the order of civilization of races of mixed blood, or else they cannot be sold. Reductions of 25 or 50 per cent in the tariff schedules will not serve to introduce anything that is not wanted, especially when European merchants have been on the ground for thirty years and furnish what is wanted. Even if with the advantage of preferential tariff schedules a superior article can be provided at an inferior price, it must be intelligently introduced and carried in stock in wholesale houses. The real explanation of the supremacy of English, French and German manufactures in Southern markets lies in the fact that maritime Europe has systematically cultivated trade relations in that quarter of the world, while Americans have neglected and abandoned the field. European agents have learned what the motley population of Brazil has required, and the manufacturers have produced what was called for. If the Portuguese traders have asked for goods of narrower width, these have been supplied, even if extensive alterations have been involved in the Manchester mills. If they have complained of prices and demanded cheaper cotton prints, the German manufacturers have sent out goods of a quality which the poorest customers at home would have been ashamed to wear. Europeans have labored persistently and successfully to make the import trade of Tropical America their own. Americans cannot hope to wrest it from them, or to obtain even a fair share of it, without patiently devoting themselves to the business of competition with equal intelligence and systematic effort.

By the Reciprocity conventions with Brazil and the Spanish West Indies the schedules on American cotton goods have been reduced 25 per cent. This preferential rate offers a marked advantage over English and German manufactures, but unless special lines of goods of the cheapest grade are supplied for Southern trade, there will be only meagre results. The exports of American cotton goods to Brazil now amount to less than $700,000 a year, chiefly in the form of coarse drilling. At the same time Europe ships to that country cottons amounting to nearly $27,000,000. It is a trade worth competing for, but it cannot be secured without a struggle. English manufacturers do not attempt to sell cotton goods by sample or through commercial travellers. They have in the principal coast towns wholesale houses where retail dealers can replenish their stocks. A similar system would largely increase American trade both in Brazil and in Cuba. When duties are levied on gross weight, as is ordinarily done in Spanish-America, 20 per cent may be added to the cost of the goods from their being placed in heavy boxes. Southern merchants never know what American goods will cost until they have them on their counters, for they cannot forecast the blunders which may be made in invoicing and packing them. Here comes in the great advantage of American wholesale houses established in the centres of population in tropical countries. Merchants on the ground will be familiar with all the details of customs law, interior transportation, credits and the requirements of public taste. They can carry assorted stocks and orders can be filled without costly blunders in packing. They will not antagonize the native retail merchants, but will enable them to buy American goods on the ground as they want them. A house of this kind representing a syndicate of Massachusetts manufacturers is now successfully introducing American boots and shoes in the British West Indies and is driving out English goods. A similar series of houses properly supported by the cotton manufacturers of New-England, with 25 per cent in duties in their favor, would make heavy inroads upon Manchester trade in the South.

Manufacturers of iron and steel are favored 25 per cent in the Brazilian and 50 per cent in the Spanish convention, and in both Reciprocity agreements, as well as in those negotiated with the British West Indies and San Domingo, engines and machinery are included in the free lists. The result in the case of Brazil was shown in an increase of over $1,000,000 in the importations of American machinery during the first five months of Reciprocity. For the Spanish West Indies since October the statistics already disclose a similar gain. Every steamer sailing from New-York for Havana or Cienfuegos has carried engines and improved machinery for sugar works, builders' hardware, iron castings and similar manufactures. Under existing conditions of free labor and competition the economical production of tropical staples like coffee and sugar is dependent upon superior mechanical plant. I met in Cuba last year engineers and designers who were visiting sugar plantations and making estimates for improved machinery from the United States. This is the most practical method of securing a larger market for American engines and machinery. It ought to be extended to the British West Indies, and especially to Brazil and Venezuela, where cheap Belgian boilers with tubes badly set are everywhere in use, and where English engines and mechanism have been introduced without adequate competition from America. The coffee industry requires complex hydraulic and steam machinery and it can be greatly improved by American inventive talent. In Mexico all the rolling stock on the railways, the improved agricultural implements in the fields, and the machinery in mines and smelters comes from the United States; but elsewhere in Spanish America England is largely supplying the mechanical plant for railway construction, mining industry and material progress. In the heart of Central America, in the mountains of Peru, in the desert of Tarapaca and in the broad stretches of the Argentine pampas, I have met English mechanical engineers who had been sent out to design machinery and to make contracts on the ground for its introduction. This is a field where American manufacturers are known to excel European rivals. They have only to take possession of it by sending expert talent into Southern countries.

I have referred to two large classes of manufactures, which are directly favored by the Reciprocity policy. There are many other classes, such as manufactures of leather, rubber, glass, paper and wood, which have a discrimination of 25 or 30 per cent in their favor in some of the conventions, or are on the free lists in other treaties. In the face of these preferential rates the time-worn objection that without free raw materials it will be impossible for Americans to compete with European manufacturers loses its force. But without reference to these discriminations it may be confidently asserted that at least 75 per cent. of the imports of Tropical America are manufactures which either have free raw materials already in the United States or have been so greatly cheapened in price by competition under the protective system as to be on a level with European goods. Few of those goods which are most heavily protected in the United States are taken from Europe at any price. Jamaica, for example, imports $1,500,000 of cotton goods and less than $140,000 of woollens, and the proportion in favor of cottons is even larger in Brazil and Venezuela. Blankets, heavy cloths, carpets, upholstered furniture, felts, linens and silks are imported most sparingly. With their abundant supplies of cotton, leather, hides, rubber, fibre, wood, iron and copper, Americans do not need to modify their tariff before making a vigorous effort to supply the Southern markets with what is needed there. It is not their tariff which stands in their way. It is ignorance of the requirements and conditions of Southern trade that is the chief obstacle to the development of their export trade. Maritime energy by which a commercial marine can be brought into existence is lacking. Banking facilities have not been supplied. Mercantile enterprise and intelligence have been confined almost wholly to the home market.

Let me take one of your most conspicuous manufacturing specialties as an illustration—manufactures of silver and jewelry of all kinds. Chili, Peru and Mexico are silver countries, and Brazil is rich in precious stones; but they have no mechanical arts for the working of metals. The shops of Rio, Montevideo, Buenos Ayres, Santiago, Valparaiso, Lima and Caracas will be ransacked in vain for samples of native manufacturing of metal. The silversmith's art is a lost art in countries where it was once conducted with refinement of ingenuity. The taste of the mixed races for ornament, finery and jewelry remains, and the most pretentious shops in their capitals and the most attractive corners of their markets are occupied by English, German and French jewellers. I do not believe that your Rhode Island silversmiths and jewelry manufacturers would have any difficulty in competing for this trade if they made the effort to do it. They would have to introduce cheaper and more tawdry lines of goods than they now make, but with their improved mechanical appliances they would have great resources for competition.

Senator Allison was next introduced and was most heartily greeted. He spoke of the effect of legislation on trade relations of this country. In prefacing his remarks he alluded pleasantly to his long acquaintance with Senator Aldrich, and to that gentleman's industry and aptness as a legislator. He also spoke of the fact that "Rhode Island in its simplicity and generosity voted for me at Chicago for President of the United States." He believed that recent legislation in Congress was conceived and executed with a purpose to benefit the people. Said he: "It happens in legislation that we are confronted with population scattered over 3,000,000 square miles. It is the business of the wise legislator to secure the greatest good and least harm. All legislation, in a sense, is compromise legislation. In the compromises that must exist you are willing to give up a little that may be for your special interests in order to benefit the country at large. So we in Iowa have to accept some things that bear hard on our agricultural community. The interests of people of the United States should be preferred to those of any other people. Notwithstanding all that is said, Iowans are in a reasonably prosperous condition. They may owe you some money, but they will pay it, and they do not want to pay it in a depreciated currency.

"The question of raising revenue for a government is a great question. Recent legislation not only dealt with currency, but also with that larger question of raising revenue. I with Senator Aldrich spent days and nights in 1888 to devise a revenue scheme which we thought would place laborers in this country in a better position than the laborers in the same vocations in other countries. The result was, in 1890, the McKinley Tariff bill, so-called. It was not a perfect bill, but it was the best bill that could be devised at that time to protect the labor of the people of the United States."

Senator Aldrich spoke of the compliment which Germany had paid the protective system of America by the words of its statesmen and the acts of its Parliament. He then went on to speak in general terms of the causes which led up to the Reciprocity legislation. He believed that this was but the beginning of a departure which would have great beneficial and far-reaching results.